Python Deep Learning Cookbook

Over 75 practical recipes on neural network modeling, reinforcement learning, and transfer learning using Python

Indra den Bakker

BIRMINGHAM - MUMBAI

Python Deep Learning Cookbook

First published: October 2017

Production reference: 1261017

Published by Packt Publishing Ltd.
Livery Place
35 Livery Street
Birmingham
B3 2PB, UK.

ISBN 978-1-78712-519-3

www.packtpub.com

Credits

Author
Indra den Bakker

Reviewer
Radovan Kavicky

Commissioning Editor
Veena Pagare

Acquisition Editor
Vinay Argekar

Content Development Editor
Cheryl Dsa

Technical Editor
Suwarna Patil

Copy Editors
Vikrant Phadkay
Alpha Singh

Project Coordinator
Nidhi Joshi

Proofreader
Safis Editing

Indexer
Tejal Daruwale Soni

Graphics
Tania Dutta

Production Coordinator
Nilesh Mohite

About the Author

Indra den Bakker is an experienced deep learning engineer and mentor. He is the founder of 23insights—part of NVIDIA's Inception program—a machine learning start-up building solutions that transform the world's most important industries. For Udacity, he mentors students pursuing a Nanodegree in deep learning and related fields, and he is also responsible for reviewing student projects. Indra has a background in computational intelligence and worked for several years as a data scientist for IPG Mediabrands and Screen6 before founding 23insights.

About the Reviewer

Radovan Kavicky is the principal data scientist and President at GapData Institute (`https://www.gapdata.org`) based in Bratislava, Slovakia, where he harnesses the power of data and the wisdom of economics for public good.

A macroeconomist by education/academic background and a consultant and analyst by profession (with more than 8 years of experience in consulting for clients from the public and private sector), with strong mathematical and analytical skills, he is able to deliver top-level research and analytical work. From MATLAB, SAS, and Stata, he switched to Python, R, and Tableau.

He is a member of the Slovak Economic Association and an evangelist of open data, open budget initiatives, and open government partnership. He is the founder of PyData Bratislava, R <- Slovakia, and SK/CZ Tableau User Group (skczTUG). He has been a speaker at TechSummit (Bratislava, 2017) and at PyData (Berlin, 2017), and a member of the global Tableau #DataLeader network (2017). You can follow him on Twitter at @radovankavicky, @GapDataInst, or @PyDataBA. His full profile and experience is available at `https://www.linkedin.com/in/radovankavicky/` and `https://github.com/radovankavicky`.

www.PacktPub.com

For support files and downloads related to your book, please visit www.PacktPub.com.

Did you know that Packt offers eBook versions of every book published, with PDF and ePub files available? You can upgrade to the eBook version at www.PacktPub.com and as a print book customer, you are entitled to a discount on the eBook copy. Get in touch with us at service@packtpub.com for more details.

At www.PacktPub.com, you can also read a collection of free technical articles, sign up for a range of free newsletters and receive exclusive discounts and offers on Packt books and eBooks.

https://www.packtpub.com/mapt

Get the most in-demand software skills with Mapt. Mapt gives you full access to all Packt books and video courses, as well as industry-leading tools to help you plan your personal development and advance your career.

Why subscribe?

- Fully searchable across every book published by Packt
- Copy and paste, print, and bookmark content
- On demand and accessible via a web browser

Customer Feedback

Thanks for purchasing this Packt book. At Packt, quality is at the heart of our editorial process. To help us improve, please leave us an honest review on this book's Amazon page at `http://www.amazon.com/dp/178712519X`.

If you'd like to join our team of regular reviewers, you can e-mail us at `customerreviews@packtpub.com`. We award our regular reviewers with free eBooks and videos in exchange for their valuable feedback. Help us be relentless in improving our products!

Table of Contents

Preface

Deep learning is revolutionizing a wide range of industries. For many applications, deep learning has proven to outperform humans by making faster and more accurate predictions. This book provides a top-down and bottom-up approach to demonstrate deep learning solutions to real-world problems in different areas. These applications include computer vision, natural language processing, time series, and robotics.

What this book covers

Chapter 1, *Programming Environments, GPU Computing, Cloud Solutions, and Deep Learning Frameworks*, includes information and recipes related to environments and GPU computing. It is a must-read for readers who have issues in setting up their environment on different platforms.

Chapter 2, *Feed-Forward Neural Networks*, provides a collection of recipes related to feed-forward neural networks and forms the basis for the other chapters. The focus of this chapter is to provide solutions to common implementation problems for different network topologies.

Chapter 3, *Convolutional Neural Networks*, focuses on convolutional neural networks and their application in computer vision. It provides recipes on techniques and optimizations used in CNNs.

Chapter 4, *Recurrent Neural Networks*, provides a collection of recipes related to recurrent neural networks. These include LSTM networks and GRUs. The focus of this chapter is to provide solutions to common implementation problems for recurrent neural networks.

Chapter 5, *Reinforcement Learning*, covers recipes for reinforcement learning with neural networks. The recipes in this chapter introduce the concepts of deep reinforcement learning in a single-agent world.

Chapter 6, *Generative Adversarial Networks*, provides a collection of recipes related to unsupervised learning problems. These include generative adversarial networks for image generation and super resolution.

Chapter 7, *Computer Vision*, contains recipes related to processing data encoded as images, including video frames. Classic techniques of processing image data using Python will be provided, along with best-of-class solutions for detection, classification, and segmentation.

Chapter 8, *Natural Language Processing*, contains recipes related to textual data processing. This includes recipes related to textual feature representation and processing, including word embeddings and text data storage.

Chapter 9, *Speech Recognition and Video Analysis*, covers recipes related to stream data processing. This includes audio, video, and frame sequences

Chapter 10, *Time Series and Structured Data*, provides recipes related to number crunching. This includes sequences and time series.

Chapter 11, *Game Playing Agents and Robotics*, focuses on state-of-the-art deep learning research applications. This includes recipes related to game-playing agents in a multi-agent environment (simulations) and autonomous vehicles.

Chapter 12, *Hyperparameter Selection, Tuning, and Neural Network Learning*, illustrates recipes on the many aspects involved in the learning process of a neural network. The overall objective of the recipes is to provide very neat and specific tricks to boost network performance.

Chapter 13, *Network Internals*, covers the internals of a neural network. This includes tensor decomposition, weight initialization, topology storage, bottleneck features, and corresponding embedding.

Chapter 14, *Pretrained Models*, covers popular deep learning models such as VGG-16 and Inception V4.

What you need for this book

This book is focused on AI in Python, as opposed to Python itself. We have used Python 3 to build various applications. We focus on how to utilize various Python libraries in the best possible way to build real-world applications. In that spirit, we have tried to keep all of the code as friendly and readable as possible. We feel that this will enable our readers to easily understand the code and readily use it in different scenarios.

Who this book is for

This book is intended for machine learning professionals who are looking to use deep learning algorithms to create real-world applications using Python. A thorough understanding of machine learning concepts and Python libraries such as NumPy, SciPy, and scikit-learn is expected. Additionally, basic knowledge of linear algebra and calculus is desired.

Conventions

In this book, you will find a number of text styles that distinguish between different kinds of information. Here are some examples of these styles and an explanation of their meaning.

Code words in text, database table names, folder names, filenames, file extensions, pathnames, dummy URLs, user input, and Twitter handles are shown as follows: "To provide a dummy dataset, we will use numpy and the following code."

A block of code is set as follows:

```
import numpy as np
x_input = np.array([[1,2,3,4,5]])
y_input = np.array([[10]])
```

Any command-line input or output is written as follows:

```
curl -O
http://developer.download.nvidia.com/compute/cuda/repos/ubuntu1604/
x86_64/cuda-repo-ubuntu1604_8.0.61-1_amd64.deb
```

New terms and **important words** are shown in bold.

Words that you see on the screen, for example, in menus or dialog boxes, appear in the text like this:

Warnings or important notes appear like this.

Tips and tricks appear like this.

Reader feedback

Feedback from our readers is always welcome. Let us know what you think about this book-what you liked or disliked. Reader feedback is important for us as it helps us develop titles that you will really get the most out of. To send us general feedback, simply email feedback@packtpub.com, and mention the book's title in the subject of your message. If there is a topic that you have expertise in and you are interested in either writing or contributing to a book, see our author guide at www.packtpub.com/authors.

Customer support

Now that you are the proud owner of a Packt book, we have a number of things to help you to get the most from your purchase.

Downloading the example code

You can download the example code files for this book from your account at `http://www.packtpub.com`. If you purchased this book elsewhere, you can visit `http://www.packtpub.com/support` and register to have the files emailed directly to you. You can download the code files by following these steps:

1. Log in or register to our website using your email address and password.
2. Hover the mouse pointer on the **SUPPORT** tab at the top.
3. Click on **Code Downloads & Errata**.

4. Enter the name of the book in the **Search** box.
5. Select the book for which you're looking to download the code files.
6. Choose from the drop-down menu where you purchased this book from.
7. Click on **Code Download**.

Once the file is downloaded, please make sure that you unzip or extract the folder using the latest version of:

- WinRAR / 7-Zip for Windows
- Zipeg / iZip / UnRarX for Mac
- 7-Zip / PeaZip for Linux

The code bundle for the book is also hosted on GitHub at `https://github.com/PacktPublishing/Python-Deep-Learning-Cookbook`. We also have other code bundles from our rich catalog of books and videos available at `https://github.com/PacktPublishing/`. Check them out!

Errata

Although we have taken every care to ensure the accuracy of our content, mistakes do happen. If you find a mistake in one of our books-maybe a mistake in the text or the code-we would be grateful if you could report this to us. By doing so, you can save other readers from frustration and help us improve subsequent versions of this book. If you find any errata, please report them by visiting http://www.packtpub.com/submit-errata, selecting your book, clicking on the **Errata Submission Form** link, and entering the details of your errata. Once your errata are verified, your submission will be accepted and the errata will be uploaded to our website or added to any list of existing errata under the Errata section of that title. To view the previously submitted errata, go to https://www.packtpub.com/books/content/support and enter the name of the book in the search field. The required information will appear under the **Errata** section.

Piracy

Piracy of copyrighted material on the internet is an ongoing problem across all media. At Packt, we take the protection of our copyright and licenses very seriously. If you come across any illegal copies of our works in any form on the internet, please provide us with the location address or website name immediately so that we can pursue a remedy. Please contact us at copyright@packtpub.com with a link to the suspected pirated material. We appreciate your help in protecting our authors and our ability to bring you valuable content.

Questions

If you have a problem with any aspect of this book, you can contact us at questions@packtpub.com, and we will do our best to address the problem.

1
Programming Environments, GPU Computing, Cloud Solutions, and Deep Learning Frameworks

This chapter focuses on technical solutions to set up popular deep learning frameworks. First, we provide solutions to set up a stable and flexible environment on local machines and with cloud solutions. Next, all popular Python deep learning frameworks are discussed in detail:

- Setting up a deep learning environment
- Launching an instance on Amazon Web Services (AWS)
- Launching an instance on Google Cloud Platform (GCP)
- Installing CUDA and cuDNN
- Installing Anaconda and libraries
- Connecting with Jupyter Notebook on a server
- Building state-of-the-art, production-ready models with TensorFlow
- Intuitively building networks with Keras
- Using PyTorch's dynamic computation graphs for RNNs
- Implementing high-performance models with CNTK
- Building efficient models with MXNet
- Defining networks using simple and efficient code with Gluon

Introduction

The recent advancements in deep learning can be, to some extent, attributed to the advancements in computing power. The increase in computing power, more specifically the use of GPUs for processing data, has contributed to the leap from shallow neural networks to deeper neural networks. In this chapter, we lay the groundwork for all following chapters by showing you how to set up stable environments for different deep learning frameworks used in this cookbook. There are many open source deep learning frameworks that are used by researchers and in the industry. Each framework has its own benefits and most of them are supported by some big tech company.

By following the steps in this first chapter carefully, you should be able to use local or cloud-based CPUs and GPUs to leverage the recipes in this book. For this book, we've used Jupyter Notebooks to execute all code blocks. These notebooks provide interactive feedback per code block in such a way that it's perfectly suited for storytelling.

The download links in this recipe are intended for an Ubuntu machine or server with a supported NVIDIA GPU. Please change the links and filenames accordingly if needed. You are free to use any other environment, package managers (for example, Docker containers), or versions if needed. However, additional steps may be required.

Setting up a deep learning environment

Before we get started with training deep learning models, we need to set up our deep learning environment. While it is possible to run deep learning models on CPUs, the speed achieved with GPUs is significantly higher and necessary when running deeper and more complex models.

How to do it...

1. First, you need to check whether you have access to a CUDA-enabled NVIDIA GPU on your local machine. You can check the overview at `https://developer.nvidia.com/cuda-gpus`.

2. If your GPU is listed on that page, you can continue installing `CUDA` and `cuDNN` if you haven't done that already. Follow the steps in the *Installing CUDA and cuDNN* section.

3. If you don't have access to an NVIDIA GPU on your local machine, you can decide to use a cloud solution. Follow the steps in the *Launching a cloud solution* section.

Launching an instance on Amazon Web Services (AWS)

Amazon Web Services (**AWS**) is the most popular cloud solution. If you don't have access to a local GPU or if you prefer to use a server, you can set up an EC2 instance on AWS. In this recipe, we provide steps to launch a GPU-enabled server.

Getting ready

Before we move on with this recipe, we assume that you already have an account on Amazon AWS and that you are familiar with its platform and the accompanying costs.

How to do it...

1. Make sure the region you want to work in gives access to P2 or G3 instances. These instances include **NVIDIA K80** GPUs and **NVIDIA Tesla M60** GPUs, respectively. The K80 GPU is faster and has more GPU memory than the M60 GPU: 12 GB versus 8 GB.

While the NVIDIA K80 and M60 GPUs are powerful GPUs for running deep learning models, these should not be considered state-of-the-art. Other faster GPUs have already been launched by NVIDIA and it takes some time before these are added to cloud solutions. However, a big advantage of these cloud machines is that it is straightforward to scale the number of GPUs attached to a machine; for example, Amazon's **p2.16xlarge** instance has 16 GPUs.

2. There are two options when launching an AWS instance. **Option 1**: You build everything from scratch. **Option 2**: You use a preconfigured **Amazon Machine Image** (**AMI**) from the AWS marketplace. If you choose option 2, you will have to pay additional costs. For an example, see this AMI at `https://aws.amazon.com/marketplace/pp/B06VSPXKDX`.

3. Amazon provides a detailed and up-to-date overview of steps to launch the deep learning AMI at `https://aws.amazon.com/blogs/ai/get-started-with-deep-learning-using-the-aws-deep-learning-ami/`.

4. If you want to build the server from scratch, launch a P2 or G3 instance and follow the steps under the *Installing CUDA and cuDNN* and *Installing Anaconda and Libraries* recipes.

5. Always make sure you stop the running instances when you're done to prevent unnecessary costs.

A good option to save costs is to use AWS Spot instances. This allows you to bid on spare Amazon EC2 computing capacity.

Launching an instance on Google Cloud Platform (GCP)

Another popular cloud provider is Google. Its **Google Cloud Platform** (**GCP**) is getting more popular and has as a major benefit—it includes a newer GPU type, NVIDIA P100, with 16 GB of GPU memory. In this recipe, we provide the steps to launch a GPU-enabled compute machine.

Getting ready

Before proceeding with this recipe, you should be familiar with GCP and its cost structure.

How to do it...

1. You need to request an increase in the GPU quota before you launch a compute instance with a GPU for the first time. Go to `https://console.cloud.google.com/projectselector/iam-admin/quotas`.

2. First, select the project you want to use and apply the **Metric** and **Region** filters accordingly. The GPU instances should show up as follows:

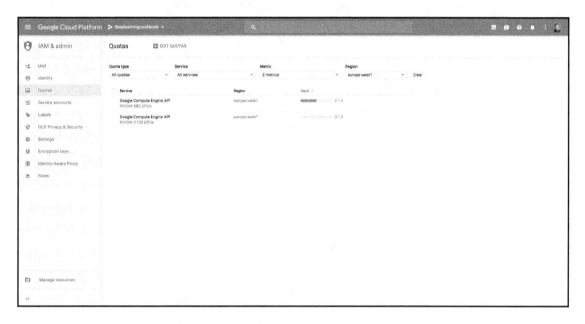

Figure 1.1: Google Cloud Platform dashboard for increasing the GPU quotas

3. Select the quota you want to change, click on EDIT QUOTAS, and follow the steps.
4. You will get an e-mail confirmation when your quota has been increased.
5. Afterwards, you can create a GPU-enabled machine.
6. When launching a machine, make sure you tick the **Allow HTTP traffic** and **Allow HTTPs traffic** boxes if you want to use a Jupyter notebook.

Installing CUDA and cuDNN

This part is essential if you want to leverage NVIDIA GPUs for deep learning. The CUDA toolkit is specially designed for GPU-accelerated applications, where the compiler is optimized for using math operations. In addition, the cuDNN library—short for CUDA Deep Neural Network library—is a library that accelerates deep learning routines such as convolutions, pooling, and activation on GPUs.

Getting ready

Make sure you've registered for **Nvidia's Accelerated Computing Developer Program** at https://developer.nvidia.com/cudnn before starting with this recipe. Only after registration will you have access to the files needed to install the cuDNN library.

How to do it...

1. We start by downloading NVIDIA with the following command in the terminal (adjust the download link accordingly if needed; make sure you use CUDA 8 and not CUDA 9 for now):

```
curl -O
http://developer.download.nvidia.com/compute/cuda/repos/ubuntu1604/
x86_64/cuda-repo-ubuntu1604_8.0.61-1_amd64.deb
```

2. Next, we unpack the file and update all all packages in the package lists. Afterwards, we remove the downloaded file:

```
sudo dpkg -i cuda-repo-ubuntu1604_8.0.61-1_amd64.deb
sudo apt-get update
rm cuda-repo-ubuntu1604_8.0.61-1_amd64.deb
```

3. Now, we're ready to install CUDA with the following command:

```
sudo apt-get install cuda-8-0
```

4. Next, we need to set the environment variables and add them to the shell script .bashrc:

```
echo 'export CUDA_HOME=/usr/local/cuda' >> ~/.bashrc
echo 'export PATH=$PATH:$CUDA_HOME/bin' >> ~/.bashrc
echo 'export LD_LIBRARY_PATH=$LD_LIBRARY_PATH:$CUDA_HOME/lib64' >>
~/.bashrc
```

5. Make sure to reload the shell script afterwards with the following command:

```
source ~/.bashrc
```

6. You can check whether the CUDA 8.0 driver and toolkit are correctly installed using the following commands in your terminal:

```
nvcc --version
nvidia-smi
```

The output of the last command should look something like this:

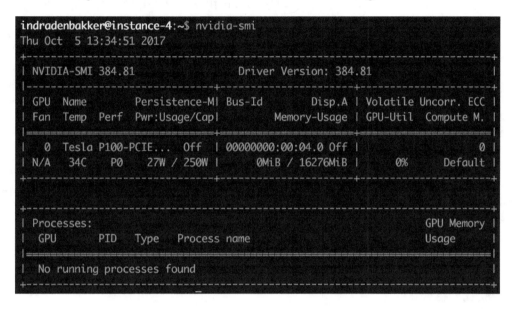

Figure 1.2: Example output of nvidia-smi showing the connected GPU

7. Here, we can see that an NVIDIA P100 GPU with 16 GB of memory is correctly connected and ready to use.

8. We are now ready to install cuDNN. Make sure the NVIDIA cuDNN file is available on the machine, for example, by copying from your local machine to the server if needed. For Google cloud compute engine (make sure you've set up gcloud and the project and zone are set up correctly), you can use the following command (replace local-directory and instance-name with your own settings):

```
gcloud compute scp local-directory/cudnn-8.0-linux-x64-v6.0.tgz
instance-name
```

9. First we unpack the file before copying to the right directory as root:

```
cd
tar xzvf cudnn-8.0-linux-x64-v6.0.tgz
sudo cp cuda/lib64/* /usr/local/cuda/lib64/
sudo cp cuda/include/cudnn.h /usr/local/cuda/include/
```

10. To clean up our space, we can remove the files we've used for installation, as follows:

```
rm -rf ~/cuda
rm cudnn-8.0-linux-x64-v5.1.tgz
```

Installing Anaconda and libraries

One of the most popular environment managers for Python users is Anaconda. With Anaconda, it's straightforward to set up, switch, and delete environments. Therefore, one can easily run Python 2 and Python 3 on the same machine and switch between different installed versions of installed libraries if needed. In this book, we purely focus on Python 3 and every recipe can be run within one environment: `environment-python-deep-learning-cookbook`.

How to do it...

1. You can directly download the installation file for Anaconda on your machine as follows (adjust your Anaconda file accordingly):

```
curl -O
https://repo.continuum.io/archive/Anaconda3-4.3.1-Linux-x86_64.sh
```

2. Next, run the bash script (if necessary, adjust the filename accordingly):

```
bash Anaconda3-4.3.1-Linux-x86_64.sh
```

Follow all prompts and choose 'yes' when you're asked to to add the PATH to the `.bashrc` file (the default is 'no').

3. Afterwards, reload the file:

```
source ~/.bashrc
```

4. Now, let's set up an Anaconda environment. Let's start with copying the files from the GitHub repository and opening the directory:

```
git clone
https://github.com/indradenbakker/Python-Deep-Learning-Cookbook-Kit
.git
cd Python-Deep-Learning-Cookbook-Kit
```

5. Create the environment with the following command:

```
conda env create -f environment-deep-learning-cookbook.yml
```

6. This creates an environment named `environment-deep-learning-cookbook` and installs all libraries and dependencies included in the `.yml` file. All libraries used in this book are included, for example, NumPy, OpenCV, Jupyter, and scikit-learn.

7. Activate the environment:

```
source activate environment-deep-learning-cookbook
```

8. You're now ready to run Python. Follow the next recipe to install Jupyter and the deep learning frameworks used in this book.

Connecting with Jupyter Notebooks on a server

As mentioned in the introduction, Jupyter Notebooks have gained a lot of traction in the last couple of years. Notebooks are an intuitive tool for running blocks of code. When creating the Anaconda environment in the *Installing Anaconda and Libraries* recipe, we included Jupyter in our list of libraries to install.

How to do it...

1. If you haven't installed Jupyter yet, you can use the following command in your activated Anaconda environment on the server:

```
conda install jupyter
```

2. Next, we move back to the terminal on our local machine.

3. One option is to access the Jupyter Notebook running on a server using SSH-tunnelling. For example, when using Google Cloud Platform:

```
gcloud compute ssh --ssh-flag="-L 8888:localhost:8888"  --zone
"europe-west1-b" "instance-name"
```

You're now logged in to the server and port `8888` on your local machine will forward to the server with port `8888`.

4. Make sure to activate the correct Anaconda environment before proceeding (adjust the name of your environment accordingly):

```
source activate environment-deep-learning-cookbook
```

5. You can create a dedicated directory for your Jupyter notebooks:

```
mkdir notebooks
cd notebooks
```

6. You can now start the Jupyter environment as follows:

```
jupyter notebook
```

This will start Jupyter Notebook on your server. Next, you can go to your local browser and access the notebook with the link provided after starting the notebook, for example, `http://localhost:8888/?token=1fa4e9aea99cd7be2b974557eee3d344ca3c992f58 61834f.`

Building state-of-the-art, production-ready models with TensorFlow

One of the most—if not the most—popular frameworks at the moment is TensorFlow. The TensorFlow framework is created, maintained, and used internally by Google. This general open source framework can be used for any numerical computation by using data flow graphs. One of the biggest advantages of using TensorFlow is that you can use the same code and deploy it on your local CPU, cloud GPU, or Android device. TensorFlow can also be used to run your deep learning model across multiple GPUs and CPUs.

How to do it...

1. First, we will show how to install TensorFlow from your terminal (make sure that you adjust the link to the TensorFlow wheel for your platform and Python version accordingly):

   ```
   pip install --ignore-installed --upgrade
   https://storage.googleapis.com/tensorflow/linux/gpu/tensorflow_gpu-
   1.3.0-cp35-cp35m-linux_x86_64.whl
   ```

   This will install the GPU-enabled version of TensorFlow and the correct dependencies.

2. You can now import the TensorFlow library into your Python environment:

   ```
   import tensorflow as tf
   ```

3. To provide a dummy dataset, we will use numpy and the following code:

   ```
   import numpy as np
   x_input = np.array([[1,2,3,4,5]])
   y_input = np.array([[10]])
   ```

4. When defining a TensorFlow model, you cannot feed the data directly to your model. You should create a placeholder that acts like an entry point for your data feed:

   ```
   x = tf.placeholder(tf.float32, [None, 5])
   y = tf.placeholder(tf.float32, [None, 1])
   ```

5. Afterwards, you apply some operations to the placeholder with some variables. For example:

   ```
   W = tf.Variable(tf.zeros([5, 1]))
   b = tf.Variable(tf.zeros([1]))
   y_pred = tf.matmul(x, W)+b
   ```

6. Next, define a loss function as follows:

   ```
   loss = tf.reduce_sum(tf.pow((y-y_pred), 2))
   ```

7. We need to specify the optimizer and the variable that we want to minimize:

   ```
   train = tf.train.GradientDescentOptimizer(0.0001).minimize(loss)
   ```

8. In TensorFlow, it's important that you initialize all variables. Therefore, we create a variable called `init`:

```
init = tf.global_variables_initializer()
```

We should note that this command doesn't initialize the variables yet; this is done when we run a session.

9. Next, we create a session and run the training for 10 epochs:

```
sess = tf.Session()
sess.run(init)

for i in range(10):
    feed_dict = {x: x_input, y: y_input}
    sess.run(train, feed_dict=feed_dict)
```

10. If we also want to extract the costs, we can do so by adding it as follows:

```
sess = tf.Session()
sess.run(init)

for i in range(10):
    feed_dict = {x: x_input, y: y_input}
    _, loss_value = sess.run([train, loss], feed_dict=feed_dict)
    print(loss_value)
```

11. If we want to use multiple GPUs, we should specify this explicitly. For example, take this part of code from the TensorFlow documentation:

```
c = []
for d in ['/gpu:0', '/gpu:1']:
    with tf.device(d):
        a = tf.constant([1.0, 2.0, 3.0, 4.0, 5.0, 6.0], shape=[2,
3])
        b = tf.constant([1.0, 2.0, 3.0, 4.0, 5.0, 6.0], shape=[3,
2])
    c.append(tf.matmul(a, b))
with tf.device('/cpu:0'):
    sum = tf.add_n(c)
# Creates a session with log_device_placement set to True.
sess = tf.Session(config=tf.ConfigProto(log_device_placement=True))
# Runs the op.
print(sess.run(sum))
```

As you can see, this gives a lot of flexibility in how the computations are handled and by which device.

 This is just a brief introduction to how TensorFlow works. The granular level of model implementation gives the user a lot of flexibility when implementing networks. However, if you're new to neural networks, it might be overwhelming. That is why the Keras framework--a wrapper on top of TensorFlow—can be a good alternative for those who want to start building neural networks without getting too much into the details. Therefore, in this book, the first few chapters will mainly focus on Keras, while the more advanced chapters will include more recipes that use other frameworks such as TensorFlow.

Intuitively building networks with Keras

Keras is a deep learning framework that is widely known and adopted by deep learning engineers. It provides a wrapper around the TensorFlow, CNTK, and the Theano frameworks. This wrapper you gives the ability to easily create deep learning models by stacking different types of layers. The power of Keras lies in its simplicity and readability of the code. If you want to use multiple GPUs during training, you need to set the devices in the same way as with TensorFlow.

How to do it...

1. We start by installing Keras on our local Anaconda environment as follows:

```
conda install -c conda-forge keras
```

Make sure your deep learning environment is activated before executing this command.

2. Next, we import `keras` library into our Python environment:

```
from keras.models import Sequential
from keras.layers import Dense
```

This command outputs the backend used by Keras. By default, the TensorFlow framework is used:

```
In [1]:  from keras.models import Sequential
         from keras.layers import Dense

         Using TensorFlow backend.
```

Figure 1.3: Keras prints the backend used

3. To provide a dummy dataset, we will use numpy and the following code:

```
import numpy as np
x_input = np.array([[1,2,3,4,5]])
y_input = np.array([[10]])
```

4. When using sequential mode, it's straightforward to stack multiple layers in Keras. In this example, we use one hidden layer with 32 units and an output layer with one unit:

```
model = Sequential()
model.add(Dense(units=32, input_dim=x_input.shape[1]))
model.add(Dense(units=1))
```

5. Next, we need to compile our model. While compiling, we can set different settings such as loss function, optimizer, and metrics:

```
model.compile(loss='mse',
              optimizer='sgd',
              metrics=['accuracy'])
```

6. In Keras, you can easily print a summary of your model. It will also show the number of parameters within the defined model:

```
model.summary()
```

In the following figure, you can see the model summary of our build model:

```
In [5]:  model.summary()

         Layer (type)                Output Shape              Param #
         =========================================================
         dense_1 (Dense)             (None, 32)                192
         _____
         dense_2 (Dense)             (None, 1)                 33
         =========================================================
         Total params: 225
         Trainable params: 225
         Non-trainable params: 0
         _____
```

Figure 1.4: Example of a Keras model summary

7. Training the model is straightforward with one command, while simultaneously saving the results to a variable called `history`:

```
history = model.fit(x_input, y_input, epochs=10, batch_size=32)
```

8. For testing, the prediction function can be used after training:

```
pred = model.predict(x_input, batch_size=128)
```

 In this short introduction to Keras, we have demonstrated how easy it is to implement a neural network in just a couple of lines of code. However, don't confuse simplicity with power. The Keras framework provides much more than we've just demonstrated here and one can adjust their model up to a granular level if needed.

Using PyTorch's dynamic computation graphs for RNNs

PyTorch is the Python deep learning framework and it's getting a lot of traction lately. **PyTorch** is the Python implementation of Torch, which uses **Lua**. It is backed by Facebook and is fast thanks to GPU-accelerated tensor computations. A huge benefit of using PyTorch over other frameworks is that graphs are created on the fly and are not static. This means networks are dynamic and you can adjust your network without having to start over again. As a result, the graph that is created on the fly can be different for each example. PyTorch supports multiple GPUs and you can manually set which computation needs to be performed on which device (CPU or GPU).

How to do it...

1. First, we install PyTorch in our Anaconda environment, as follows:

   ```
   conda install pytorch torchvision cuda80 -c soumith
   ```

   If you want to install PyTorch on another platform, you can have a look at the PyTorch website for clear guidance: http://pytorch.org/.

2. Let's import PyTorch into our Python environment:

   ```
   import torch
   ```

3. While Keras provides higher-level abstraction for building neural networks, PyTorch has this feature built in. This means one can build with higher-level building blocks or can even build the forward and backward pass manually. In this introduction, we will use the higher-level abstraction. First, we need to set the size of our random training data:

   ```
   batch_size = 32
   input_shape = 5
   output_shape = 10
   ```

4. To make use of GPUs, we will cast the tensors as follows:

   ```
   torch.set_default_tensor_type('torch.cuda.FloatTensor')
   ```

   This ensures that all computations will use the attached GPU.

5. We can use this to generate random training data:

   ```
   from torch.autograd import Variable
   X = Variable(torch.randn(batch_size, input_shape))
   y = Variable(torch.randn(batch_size, output_shape),
   requires_grad=False)
   ```

6. We will use a simple neural network having one hidden layer with 32 units and an output layer:

   ```
   model = torch.nn.Sequential(
           torch.nn.Linear(input_shape, 32),
           torch.nn.Linear(32, output_shape),
       ).cuda()
   ```

   We use the .cuda() extension to make sure the model runs on the GPU.

7. Next, we define the MSE loss function:

```
loss_function = torch.nn.MSELoss()
```

8. We are now ready to start training our model for 10 epochs with the following code:

```
learning_rate = 0.001
for i in range(10):
    y_pred = model(x)
    loss = loss_function(y_pred, y)
    print(loss.data[0])
    # Zero gradients
    model.zero_grad()
    loss.backward()

    # Update weights
    for param in model.parameters():
        param.data -= learning_rate * param.grad.data
```

 The PyTorch framework gives a lot of freedom to implement simple neural networks and more complex deep learning models. What we didn't demonstrate in this introduction, is the use of dynamic graphs in PyTorch. This is a really powerful feature that we will demonstrate in other chapters of this book.

Implementing high-performance models with CNTK

Microsoft also introduced its open source deep learning framework not too long ago: Microsoft Cognitive Toolkit. This framework is better known as CNTK. CNTK is written in C++ for performance reasons and has a Python API. CNTK supports GPUs and multi-GPU usage.

How to do it...

1. First, we install CNTK with pip as follows:

```
pip install
https://cntk.ai/PythonWheel/GPU/cntk-2.2-cp35-cp35m-linux_x86_64.wh
l
```

Adjust the wheel file if necessary (see `https://docs.microsoft.com/en-us/cognitive-toolkit/Setup-Linux-Python?tabs=cntkpy22`).

2. After installing CNTK, we can import it into our Python environment:

```
import cntk
```

3. Let's create some simple dummy data that we can use for training:

```
import numpy as np
x_input = np.array([[1,2,3,4,5]], np.float32)
y_input = np.array([[10]], np.float32)
```

4. Next, we need to define the placeholders for the input data:

```
X = cntk.input_variable(5, np.float32)
y = cntk.input_variable(1, np.float32)
```

5. With CNTK, it's straightforward to stack multiple layers. We stack a dense layer with 32 inputs on top of an output layer with 1 output:

```
from cntk.layers import Dense, Sequential
model = Sequential([Dense(32),
                    Dense(1)])(X)
```

6. Next, we define the loss function:

```
loss = cntk.squared_error(model, y)
```

7. Now, we are ready to finalize our model with an optimizer:

```
learning_rate = 0.001
trainer = cntk.Trainer(model, (loss),
cntk.adagrad(model.parameters, learning_rate))
```

8. Finally, we can train our model as follows:

```
for epoch in range(10):
        trainer.train_minibatch({X: x_input, y: y_input})
```

As we have demonstrated in this introduction, it is straightforward to build models in CNTK with the appropriate high-level wrappers. However, just like TensorFlow and PyTorch, you can choose to implement your model on a more granular level, which gives you a lot of freedom.

Building efficient models with MXNet

The MXNet deep learning framework allows you to build efficient deep learning models in Python. Next to Python, it also let you build models in popular languages as R, Scala, and Julia. Apache MXNet is supported by Amazon and Baidu, amongst others. MXNet has proven to be fast in benchmarks and it supports GPU and multi-GPU usages. By using lazy evaluation, MXNet is able to automatically execute operations in parallel. Furthermore, the MXNet frameworks uses a symbolic interface, called Symbol. This simplifies building neural network architectures.

How to do it...

1. To install MXNet on Ubuntu with GPU support, we can use the following command in the terminal:

   ```
   pip install mxnet-cu80==0.11.0
   ```

   For other platforms and non-GPU support, have a look at https://mxnet.incubator.apache.org/get_started/install.html.

2. Next, we are ready to import mxnet in our Python environment:

   ```
   import mxnet as mx
   ```

3. We create some simple dummy data that we assign to the GPU and CPU:

   ```
   import numpy as np
   x_input = mx.nd.empty((1, 5), mx.gpu())
   x_input[:] = np.array([[1,2,3,4,5]], np.float32)

   y_input = mx.nd.empty((1, 5), mx.cpu())
   y_input[:] = np.array([[10, 15, 20, 22.5, 25]], np.float32)
   ```

4. We can easily copy and adjust the data. Where possible MXNet will automatically execute operations in parallel:

   ```
   x_input
   w_input = x_input
   z_input = x_input.copyto(mx.cpu())
   x_input += 1
   w_input /= 2
   z_input *= 2
   ```

5. We can print the output as follows:

```
print(x_input.asnumpy())
print(w_input.asnumpy())
print(z_input.asnumpy())
```

6. If we want to feed our data to a model, we should create an iterator first:

```
batch_size = 1
train_iter = mx.io.NDArrayIter(x_input, y_input, batch_size,
shuffle=True, data_name='input', label_name='target')
```

7. Next, we can create the symbols for our model:

```
X = mx.sym.Variable('input')
Y = mx.symbol.Variable('target')
fc1 = mx.sym.FullyConnected(data=X, name='fc1', num_hidden = 5)
lin_reg = mx.sym.LinearRegressionOutput(data=fc1, label=Y,
name="lin_reg")
```

8. Before we can start training, we need to define our model:

```
model = mx.mod.Module(
    symbol = lin_reg,
    data_names=['input'],
    label_names = ['target']
)
```

9. Let's start training:

```
model.fit(train_iter,
          optimizer_params={'learning_rate':0.01, 'momentum': 0.9},
          num_epoch=100,
          batch_end_callback = mx.callback.Speedometer(batch_size, 2))
```

10. To use the trained model for prediction we:

```
model.predict(train_iter).asnumpy()
```

 We've shortly introduced the MXNet framework. In this introduction, we've demonstrated how easily one can assign variables and computations to a CPU or GPU and how to use the Symbol interface. However, there is much more to explore and the MXNet is a powerful framework for building flexible and efficient deep learning models.

Defining networks using simple and efficient code with Gluon

The newest addition to the broad range of deep learning frameworks is Gluon. Gluon is recently launched by AWS and Microsoft to provide an API with simple, easy-to-understand code without the loss of performance. Gluon is already included in the latest release of MXNet and will be available in future releases of CNTK (and other frameworks). Just like Keras, Gluon is a wrapper around other deep learning frameworks. The main difference between Keras and Gluon, is that Gluon will (at first) focus on imperative frameworks.

How to do it...

1. At the moment, gluon is included in the latest release of MXNet (follow the steps in *Building efficient models with MXNet* to install MXNet).

2. After installing, we can directly import gluon as follows:

```
from mxnet import gluon
```

3. Next, we create some dummy data. For this we need the data to be in MXNet's NDArray or Symbol:

```
import mxnet as mx
import numpy as np
x_input = mx.nd.empty((1, 5), mx.gpu())
x_input[:] = np.array([[1,2,3,4,5]], np.float32)

y_input = mx.nd.empty((1, 5), mx.gpu())
y_input[:] = np.array([[10, 15, 20, 22.5, 25]], np.float32)
```

4. With Gluon, it's really straightforward to build a neural network by stacking layers:

```
net = gluon.nn.Sequential()
with net.name_scope():
    net.add(gluon.nn.Dense(16, activation="relu"))
    net.add(gluon.nn.Dense(len(y_input)))
```

5. Next, we initialize the parameters and we store these on our GPU as follows:

```
net.collect_params().initialize(mx.init.Normal(), ctx=mx.gpu())
```

6. With the following code we set the loss function and the optimizer:

```
softmax_cross_entropy = gluon.loss.SoftmaxCrossEntropyLoss()
trainer = gluon.Trainer(net.collect_params(), 'adam',
{'learning_rate': .1})
```

7. We're ready to start training or model:

```
n_epochs = 10

for e in range(n_epochs):
    for i in range(len(x_input)):
        input = x_input[i]
        target = y_input[i]
        with mx.autograd.record():
            output = net(input)
            loss = softmax_cross_entropy(output, target)
            loss.backward()
        trainer.step(input.shape[0])
```

We've shortly demonstrated how to implement a neural network architecture with Gluon. Gluon is a powerful extension that can be used to implement deep learning architectures with clean code. At the same time, there is almost no performance loss when using Gluon.

2
Feed-Forward Neural Networks

In this chapter, we will implement **Feed-Forward Neural Networks** (**FNN**) and discuss the building blocks for deep learning:

- Understanding the perceptron
- Implementing a single-layer neural network
- Building a multi-layer neural network
- Getting started with activation functions
- Hidden layers and hidden units
- Implementing an autoencoder
- Tuning the loss function
- Experimenting with different optimizers
- Improving generalization with regularization
- Adding dropout to prevent overfitting

Introduction

The focus of this chapter is to provide solutions to common implementation problems for FNN and other network topologies. The techniques discussed in this chapter also apply to the following chapters.

FNNs are networks where the information only moves in one direction and does not cycle (as we will see in Chapter 4, *Recurrent Neural Networks*). FNNs are mainly used for supervised learning where the data is not sequential or time-dependent, for example for general classification and regression tasks. We will start by introducing a perceptron and we will show how to implement a perceptron with NumPy. A perceptron demonstrates the mechanics of a single unit. Next, we will increase the complexity by increasing the number of units and introduce single-layer and multi-layer neural networks. The high number of units, in combination with a high number of layers, gives the depth of the architecture and is responsible for the name deep learning.

Understanding the perceptron

First, we need to understand the basics of neural networks. A neural network consists of one or multiple layers of **neurons**, named after the biological neurons in human brains. We will demonstrate the mechanics of a single neuron by implementing a perceptron. In a perceptron, a single unit (neuron) performs all the computations. Later, we will scale the number of units to create deep neural networks:

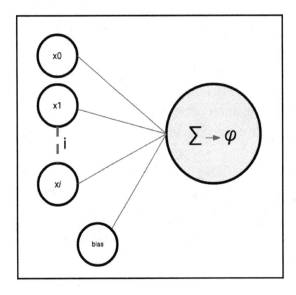

Figure 2.1: Perceptron

A perceptron can have multiple inputs. On these inputs, the unit performs some computations and outputs a single value, for example a binary value to classify two classes. The computations performed by the unit are a simple matrix multiplication of the input and the weights. The resulting values are summed up and a bias is added:

$$\sum_i w_i x_i + b$$

These computations can easily be scaled to high dimensional input. An **activation function** (φ) determines the final output of the perceptron in the **forward pass**:

$$\varphi(x) = \begin{cases} 1 & if\, x < 0.5 \\ 0 & if\, x \geq 0.5 \end{cases}$$

The weights and bias are randomly initialized. After each **epoch** (iteration over the training data), the weights are updated based on the difference between the output and the desired output (**error**) multiplied by the **learning rate**. As a consequence, the weights will be updated towards the training data (**backward pass**) and the accuracy of the output will improve. Basically, the perceptron is a linear combination optimized on the training data. As an activation function we will use a unit step function: if the output is above a certain threshold the output will be activated (hence a 0 versus 1 binary classifier). A perceptron is able to classify classes with 100% accuracy if the classes are linearly separable. In the next recipe, we will show you how to implement a perceptron with NumPy.

How to do it...

1. Import the libraries and dataset as follows:

```
import numpy as np
from sklearn.model_selection import train_test_split
import matplotlib.pyplot as plt
# We will be using the Iris Plants Database
from sklearn.datasets import load_iris

SEED = 2017
```

2. First, we subset the imported data as shown here:

```
# The first two classes (Iris-Setosa and Iris-Versicolour) are
linear separable
iris = load_iris()
idxs = np.where(iris.target<2)
X = iris.data[idxs]
y = iris.target[idxs]
```

3. Let's plot the data for two of the four variables with the following code snippet:

```
plt.scatter(X[Y==0][:,0],X[Y==0][:,2], color='green', label='Iris-
Setosa')
plt.scatter(X[Y==1][:,0],X[Y==1][:,2], color='red', label='Iris-
Versicolour')
plt.title('Iris Plants Database')
plt.xlabel('sepal length in cm')
plt.ylabel('sepal width in cm')
plt.legend()
plt.show()
```

In the following graph, we've plotted the distribution of the two classes:

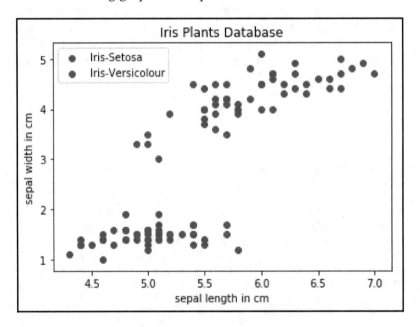

Figure 2.2: Iris plants database (two classes)

4. To validate our results, we split the data into training and validation sets as follows:

```
X_train, X_val, y_train, y_val = train_test_split(X, y,
test_size=0.2, random_state=SEED)
```

5. Next, we initialize the `weights` and the `bias` for the perceptron:

```
weights = np.random.normal(size=X_train.shape[1])
bias = 1
```

6. Before training, we need to define the hyperparameters:

```
learning_rate = 0.1
n_epochs = 15
```

7. Now, we can start training our perceptron with a `for` loop:

```
del_w = np.zeros(weights.shape)
hist_loss = []
hist_accuracy = []

for i in range(n_epochs):
    # We apply a simple step function, if the output is > 0.5 we
predict 1, else 0
    output = np.where((X_train.dot(weights)+bias)>0.5, 1, 0)

    # Compute MSE
    error = np.mean((y_train-output)**2)

    # Update weights and bias
    weights-= learning_rate * np.dot((output-y_train), X_train)
    bias += learning_rate * np.sum(np.dot((output-y_train),
X_train))

    # Calculate MSE
    loss = np.mean((output - y_train) ** 2)
    hist_loss.append(loss)

    # Determine validation accuracy
    output_val = np.where(X_val.dot(weights)>0.5, 1, 0)
    accuracy = np.mean(np.where(y_val==output_val, 1, 0))
    hist_accuracy.append(accuracy)
```

8. We've saved the training loss and validation accuracy so that we can plot them:

```
fig = plt.figure(figsize=(8, 4))
a = fig.add_subplot(1,2,1)
imgplot = plt.plot(hist_loss)
plt.xlabel('epochs')
a.set_title('Training loss')

a=fig.add_subplot(1,2,2)
imgplot = plt.plot(hist_accuracy)
plt.xlabel('epochs')
a.set_title('Validation Accuracy')
plt.show()
```

In the following screenshot, the resulting training loss and validation accuracy are shown:

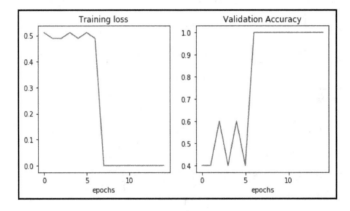

Figure 2.3: Training loss and validation accuracy

Implementing a single-layer neural network

Now we can move on to **neural networks**. We will start by implementing the simplest form of a neural network: a single-layer neural network. The difference from a perceptron is that the computations are done by multiple units (neurons), hence a network. As you may expect, adding more units will increase the number of problems that can be solved. The units perform their computations separately and are stacked in a layer; we call this layer the **hidden layer**. Therefore, we call the units stacked in this layer the **hidden units**. For now, we will only consider a single hidden layer. The output layer performs as a perceptron. This time, as input we have the hidden units in the hidden layer instead of the input variables:

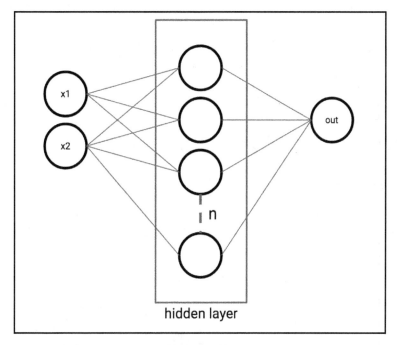

Figure 2.4: Single-layer neural network with two input variables, *n* hidden units, and a single output unit

In our implementation of the perceptron, we've used a unit step function to determine the class. In the next recipe, we will use a non-linear activation function sigmoid for the hidden units and the output function. By replacing the step function with a non-linear activation function, the network will be able to uncover non-linear patterns as well. More on this later in the *Activation functions* section. In the backward pass, we use the derivative of the sigmoid to update the weights.

In the following recipe, we will classify two non-linearly separable classes with NumPy.

How to do it...

1. Import libraries and dataset:

```
import numpy as np
from sklearn.model_selection import train_test_split
import matplotlib.pyplot as plt
# We will be using make_circles from scikit-learn
from sklearn.datasets import make_circles

SEED = 2017
```

2. First, we need to create the training data:

```
# We create an inner and outer circle
X, y = make_circles(n_samples=400, factor=.3, noise=.05,
random_state=2017)
outer = y == 0
inner = y == 1
```

3. Let's plot the data to show the two classes:

```
plt.title("Two Circles")
plt.plot(X[outer, 0], X[outer, 1], "ro")
plt.plot(X[inner, 0], X[inner, 1], "bo")
plt.show()
```

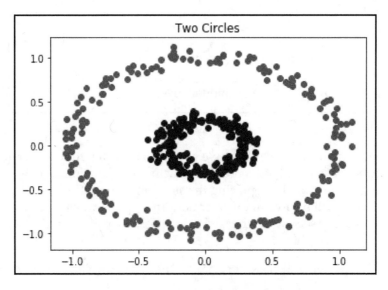

Figure 2.5: Example of non-linearly separable data

4. We normalize the data to make sure the center of both circles is *(1,1)*:

```
X = X+1
```

5. To determine the performance of our algorithm we split our data:

```
X_train, X_val, y_train, y_val = train_test_split(X, y,
test_size=0.2, random_state=SEED)
```

6. A linear activation function won't work in this case, so we'll be using a `sigmoid` function:

```
def sigmoid(x):
  return 1 / (1 + np.exp(-x))
```

7. Next, we define the hyperparameters:

```
n_hidden = 50 # number of hidden units
n_epochs = 1000
learning_rate = 1
```

8. Initialize the weights and other variables:

```
# Initialise weights
weights_hidden = np.random.normal(0.0, size=(X_train.shape[1],
n_hidden))
weights_output = np.random.normal(0.0, size=(n_hidden))

hist_loss = []
hist_accuracy = []
```

9. Run the single-layer neural network and output the statistics:

```
for e in range(n_epochs):
  del_w_hidden = np.zeros(weights_hidden.shape)
  del_w_output = np.zeros(weights_output.shape)

  # Loop through training data in batches of 1
  for x_, y_ in zip(X_train, y_train):
   # Forward computations
   hidden_input = np.dot(x_, weights_hidden)
   hidden_output = sigmoid(hidden_input)
   output = sigmoid(np.dot(hidden_output, weights_output))

   # Backward computations
   error = y_ - output
   output_error = error * output * (1 - output)
   hidden_error = np.dot(output_error, weights_output) *
hidden_output
                    * (1 - hidden_output)
   del_w_output += output_error * hidden_output
```

```
        del_w_hidden += hidden_error * x_[:, None]

    # Update weights
    weights_hidden += learning_rate * del_w_hidden / X_train.shape[0]
    weights_output += learning_rate * del_w_output / X_train.shape[0]

    # Print stats (validation loss and accuracy)
    if e % 100 == 0:
      hidden_output = sigmoid(np.dot(X_val, weights_hidden))
      out = sigmoid(np.dot(hidden_output, weights_output))
      loss = np.mean((out - y_val) ** 2)
      # Final prediction is based on a threshold of 0.5
      predictions = out > 0.5
      accuracy = np.mean(predictions == y_val)
      print("Epoch: ", '{:>4}'.format(e),
            "; Validation loss: ", '{:>6}'.format(loss.round(4)),
            "; Validation accuracy: ",
    '{:>6}'.format(accuracy.round(4)))
```

In the following screenshot, the output during training is shown:

```
Epoch:      0 ; Validation loss:   0.4194 ; Validation accuracy:      0.3
Epoch:    100 ; Validation loss:   0.2034 ; Validation accuracy:   0.8167
Epoch:    200 ; Validation loss:   0.1519 ; Validation accuracy:   0.8667
Epoch:    300 ; Validation loss:   0.1165 ; Validation accuracy:      0.9
Epoch:    400 ; Validation loss:   0.0926 ; Validation accuracy:     0.95
Epoch:    500 ; Validation loss:   0.0761 ; Validation accuracy:      1.0
Epoch:    600 ; Validation loss:   0.0643 ; Validation accuracy:      1.0
Epoch:    700 ; Validation loss:   0.0555 ; Validation accuracy:      1.0
Epoch:    800 ; Validation loss:   0.0488 ; Validation accuracy:      1.0
Epoch:    900 ; Validation loss:   0.0436 ; Validation accuracy:      1.0
```

Figure 2.6: Training statistics

Building a multi-layer neural network

What we've created in the previous recipe is actually the simplest form of an FNN: a neural network where the information flows only in one direction. For our next recipe, we will extend the number of hidden layers from one to multiple layers. Adding additional layers increases the power of a network to learn complex non-linear patterns.

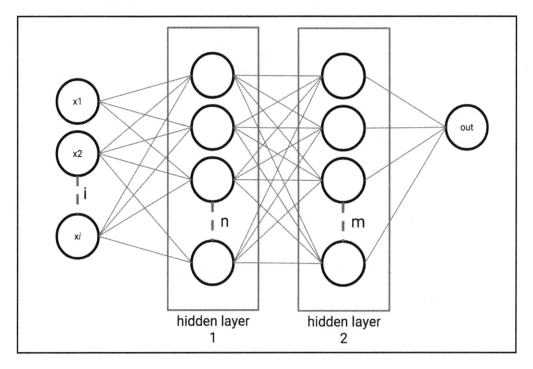

Figure 2.7: Two-layer neural network with *i* input variables, *n* hidden units, and *m* hidden units respectively, and a single output unit

As you can see in *Figure 2-7*, by adding an additional layer the number of connections (weights), also called trainable parameters, increases exponentially. In the next recipe, we will create a network with two hidden layers to predict wine quality. This is a regression task, so we will be using a linear activation for the output layer. For the hidden layers, we use ReLU activation functions. This recipe uses the Keras framework to implement the feed-forward network.

How to do it...

1. We start by import the libraries as follows:

```
import numpy as np
import pandas as pd
from sklearn.model_selection import train_test_split

from keras.models import Sequential
from keras.layers import Dense
from keras.callbacks import EarlyStopping, ModelCheckpoint
```

```
from keras.optimizers import Adam

from sklearn.preprocessing import StandardScaler

SEED = 2017
```

2. Load dataset:

```
data = pd.read_csv('Data/winequality-red.csv', sep=';')
y = data['quality']
X = data.drop(['quality'], axis=1)
```

3. Split data for training and testing:

```
X_train, X_test, y_train, y_test = train_test_split(X, y,
test_size=0.2, random_state=SEED)
```

4. Print average quality and first rows of training set:

```
print('Average quality training set:
{:.4f}'.format(y_train.mean()))
X_train.head()
```

In the following screenshot, we can see an example of the output of the training data:

```
Average quality training set:   5.623143
```

	fixed acidity	volatile acidity	citric acid	residual sugar	chlorides	free sulfur dioxide	total sulfur dioxide	density	pH	sulphates	alcohol
0	7.4	0.70	0.00	1.9	0.076	11.0	34.0	0.9978	3.51	0.56	9.4
1	7.8	0.88	0.00	2.6	0.098	25.0	67.0	0.9968	3.20	0.68	9.8
2	7.8	0.76	0.04	2.3	0.092	15.0	54.0	0.9970	3.26	0.65	9.8
3	11.2	0.28	0.56	1.9	0.075	17.0	60.0	0.9980	3.16	0.58	9.8
4	7.4	0.70	0.00	1.9	0.076	11.0	34.0	0.9978	3.51	0.56	9.4

Figure 2-8: Training data

5. An important next step is to normalize the input data:

```
scaler = StandardScaler().fit(X_train)
X_train = pd.DataFrame(scaler.transform(X_train))
X_test = pd.DataFrame(scaler.transform(X_test))
```

6. Determine baseline predictions:

```
# Predict the mean quality of the training data for each validation
input
print('MSE:', np.mean((y_test - ([y_train.mean()] *
y_test.shape[0])) ** 2).round(4))
## MSE: 0.594
```

7. Now, let's build our neural network by defining the network architecture:

```
model = Sequential()
# First hidden layer with 100 hidden units
model.add(Dense(200, input_dim=X_train.shape[1],
activation='relu'))
# Second hidden layer with 50 hidden units
model.add(Dense(25, activation='relu'))
# Output layer
model.add(Dense(1, activation='linear'))
# Set optimizer
opt = Adam()
# Compile model
model.compile(loss='mse', optimizer=opt, metrics=['accuracy'])
```

8. Let's define the callback for early stopping and saving the best model:

```
callbacks = [
            EarlyStopping(monitor='val_acc', patience=20,
verbose=2),
ModelCheckpoint('checkpoints/multi_layer_best_model.h5',
monitor='val_acc', save_best_only=True, verbose=0)
            ]
```

9. Run the model with a batch size of 64, 5,000 epochs, and a validation split of 20%:

```
batch_size = 64
n_epochs = 5000
model.fit(X_train.values, y_train, batch_size=batch_size,
epochs=n_epochs, validation_split=0.2,
          verbose=2,
          callbacks=callbacks)
```

10. We can now print the performance on the test set after loading the optimal weights:

```
best_model = model
best_model.load_weights('checkpoints/multi_layer_best_model.h5')
best_model.compile(loss='mse', optimizer='adam',
```

```
              metrics=['accuracy'])

              # Evaluate on test set
              score = best_model.evaluate(X_test.values, y_test, verbose=0)
              print('Test accuracy: %.2f%%' % (score[1]*100))

              ## Test accuracy: 66.25%
              ## Benchmark accuracy on dataset 62.4%
```

 With a small dataset, it's advisable to retrain on the complete training set (without validation set) and increase the number of epochs proportional to the additional data. Another option, is to use cross-validation and average the results when making predictions.

Getting started with activation functions

If we only use linear activation functions, a neural network would represent a large collection of linear combinations. However, the power of neural networks lies in their ability to model complex nonlinear behavior. We briefly introduced the non-linear activation functions sigmoid and ReLU in the previous recipes, and there are many more popular nonlinear activation functions, such as **ELU**, **Leaky ReLU**, **TanH**, and **Maxout**.

There is no general rule as to which activation works best for the hidden units. Deep learning is a relatively new field and most results are obtained by trial and error instead of mathematical proofs. For the output unit, we use a single output unit and a linear activation function for regression tasks. For classification tasks with n classes, we use *n* output nodes and a softmax activation function. The softmax function forces the network to output probabilities between *0* and *1* for mutually exclusive classes and the probabilities sum up to *1*. For binary classification, we can also use a single output node and a sigmoid activation function to output probabilities.

Choosing the correct activation function for the hidden units can be crucial. In the backward pass, the updates are dependent on the derivative of the activation function. For deep neural networks, the gradients of the updated weights can go to zero in the first couple of layers (also known as the **vanishing gradients** problem) or can grow exponentially big (also known as the **exploding gradients** problem). This holds especially when activation functions have a derivative that only takes on small values (for example the sigmoid activation function) or activation functions that have a derivative that can take values that are larger than *1*.

Activation functions such as the ReLU prevents such cases. The ReLU has a derivative of *1* when the output is positive and is *0* otherwise. When using a ReLU activation function, a sparse network is generated with a relatively small number of activated connections. The loss that is passed through the network seems more useful in such cases. In some cases, the ReLU causes too many of the neurons to die; in such cases, you should try a variant such as Leaky ReLU. In our next recipe, we will compare the difference in results between a sigmoid and a ReLU activation function when classifying handwritten digits with a deep FNN.

How to do it...

1. Import the libraries as follows:

```
import numpy as np
import pandas as pd
from sklearn.model_selection import train_test_split
import matplotlib.pyplot as plt

from keras.models import Sequential
from keras.layers import Dense
from keras.utils import to_categorical
from keras.callbacks import Callback

from keras.datasets import mnist

SEED = 2017
```

2. Load the MNIST dataset:

```
(X_train, y_train), (X_val, y_val) = mnist.load_data()
```

3. Show an example of each label and print the count per label:

```
# Plot first image of each label
unique_labels = set(y_train)
plt.figure(figsize=(12, 12))

i = 1
for label in unique_labels:
 image = X_train[y_train.tolist().index(label)]
 plt.subplot(10, 10, i)
 plt.axis('off')
 plt.title("{0}: ({1})".format(label,
y_train.tolist().count(label)))
```

```
i += 1
_ = plt.imshow(image, cmap='gray')
plt.show()
```

We obtain the following result:

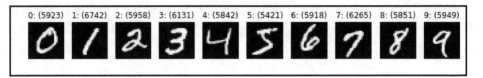

Figure 2.9: Examples of labels (and count) in the MNIST dataset

4. Preprocess the data:

```
# Normalize data
X_train = X_train.astype('float32')/255.
X_val = X_val.astype('float32')/255.

# One-Hot-Encode labels
y_train = np_utils.to_categorical(y_train, 10)
y_val = np_utils.to_categorical(y_val, 10)

# Flatten data - we threat the image as a sequential array of
values
X_train = np.reshape(X_train, (60000, 784))
X_val = np.reshape(X_val, (10000, 784))
```

5. Define the model with the sigmoid activation function:

```
model_sigmoid = Sequential()
model_sigmoid.add(Dense(700, input_dim=784, activation='sigmoid'))
model_sigmoid.add(Dense(700, activation='sigmoid'))
model_sigmoid.add(Dense(700, activation='sigmoid'))
model_sigmoid.add(Dense(700, activation='sigmoid'))
model_sigmoid.add(Dense(700, activation='sigmoid'))
model_sigmoid.add(Dense(350, activation='sigmoid'))
model_sigmoid.add(Dense(100, activation='sigmoid'))
model_sigmoid.add(Dense(10, activation='softmax'))

# Compile model with SGD
model_sigmoid.compile(loss='categorical_crossentropy',
optimizer='sgd', metrics=['accuracy'])
```

6. Define the model with the ReLU activation function:

```
model_relu = Sequential()
model_relu.add(Dense(700, input_dim=784, activation='relu'))
model_relu.add(Dense(700, activation='relu'))
model_relu.add(Dense(700, activation='relu'))
model_relu.add(Dense(700, activation='relu'))
model_relu.add(Dense(700, activation='relu'))
model_relu.add(Dense(350, activation='relu'))
model_relu.add(Dense(100, activation='relu'))
model_relu.add(Dense(10, activation='softmax'))

# Compile model with SGD
model_relu.compile(loss='categorical_crossentropy',
optimizer='sgd', metrics=['accuracy'])
```

7. Create a callback function to store the loss values per batch:

```
class history_loss(cb.Callback):
 def on_train_begin(self, logs={}):
 self.losses = []

 def on_batch_end(self, batch, logs={}):
 batch_loss = logs.get('loss')
 self.losses.append(batch_loss)
```

8. Run models:

```
n_epochs = 10
batch_size = 256
validation_split = 0.2

history_sigmoid = history_loss()
model_sigmoid.fit(X_train, y_train, epochs=n_epochs,
batch_size=batch_size,
 callbacks=[history_sigmoid],
 validation_split=validation_split, verbose=2)

history_relu = history_loss()
model_relu.fit(X_train, y_train, epochs=n_epochs,
batch_size=batch_size,
 callbacks=[history_relu],
 validation_split=validation_split, verbose=2)
```

9. Plot losses:

```
plt.plot(np.arange(len(history_sigmoid.losses)), sigmoid,
label='sigmoid')
plt.plot(np.arange(len(history_relu.losses)), relu, label='relu')
plt.title('Losses')
plt.xlabel('number of batches')
plt.ylabel('loss')
plt.legend(loc=1)
plt.show()
```

This code gives us the following result:

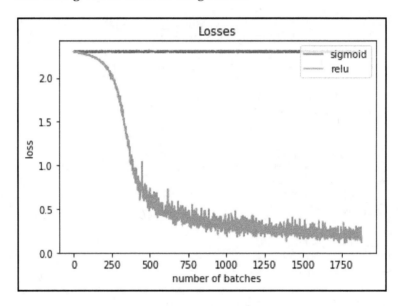

Figure 2.10: Losses for sigmoid and ReLU model

10. Extract the maximum weights of each model per layer:

```
w_sigmoid = []
w_relu = []
for i in range(len(model_sigmoid.layers)):
    w_sigmoid.append(max(model_sigmoid.layers[i].get_weights()[1]))
    w_relu.append(max(model_relu.layers[i].get_weights()[1]))
```

11. Plot the weights of both models:

```
fig, ax = plt.subplots()

index = np.arange(len(model_sigmoid.layers))
bar_width = 0.35

plt.bar(index, w_sigmoid, bar_width, label='sigmoid',
color='b', alpha=0.4)
plt.bar(index + bar_width, w_relu, bar_width, label='relu',
color='r', alpha=0.4)
plt.title('Weights across layers')
plt.xlabel('layer number')
plt.ylabel('maximum weight')
plt.legend(loc=0)

plt.xticks(index + bar_width / 2, np.arange(8))
plt.show()
```

We obtain the following result:

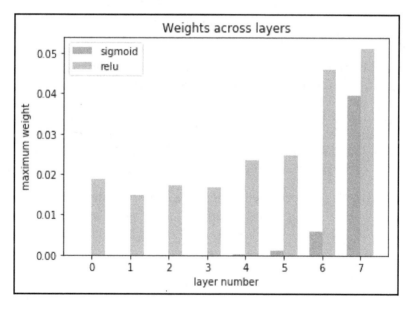

Figure 2.11: Maximum weights across layers for sigmoid and ReLU activation functions

In Chapter 3, *Convolutional Neural Networks*, we will show you how to get over 99% accuracy on the MNIST dataset.

Experiment with hidden layers and hidden units

The most commonly used layers in general neural networks are fully-connected layers. In fully-connected layers, the units in two successive layers are all pairwise connected. However, the units within a layer don't share any connections. As stated before, the connections between the layers are also called trainable parameters. The weights of these connections are trained by the network. The more connections, the more parameters and the more complex patterns can be modeled. Most state-of-the-art models have 100+ million parameters. However, a deep neural network with many layers and units takes more time to train. Also, with extremely deep models the time to infer predictions takes significantly longer (which can be problematic in a real-time environment). In the following chapters, we will introduce other popular layer types that are specific to their network types.

Picking the correct number of hidden layers and hidden units can be important. When using too few nodes, the model won't be able to pick up all the signals, resulting in a low accuracy and poor predictive performance (underfitting). Using too many nodes, the model will tend to overfit on the training data (see regularization for techniques to prevent overfitting) and won't be able to generalize well. Therefore, we always have to look at the performance on the validation data to find the right balance. In the next recipe, we will show an example of overfitting and output the number of trainable parameters.

Deep FNNs perform well if there is a lot of high dimensional training data available. For simple classification or regression tasks, often a single-layer neural network performs best.

How to do it...

1. Import libraries as follows:

```
import numpy as np
import pandas as pd
import matplotlib.pyplot as plt
from sklearn.model_selection import train_test_split
from sklearn.preprocessing import StandardScaler

from keras.models import Sequential
from keras.layers import Dense
from keras.optimizers import SGD

SEED = 2017
```

2. Load the dataset:

```
data = pd.read_csv('Data/winequality-red.csv', sep=';')
y = data['quality']
X = data.drop(['quality'], axis=1)
```

3. Split the dataset into training and testing:

```
X_train, X_test, y_train, y_test = train_test_split(X, y,
test_size=0.2, random_state=SEED)
```

4. Normalize the input data:

```
scaler = StandardScaler().fit(X_train)
X_train = pd.DataFrame(scaler.transform(X_train))
X_test = pd.DataFrame(scaler.transform(X_test))
```

5. Define the model and optimizer and compile:

```
model = Sequential()
model.add(Dense(1024, input_dim=X_train.shape[1],
activation='relu'))
model.add(Dense(1024, activation='relu'))
model.add(Dense(512, activation='relu'))
model.add(Dense(512, activation='relu'))
# Output layer
model.add(Dense(1, activation='linear'))
# Set optimizer
opt = SGD()
# Compile model
model.compile(loss='mse', optimizer=opt, metrics=['accuracy'])
```

6. Set the hyperparameters and train the model:

```
n_epochs = 500
batch_size = 256

history = model.fit(X_train.values, y_train, batch_size=batch_size,
epochs=n_epochs, validation_split=0.2, verbose=0)
```

7. Predict on the test set:

```
predictions = model.predict(X_test.values)
print('Test accuracy:
{:f>2}%'.format(np.round(np.sum([y_test==predictions.flatten().roun
d()])/y_test.shape[0]*100, 2)))
```

8. Plot the training and validation accuracy:

```
plt.plot(np.arange(len(history.history['acc'])),
history.history['acc'], label='training')
plt.plot(np.arange(len(history.history['val_acc'])),
history.history['val_acc'], label='validation')
plt.title('Accuracy')
plt.xlabel('epochs')
plt.ylabel('accuracy ')
plt.legend(loc=0)
plt.show()
```

The following graph is obtained:

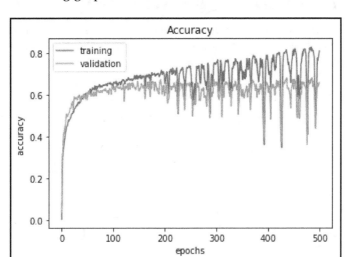

Figure 2.12: Training and validation accuracy

We should focus on the validation accuracy and use **early stopping** to stop the training after around 450 epochs. This results in the highest validation accuracy. in the sections *Improving generalization with regularization* and *A`dding dropout to prevent overfitting*, we will introduce techniques to prevent overfitting. By using these techniques, we can create deeper models without overfitting on the training data.

There's more...

Generally, we use a decreasing number of hidden units for FNN. This means that in the first hidden layer we use the most hidden units and we decrease the number of hidden units with each additional layer. Often, the number of hidden units is divided by two in each step. Keep in mind that this is a rule of thumb and the number of hidden layers and hidden units should be obtained by trial and error, based on the validation results.

In Chapter 13, *Network Internals* and Chapter 14, *Pretrained Models*, we will introduce techniques to optimize the number of hidden layers and hidden units.

Implementing an autoencoder

For autoencoders, we use a different network architecture, as shown in the following figure. In the first couple of layers, we decrease the number of hidden units. Halfway, we start increasing the number of hidden units again until the number of hidden units is the same as the number of input variables. The middle hidden layer can be seen as an encoded variant of the inputs, where the output determines the quality of the encoded variant:

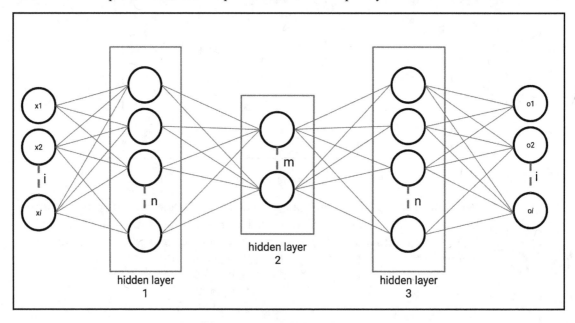

Figure 2.13: Autoencoder network with three hidden layers, with m < n

In the next recipe, we will implement an autoencoder in Keras to decode **Street View House Numbers** (**SVHN**) from 32 x 32 images to 32 floating numbers. We can determine the quality of the encoder by decoding back to 32 x 32 and comparing the images.

How to do it...

1. Import the necessary libraries with the following code:

```
import numpy as np
from matplotlib import pyplot as plt
import scipy.io
```

```
from keras.models import Sequential
from keras.layers.core import Dense
from keras.optimizers import Adam
```

2. Load the dataset and extract the data we need:

```
mat = scipy.io.loadmat('./data/train_32x32.mat')
mat = mat['X']
b, h, d, n = mat.shape
```

3. Preprocess the data:

```
# Grayscale
img_gray = np.zeros(shape =(n, b * h))

def rgb2gray(rgb):
    return np.dot(rgb[...,:3], [0.299, 0.587, 0.114])

for i in range(n):
    #Convert to greyscale
    img = rgb2gray(mat[:,:,:,i])
    img = img.reshape(1, 1024)
    img_gray[i,:] = img

# Normalize
X_train = img_gray/255.
```

4. Next, let's define the autoencoder network architecture:

```
img_size = X_train.shape[1]
model = Sequential()
model.add(Dense(256, input_dim=img_size, activation='relu'))
model.add(Dense(128, activation='relu'))
model.add(Dense(64, activation='relu'))
model.add(Dense(32, activation='relu'))

model.add(Dense(64, activation='relu'))
model.add(Dense(128, activation='relu'))
model.add(Dense(256, activation='relu'))
model.add(Dense(img_size, activation='sigmoid'))

opt = Adam()
model.compile(loss='binary_crossentropy', optimizer=opt)
```

5. Now, we can train the autencoder:

```
n_epochs = 100
batch_size = 512

model.fit(X_train, X_train, epochs=n_epochs, batch_size=batch_size,
shuffle=True, validation_split=0.2)
```

6. We want to see how our autoencoder performs on the training set:

```
pred = model.predict(X_train)
```

7. Let's plot some of the original images and their decoded versions:

```
n = 5
plt.figure(figsize=(15, 5))
for i in range(n):
    # display original
    ax = plt.subplot(2, n, i + 1)
    plt.imshow(mat[i].reshape(32, 32), cmap='gray')

    ax = plt.subplot(2, n, i + 1 + n)
    plt.imshow(pred[i].reshape(32, 32), cmap='gray')
plt.show()
```

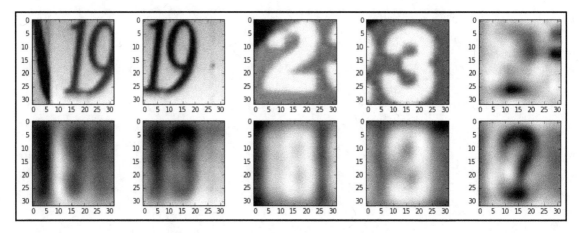

Figure 2.14: Example input and output of an autoencoder network for house numbers

In `Chapter 3`, *Convolutional Neural Networks*, we will show you how to implement a convolutional autoencoder for the SVHN dataset.

Tuning the loss function

While training a neural network for a supervised learning problem, the objective of the network is to minimize the loss function. The loss function — also known as error, cost function, or opimization function–compares the prediction with the ground truth during the forward pass. The output of this loss function is used to optimize the weights during the backward pass. Therefore, the loss function is crucial in training the network. By setting the correct loss function, we force the network to optimize towards the desired predictions. For example, for imbalanced datasets we need a different loss function.

In the previous recipes, we've used **mean squared error** (MSE) and categorical cross entropy as loss functions. There are also other popular loss functions, and another option is to create a custom loss function. A custom loss function gives the ability to optimize to the desired output. This will be more important when we will implement **Generative Adversarial Networks** (GANs). In the following recipe, we will train a network architecture with and without adjusted weights for the loss function to account for unbalanced classes.

How to do it...

1. Load the libraries with the following code:

```
import numpy as np
from matplotlib import pyplot as plt
from sklearn.metrics import confusion_matrix

from keras.datasets import mnist
from keras.models import Sequential
from keras.layers import Dense, Dropout
from keras.optimizers import Adam
from keras.callbacks import EarlyStopping
```

2. Import the MNIST dataset and create an imbalanced dataset with 9s and 4s:

```
(X_train, y_train), (X_test, y_test) = mnist.load_data()
# Extract all 9s and 100 examples of 4s
```

```
y_train_9 = y_train[y_train == 9]
y_train_4 = y_train[y_train == 4][:100]
X_train_9 = X_train[y_train == 9]
X_train_4 = X_train[y_train == 4][:100]
X_train = np.concatenate((X_train_9, X_train_4), axis=0)
y_train = np.concatenate((y_train_9, y_train_4), axis=0)

y_test_9 = y_test[y_test == 9]
y_test_4 = y_test[y_test == 4]
X_test_9 = X_test[y_test == 9]
X_test_4 = X_test[y_test == 4]
X_test = np.concatenate((X_test_9, X_test_4), axis=0)
y_test = np.concatenate((y_test_9, y_test_4), axis=0)
```

3. Normalize and flatten the data:

```
X_train = X_train.astype('float32')/255.
X_test = X_test.astype('float32')/255.
X_train = X_train.reshape(len(X_train), np.prod(X_train.shape[1:]))
X_test = X_test.reshape(len(X_test), np.prod(X_test.shape[1:]))
```

4. Turn the targets into a binary classification problem and print the counts:

```
y_train_binary = y_train == 9
y_test_binary = y_test == 9
print(np.unique(y_train_binary, return_counts=True))
```

5. Define the network architecture and compile:

```
model = Sequential()
model.add(Dense(512, input_dim=X_train.shape[1],
activation='relu'))
model.add(Dropout(0.75))
model.add(Dense(512, activation='relu'))
model.add(Dropout(0.75))
model.add(Dense(128, activation='relu'))
model.add(Dropout(0.75))
model.add(Dense(128, activation='relu'))
model.add(Dense(1, activation='sigmoid'))

opt = Adam()
model.compile(loss='binary_crossentropy', optimizer=opt,
metrics=['binary_accuracy'])
```

6. We will create a callback function to use early stopping:

```
callbacks = [EarlyStopping(monitor='val_loss', patience=5)]
```

7. Define the loss weights per class:

```
class_weight_equal = {False : 1., True: 1}
class_weight_imbalanced = {False : 100, True: 1}
```

8. Train the model with equal weights for both classes:

```
n_epochs = 1000
batch_size = 512
validation_split = 0.01

model.fit(X_train, y_train_binary, epochs=n_epochs,
batch_size=batch_size, shuffle=True,
validation_split=validation_split, class_weight=class_weight_equal,
        callbacks=callbacks, verbose=0
)
```

9. Test on the test set and output the confusion matrix:

```
preds_equal = model.predict(X_test)
confusion_matrix(y_test_binary, np.round(preds_equal),
labels=[True, False])

#array([[1009, 0],
# [ 982, 0]])
```

10. Next, we train with imbalanced weights and test on the test set:

```
model.compile(loss='binary_crossentropy', optimizer='rmsprop',
metrics=['binary_accuracy'])

model.fit(X_train, y_train_binary, epochs=n_epochs,
        batch_size=batch_size, shuffle=True,
validation_split=validation_split,
class_weight=class_weight_imbalanced,
        callbacks=callbacks, verbose=0
        )

preds_imbalanced = model.predict(X_test)
confusion_matrix(y_test_binary, np.round(preds_imbalanced),
labels=[True, False])

#array([[1009, 3],
# [ 546, 436]])
```

Experimenting with different optimizers

The most popular and well known optimizer is **Stochastic Gradient Descent (SGD)**. This technique is widely used in other machine learning models as well. SGD is a method to find minima or maxima by iteration. There are many popular variants of SGD that try to speed up convergence and less tuning by using an adaptive learning rate. The following table is an overview of the most commonly used optimizers in deep learning:

Optimizer	Hyperparameters	Comments
SGD	Learning rate, decay	+ Learning rate directly impacts performance (smaller learning rate avoids local minima) - Requires more manual tuning - Slow convergence
AdaGrad	Learning rate, epsilon, decay	+ Adaptive learning rate for all parameters (well suited for sparse data) - Learning rate becomes too small and stops learning
AdaDelta	Learning rate, rho, epsilon, decay	+ Faster convergence at start - Slows down near minimum
Adam	Learning rate, beta 1, beta 2, epsilon, decay	+ Adaptive learning rate and momentum for all parameters
RMSprop	Learning rate, rho, epsilon, decay	+- Similar to AdaDelta, but better for nonconvex problems
Momentum	Learning rate, momentum, decay	+ Faster convergence + Decreases movement in wrong direction - Oscillate around the minimum if momentum is too big
Nesterov Accelerated Gradient (NAG)	Learning rate, momentum, decay	+- Similar to momentum, but slows down earlier

The choice of the optimizer is arbitrary and largely depends on the users ability to tune the optimizer. There is no best solution that performs best for all problems. SGD gives the user the ability to avoid local optima by picking a small learning rate, but the downside is that the training time takes significantly longer. In the following recipe, we will train our network with different optimizers and compare the results.

How to do it...

1. Load the libraries:

```
import numpy as np
import pandas as pd

from sklearn.model_selection import train_test_split
from keras.models import Sequential
from keras.layers import Dense, Dropout
from keras.callbacks import EarlyStopping, ModelCheckpoint
from keras.optimizers import SGD, Adadelta, Adam, RMSprop, Adagrad,
Nadam, Adamax
```

2. Import the dataset and extract the target variable:

```
data = pd.read_csv('../Data/winequality-red.csv', sep=';')
y = data['quality']
X = data.drop(['quality'], axis=1)
```

3. Split the dataset for training, validation, and testing:

```
X_train, X_test, y_train, y_test = train_test_split(X, y,
test_size=0.2, random_state=2017)
X_train, X_val, y_train, y_val = train_test_split(X_train, y_train,
test_size=0.2, random_state=2017)
```

4. Define a function that creates the model:

```
def create_model(opt):
model = Sequential()
model.add(Dense(100, input_dim=X_train.shape[1],
activation='relu'))
model.add(Dense(50, activation='relu'))
model.add(Dense(25, activation='relu'))
model.add(Dense(10, activation='relu'))
model.add(Dense(1, activation='linear'))
return model
```

5. Create a function that defines `callbacks` we will be using during training:

```
def create_callbacks(opt):
callbacks = [
EarlyStopping(monitor='val_acc', patience=200, verbose=2),
ModelCheckpoint('best_model_' + opt + '.h5', monitor='val_acc',
save_best_only=True, verbose=0)
]
return callbacks
```

6. Create a `dict` of the optimizers we want to try:

```
opts = dict({
'sgd': SGD(),
 'sgd-0001': SGD(lr=0.0001, decay=0.00001),
 'adam': Adam(),
 'adadelta': Adadelta(),
 'rmsprop': RMSprop(),
 'rmsprop-0001': RMSprop(lr=0.0001),
 'nadam': Nadam(),
 'adamax': Adamax()
})
```

7. Train our networks and store `results`:

```
results = []
# Loop through the optimizers
for opt in opts:
 model = create_model(opt)
 callbacks = create_callbacks(opt)
 model.compile(loss='mse', optimizer=opts[opt],
metrics=['accuracy'])
 hist = model.fit(X_train.values, y_train, batch_size=128,
epochs=5000,
   validation_data=(X_val.values, y_val),
   verbose=0,
   callbacks=callbacks)
 best_epoch = np.argmax(hist.history['val_acc'])
 best_acc = hist.history['val_acc'][best_epoch]
 best_model = create_model(opt)
 # Load the model weights with the highest validation accuracy
 best_model.load_weights('best_model_' + opt + '.h5')
 best_model.compile(loss='mse', optimizer=opts[opt],
metrics=['accuracy'])
 score = best_model.evaluate(X_test.values, y_test, verbose=0)
 results.append([opt, best_epoch, best_acc, score[1]])
```

8. Compare the results:

```
res = pd.DataFrame(results)
res.columns = ['optimizer', 'epochs', 'val_accuracy',
'test_accuracy']
res
```

We obtain the following result:

	optimizer	epochs	val_accuracy	test_accuracy
0	sgd-0001	106	0.519531	0.53750
1	adam	112	0.589844	0.61250
2	sgd	0	0.000000	0.00000
3	adamax	213	0.578125	0.58750
4	rmsprop	600	0.597656	0.61250
5	adadelta	109	0.570312	0.58125
6	rmsprop-0001	38	0.539062	0.56250
7	nadam	84	0.597656	0.59375

Figure 2.15: Results of training with different optimizers on the Wine Quality dataset

In Chapter 12, *Hyperparameter Selection, Tuning, and Neural Network Learning* we will demonstrate how to use grid search for parameter tuning. Grid search can be used to find the right optimizer (in combination with other hyperparameters) to tune you neural network.

Improving generalization with regularization

Overfitting on the training data is one of the biggest challenges of machine learning. There are many machine learning algorithms that are able to train on the training data by remembering all cases. In this scenario, the algorithm might not be able to generalize and make a correct prediction on new data. This is an especially big threat for deep learning, where neural networks have large numbers of trainable parameters. Therefore, it is extremely important to create a representative validation set.

In deep learning, the general advice when tackling new problems is to overfit as much as you can on the training data first. This ensures that your model is able to train on the training data and is complex enough. Afterwards, you should regularize as much as you can to make sure the model is able to generalize on unseen data (the validation set) as well.

Most of the techniques used to prevent overfitting can be placed under **regularization**. Regularization include all techniques in machine learning that explicitly reduce the test (thus generalization) error, sometimes at the expense of a higher training error. Such techniques can be in the form of adding restrictions on the parameter space. This assumes that a model with small weights is simpler than a model with large weights. In the following recipe, we will apply **L1 regularization** to prevent the model from overfitting.

How to do it...

1. First, load all libraries:

```python
import numpy as np
import pandas as pd
from matplotlib import pyplot as plt

from keras.models import Sequential
from keras.layers import Dense, Dropout
from keras import regularizers
```

2. Import the data and extract the features:

```python
data = pd.read_csv('Data/bike-sharing/hour.csv')
# Feature engineering
ohe_features = ['season', 'weathersit', 'mnth', 'hr', 'weekday']
for feature in ohe_features:
    dummies = pd.get_dummies(data[feature], prefix=feature,
drop_first=False)
    data = pd.concat([data, dummies], axis=1)

drop_features = ['instant', 'dteday', 'season', 'weathersit',
                 'weekday', 'atemp', 'mnth', 'workingday', 'hr',
'casual', 'registered']
data = data.drop(drop_features, axis=1)
```

3. Normalize numerical data:

```
norm_features = ['cnt', 'temp', 'hum', 'windspeed']
scaled_features = {}
for feature in norm_features:
    mean, std = data[feature].mean(), data[feature].std()
    scaled_features[feature] = [mean, std]
    data.loc[:, feature] = (data[feature] - mean)/std
```

4. Split data for training, validation, and testing:

```
# Save the final month for testing
test_data = data[-31*24:]
data = data[:-31*24]
# Extract the target field
target_fields = ['cnt']
features, targets = data.drop(target_fields, axis=1),
data[target_fields]
test_features, test_targets = test_data.drop(target_fields,
axis=1), test_data[target_fields]
# Create a validation set (based on the last )
X_train, y_train = features[:-30*24], targets[:-30*24]
X_val, y_val = features[-30*24:], targets[-30*24:]
```

5. Define the network architecture:

```
model = Sequential()
model.add(Dense(250, input_dim=X_train.shape[1],
activation='relu'))
model.add(Dense(150, activation='relu'))
model.add(Dense(50, activation='relu'))
model.add(Dense(25, activation='relu'))
model.add(Dense(1, activation='linear'))

# Compile model
model.compile(loss='mse', optimizer='sgd', metrics=['mse'])
```

6. Train the network architecture on training data and use the validation set:

```
n_epochs = 4000
batch_size = 1024

history = model.fit(X_train.values, y_train['cnt'],
                validation_data=(X_val.values, y_val['cnt']),
                batch_size=batch_size, epochs=n_epochs, verbose=0
                )
```

7. Plot training and validation loss:

```
plt.plot(np.arange(len(history.history['loss'])),
history.history['loss'], label='training')
plt.plot(np.arange(len(history.history['val_loss'])),
history.history['val_loss'], label='validation')
plt.title('Overfit on Bike Sharing dataset')
plt.xlabel('epochs')
plt.ylabel('loss')
plt.legend(loc=0)
plt.show()
```

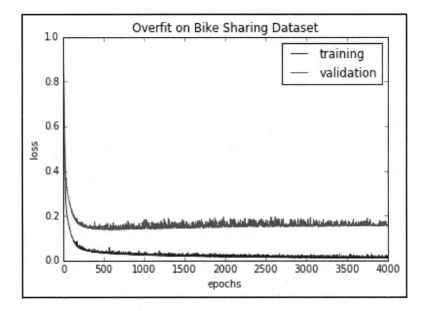

Figure 2.16: Model overfits on training data (training loss shows slightly increasing trend after 1000 epochs)

8. We also plot the minimum loss and after how many epochs this minimum has been reached:

```
print('Minimum loss: ', min(history.history['val_loss']),
        '\nAfter ', np.argmin(history.history['val_loss']), '
epochs')

# Minimum loss: 0.140975862741
# After 730 epochs
```

9. Define the network architecture with **L2 regularization**:

```
model_reg = Sequential()
model_reg.add(Dense(250, input_dim=X_train.shape[1],
activation='relu',
          kernel_regularizer=regularizers.l2(0.005)))
model_reg.add(Dense(150, activation='relu'))
model_reg.add(Dense(50, activation='relu'))
model_reg.add(Dense(25, activation='relu',
          kernel_regularizer=regularizers.l2(0.005)))
model_reg.add(Dense(1, activation='linear'))

# Compile model
model_reg.compile(loss='mse', optimizer='sgd', metrics=['mse'])
```

10. Train the adjusted network:

```
hist_reg = model_reg.fit(X_train.values, y_train['cnt'],
validation_data=(X_val.values, y_val['cnt']),
              batch_size=1024, nb_epoch=4000, verbose=0
              )
```

11. Plot the results:

```
plt.plot(np.arange(len(history_reg.history['loss'])),
history_reg.history['loss'], label='training')
plt.plot(np.arange(len(history_reg.history['val_loss'])),
history_reg.history['val_loss'], label='validation')
plt.title('Use regularisation for Bike Sharing dataset')
plt.xlabel('epochs')
plt.ylabel('loss')
plt.legend(loc=0)
plt.show()
```

We obtain the following result:

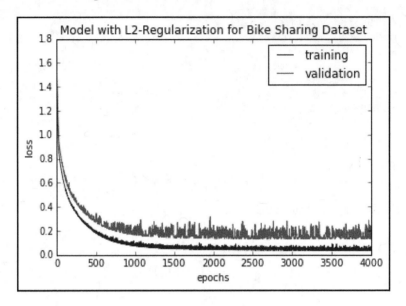

Figure 2.17: Model with L2 regularization to prevent overfitting

12. We also print the statistics of our model with regularisation:

```
print('Minimum loss: ', min(history_reg.history['val_loss']),
      '\nAfter ', np.argmin(history_reg.history['val_loss']), '
epochs')

# Minimum loss: 0.13514482975
# After 3647 epochs
```

Adding dropout to prevent overfitting

Another popular method for regularization is dropout. A dropout forces a neural network to learn multiple independent representations by randomly removing connections between neurons in the learning phase. For example, when using a dropout of 0.5, the network has to see each example twice before the connection is learned. Therefore, a network with dropout can be seen as an ensemble of networks.

In the following recipe, we will improve a model that clearly overfits the training data by adding dropouts.

How to do it...

1. Import the libraries as follows:

```
import numpy as np
import pandas as pd
from sklearn.model_selection import train_test_split

from keras.models import Sequential
from keras.layers import Dense, Dropout
from keras.wrappers.scikit_learn import KerasRegressor
from sklearn.model_selection import cross_val_score
from sklearn.model_selection import KFold
from sklearn.preprocessing import StandardScaler
from sklearn.pipeline import Pipeline


import numpy as np
from matplotlib import pyplot as plt
```

2. Load the dataset and extract features:

```
data = pd.read_csv('../Data/Bike-Sharing-Dataset/hour.csv')
# Feature engineering
ohe_features = ['season', 'weathersit', 'mnth', 'hr', 'weekday']
for feature in ohe_features:
 dummies = pd.get_dummies(data[feature], prefix=feature,
drop_first=False)
 data = pd.concat([data, dummies], axis=1)

drop_features = ['instant', 'dteday', 'season', 'weathersit',
 'weekday', 'atemp', 'mnth', 'workingday', 'hr', 'casual',
'registered']
data = data.drop(drop_features, axis=1)
```

3. Normalize features:

```
norm_features = ['cnt', 'temp', 'hum', 'windspeed']
scaled_features = {}
for feature in norm_features:
 mean, std = data[feature].mean(), data[feature].std()
 scaled_features[feature] = [mean, std]
 data.loc[:, feature] = (data[feature] - mean)/std
```

4. Split the dataset for training, validation, and testing:

```
# Save the final month for testing
test_data = data[-31*24:]
data = data[:-31*24]

# Extract the target field
target_fields = ['cnt']
features, targets = data.drop(target_fields, axis=1),
data[target_fields]
test_features, test_targets = test_data.drop(target_fields,
axis=1), test_data[target_fields]

# Create a validation set (based on the last )
X_train, y_train = features[:-30*24], targets[:-30*24]
X_val, y_val = features[-30*24:], targets[-30*24:]
```

5. Define the model:

```
model = Sequential()
model.add(Dense(250, input_dim=X_train.shape[1],
activation='relu'))
model.add(Dense(150, activation='relu'))
model.add(Dense(50, activation='relu'))
model.add(Dense(25, activation='relu'))
model.add(Dense(1, activation='linear'))

# Compile model
model.compile(loss='mse', optimizer='sgd', metrics=['mse'])
```

6. Set the hyperparameters and train the model:

```
n_epochs = 1000
batch_size = 1024

history = model.fit(X_train.values, y_train['cnt'],
    validation_data=(X_val.values, y_val['cnt']),
    batch_size=batch_size, epochs=n_epochs, verbose=0
    )
```

7. Plot the training and validation losses:

```
plt.plot(np.arange(len(history.history['loss'])),
history.history['loss'], label='training')
plt.plot(np.arange(len(history.history['val_loss'])),
history.history['val_loss'], label='validation')
plt.title('Overfit on Bike Sharing dataset')
plt.xlabel('epochs')
```

```
plt.ylabel('loss')
plt.legend(loc=0)
plt.show()
```

The result obtained is shown as follows:

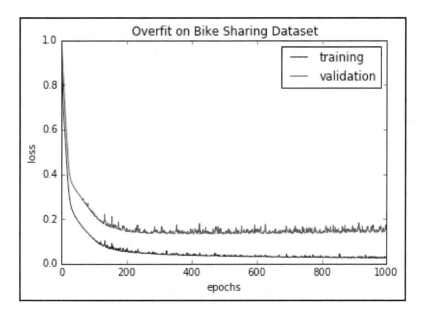

Figure 2.18: Model overfits on training data (training loss shows slightly increasing trend after 450 epochs)

8. Let's also print the minimum loss:

```
print('Minimum loss: ', min(hist.history['val_loss']),
  '\nAfter ', np.argmin(hist.history['val_loss']), ' epochs')

#Minimum loss: 0.132234960794
#After 426 epochs
```

9. Let's add dropouts to our network architecture to prevent overfitting:

```
model_drop = Sequential()
model_drop.add(Dense(250, input_dim=X_train.shape[1],
activation='relu'))
model_drop.add(Dropout(0.20))
model_drop.add(Dense(150, activation='relu'))
model_drop.add(Dropout(0.20))
model_drop.add(Dense(50, activation='relu'))
model_drop.add(Dropout(0.20))
model_drop.add(Dense(25, activation='relu'))
```

```
model_drop.add(Dropout(0.20))
model_drop.add(Dense(1, activation='linear'))

# Compile model
model_drop.compile(loss='mse', optimizer='sgd', metrics=['mse'])
```

10. Train our new model:

```
history_drop = model_drop.fit(X_train.values, y_train['cnt'],
    validation_data=(X_val.values, y_val['cnt']),
    batch_size=batch_size, epochs=n_epochs, verbose=0
    )
```

11. Plot our results:

```
plt.plot(np.arange(len(history_drop.history['loss'])),
history_drop.history['loss'], label='training')
plt.plot(np.arange(len(history_drop.history['val_loss'])),
history_drop.history['val_loss'], label='validation')
plt.title('Use dropout for Bike Sharing dataset')
plt.xlabel('epochs')
plt.ylabel('loss')
plt.legend(loc=0)
plt.show()
```

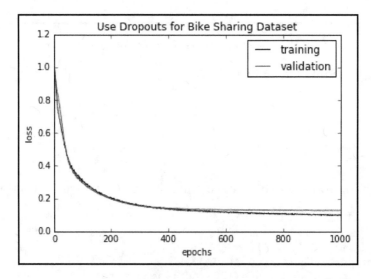

Figure 2.19: Model with dropouts to prevent overfitting

12. Finally, let's print our final statistics:

```
print('Minimum loss: ', min(history_drop.history['val_loss']),
 '\nAfter ', np.argmin(history_drop.history['val_loss']), '
epochs')

# Minimum loss: 0.126063346863
# After 998 epochs
```

3
Convolutional Neural Networks

In this chapter, we will focus on **convolutional neural networks** (**CNNs**) and cover the following topics:

- Getting started with filters and parameter sharing
- Applying pooling layers
- Optimizing with batch normalization
- Understanding padding and strides
- Experimenting with different types of initialization
- Implementing a convolutional autoencoder
- Applying a 1D CNN to text

Introduction

This chapter focuses on CNNs and their building blocks. In this chapter, we will provide recipes regarding techniques and optimizations used in CNNs. A convolutional neural network, also known as **ConvNet**, is a specific type of feed-forward neural network where the network has one or multiple convolutional layers. The convolutional layers can be complemented with fully connected layers. If the network only contains convolutional layers, we name the network architecture a **fully convolutional network** (**FCN**). Convolutional networks and computer vision are inseparable in deep learning. However, CNNs can be used in other applications, such as in a wide variety of NLP problems, as we will introduce in this chapter.

Getting started with filters and parameter sharing

Let's introduce the most important part of convolutional networks: convolutional layers. In a convolutional layer, we have blocks that convolve over the input data (like a sliding window). This technique shares parameters for each block in such a way that it can detect a feature within the block across the whole input data. The size of a block is called the kernel size or filter size. Summarized, the convolutional layer extracts local features within the total feature set. This is illustrated with an image as input data in the following figure:

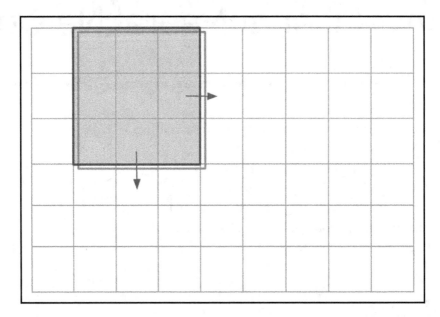

Figure 3.1: An example of a convolutional block with kernel size 3 x 3 and filter depth 2 (red and green) on a 9 x 6 x 1 input image

The input data can contain multiple different features, so this trick can be applied multiple times. This is called the number of filters or filter depth. Simply said, if we use a convolutional layer with five filters on image data, the convolutional block tries to learn five different features in the images, for example the facial features such as the nose, eyes, mouth, ears, and eyebrows. Although, these features are never explicitly specified, the network tries to learn valuable features itself.

 For convolutional neural networks, it's advised to use an increasing number of filters, for example double the number of filters for each convolutional layer: 32, 64, and 128.

In the following recipe, we will implement a convolutional neural network to classify the MNIST images that we used in the previous chapter.

How to do it...

1. Import all necessary libraries:

```
import numpy as np
from matplotlib import pyplot as plt

from keras.utils.np_utils import to_categorical
from keras.models import Sequential
from keras.layers.core import Dense, Dropout, Flatten
from keras.layers import Conv2D
from keras.optimizers import Adam
from keras.datasets import mnist
```

2. Load the `mnist` dataset:

```
from keras.datasets import mnist
(X_train, y_train), (X_test, y_test) = mnist.load_data()
```

3. Reshape the training data to represent one-channel image input:

```
img_rows, img_cols = X_train[0].shape[0], X_train[0].shape[1]
X_train = X_train.reshape(X_train.shape[0], img_rows, img_cols, 1)
X_test = X_test.reshape(X_test.shape[0], img_rows, img_cols, 1)
input_shape = (img_rows, img_cols, 1)
```

4. Normalize the input data:

```
X_train = X_train.astype('float32')/255.
X_test = X_test.astype('float32')/255.
```

5. One-hot encode the labels:

```
n_classes = len(set(y_train))
y_train = to_categorical(y_train, n_classes)
y_test = to_categorical(y_test, n_classes)
```

6. Define the CNN architecture:

```
model = Sequential()
model.add(Conv2D(32, kernel_size=(3, 3), activation='relu',
input_shape=input_shape))
```

```
model.add(Conv2D(64, kernel_size=(3, 3), activation='relu'))
model.add(Conv2D(128, kernel_size=(3, 3), activation='relu'))
model.add(Dropout(0.5))
model.add(Flatten())
model.add(Dense(128, activation='relu'))
model.add(Dropout(0.5))
model.add(Dense(n_classes, activation='softmax'))

opt = Adam()
model.compile(loss=losses.categorical_crossentropy,
              optimizer=opt,
metrics=['accuracy'])
```

7. Set network hyperparameters and the callback function:

```
batch_size = 128
n_epochs = 11

callbacks = [EarlyStopping(monitor='val_acc', patience=5)]
```

8. Train the model:

```
model.fit(X_train, y_train, batch_size=batch_size, epochs=n_epochs,
verbose=1, validation_split=0.2, callbacks=callbacks)
```

9. Show the results on the test set:

```
score = model.evaluate(X_test, y_test, verbose=0)
print('Test loss:', score[0])
print('Test accuracy:', score[1])
# Test loss: 0.0288668684929
# Test accuracy: 0.9927

# Extract predictions
preds = model.predict(X_test)

n_examples = 10
plt.figure(figsize=(15, 15))
for i in range(n_examples):
    ax = plt.subplot(2, n_examples, i + 1)
    plt.imshow(X_test[i, :, :, 0], cmap='gray')
    plt.title("Label: {}\nPredicted:
    {}".format(np.argmax(y_test[i]), np.argmax(preds[i])))
    plt.axis('off')
plt.show()
```

The output of is as follows:

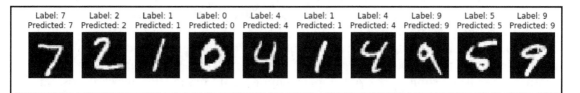

Figure 3.2: 10 examples of the truth labels, predicted labels, and input image

10. Let's also plot the misclassified images and their labels:

```
plt.        figure(figsize=(15, 15))

j=1
for i in range(len(y_test)):
    if(j==10):
        break
    label = np.argmax(y_test[i])
    pred = np.argmax(preds[i])
    if label != pred:
        ax = plt.subplot(2, n_examples, j + 1)
        plt.imshow(X_test[i, :, :, 0], cmap='gray')
        plt.title("Label: {}\nPredicted: {}".format(label, pred))
        plt.axis('off')
        j+=1
plt.show()
```

As we can see in our output, some of the misclassified examples are actually really hard to predict. For example, the 7th example with label 8 and predicted label 9:

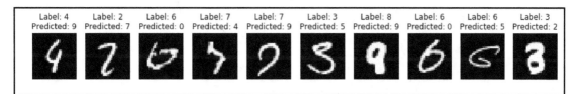

Figure 3.3: 10 examples of misclassified images

The results of this model are already quite nice. With a limited depth (three convolutional layers and one fully connected layer), and just around 11 epochs, we were able to get 99.30% accuracy on the test set. Our model has 16,230,794 trainable parameters and runs 1 epoch in around 45 seconds on a NVIDIA Tesla K80 GPU. A state-of-the-art research paper was reported to have obtained an error rate of 0.23 (which maps to an accuracy of 99.77%). The model in this paper used an ensemble of 35 deep neural networks, including image augmentation. With some of the additional techniques discussed later, we can boost our own test score for our model further.

Applying pooling layers

A popular optimization technique for CNNs is **pooling layers**. A pooling layer is a method to reduce the number of trainable parameters in a smart way. Two of the most commonly used pooling layers are average pooling and maximum (max) pooling. In the first, for a specified block size the inputs are averaged and extracted. For the latter, the maximum value within a block is extracted. These pooling layers provide a translational invariance. In other words, the exact location of a feature is less relevant. Also, by reducing the number of trainable parameters we limit the complexity of the network, which should prevent overfitting. Another benefit is that it will reduce the training and inference time significantly.

In the next recipe, we will add max pooling layers to the CNN we've implemented in the previous recipe and at the same time we will increase the number of filters in the convolutional layers.

How to do it...

1. Import all necessary libraries:

```
import numpy as np

from keras.utils import np_utils
from keras.models import Sequential
from keras.layers.core import Dense, Dropout, Flatten
from keras.callbacks import EarlyStopping, ModelCheckpoint
from keras.layers import Conv2D, MaxPooling2D
from keras.optimizers import Adam

from keras.callbacks import EarlyStopping
```

2. Load the `mnist` dataset:

```
from keras.datasets import mnist
(X_train, y_train), (X_test, y_test) = mnist.load_data()
```

3. Reshape the training data to represent grayscaled image input:

```
img_rows, img_cols = X_train[0].shape[0], X_train[0].shape[1]
X_train = X_train.reshape(X_train.shape[0], img_rows, img_cols, 1)
X_test = X_test.reshape(X_test.shape[0], img_rows, img_cols, 1)
input_shape = (img_rows, img_cols, 1)
```

4. Normalize the input data:

```
X_train = X_train.astype('float32')/255.
X_test = X_test.astype('float32')/255.
```

5. One-hot encode the labels:

```
n_classes = len(set(y_train))
y_train = np_utils.to_categorical(y_train, n_classes)
y_test = np_utils.to_categorical(y_test, n_classes)
```

6. Define the CNN architecture and output the network architecture:

```
model = Sequential()

model.add(Conv2D(64, kernel_size=(3, 3), activation='relu',
input_shape=input_shape))
model.add(MaxPooling2D(pool_size=(2, 2)))

model.add(Conv2D(128, kernel_size=(3, 3), activation='relu',
padding='same'))
model.add(MaxPooling2D(pool_size=(2, 2)))

model.add(Conv2D(256, kernel_size=(3, 3), activation='relu',
padding='same'))
model.add(MaxPooling2D(pool_size=(2, 2)))

model.add(Dropout(0.5))
model.add(Flatten())
model.add(Dense(128, activation='relu'))
model.add(Dropout(0.5))
model.add(Dense(n_classes, activation='softmax'))

model.compile(loss=losses.categorical_crossentropy,
optimizer='adam', metrics=['accuracy'])
model.summary()
```

7. Set the network hyperparameters and define the callback function:

```
batch_size = 128
n_epochs = 200

callbacks = [EarlyStopping(monitor='val_acc', patience=5)]
```

8. Train the model:

```
model.fit(X_train, y_train, batch_size=batch_size, epochs=n_epochs,
verbose=1, validation_split=0.2, callbacks=callbacks)
```

9. Show the results on the test set:

```
score = model.evaluate(X_test, y_test, verbose=0)
print('Test loss:', score[0])
print('Test accuracy:', score[1])

# Test loss: 0.0197916838032
# Test accuracy: 0.9955
```

By applying a max pooling layer after each convolutional layer, we were able to decrease our error rate to 0.45 (a decrease of 36% compared to our previous error rate of 0.70). Moreover, by applying max pooling the number of trainable parameters is reduced significantly to 665,994. As a result, 1 epoch takes just around 11 seconds.

Optimizing with batch normalization

Another well-known optimization technique for CNNs is batch normalization. This technique normalizes the inputs of the current batch before feeding it to the next layer; therefore, the mean activation for each batch is around zero and the standard deviation around one, and we can avoid internal covariate shift. By doing this, the input distribution of the data per batch has less effect on the network, and as a consequence the model is able to generalize better and train faster.

In the following recipe, we'll show you how to apply batch normalization to an image dataset with 10 classes (CIFAR-10). First, we train the network architecture without batch normalization to demonstrate the difference in performance.

How to do it...

1. Import all necessary libraries:

```python
import numpy as np
from matplotlib import pyplot as plt

from keras.utils import np_utils
from keras.models import Sequential
from keras.layers.core import Dense, Dropout, Activation, Flatten
from keras.callbacks import EarlyStopping
from keras.layers import Conv2D, MaxPooling2D
from keras.layers.normalization import BatchNormalization
```

2. Load the `cifar10` dataset:

```python
from keras.datasets import cifar10
(X_train, y_train), (X_val, y_val) = cifar10.load_data()
```

3. Normalize the input data:

```python
X_train = X_train.astype('float32')/255.
X_val = X_val.astype('float32')/255.
```

4. One-hot encode the labels:

```python
n_classes = 10
y_train = np_utils.to_categorical(y_train, n_classes)
y_val = np_utils.to_categorical(y_val, n_classes)
```

5. Define the CNN architecture and output the network architecture:

```python
input_shape = X_train[0].shape

model = Sequential()

model.add(Conv2D(32, kernel_size=(3, 3), input_shape=input_shape,
padding='same'))
model.add(Activation('relu'))
model.add(Conv2D(32, kernel_size=(3, 3), padding='same'))
model.add(Activation('relu'))
model.add(MaxPooling2D(pool_size=(2, 2), padding='same'))

model.add(Dropout(0.25))

model.add(Conv2D(64, kernel_size=(3, 3), padding='same'))
model.add(Activation('relu'))
```

```
model.add(Conv2D(64, kernel_size=(3, 3), padding='same'))
model.add(Activation('relu'))
model.add(MaxPooling2D(pool_size=(2, 2), padding='same'))

model.add(Dropout(0.25))

model.add(Conv2D(128, kernel_size=(3, 3), padding='same'))
model.add(Activation('relu'))
model.add(Conv2D(128, kernel_size=(3, 3), padding='same'))
model.add(Activation('relu'))
model.add(MaxPooling2D(pool_size=(2, 2), padding='same'))

model.add(Dropout(0.25))

model.add(Flatten())
model.add(Dense(512, activation='relu'))
model.add(Dropout(0.5))
model.add(Dense(128, activation='relu'))
model.add(Dense(n_classes, activation='softmax'))

model.compile(loss='categorical_crossentropy', optimizer='adam',
metrics=['accuracy'])
model.summary()
```

6. Define a callback to prevent overfitting:

```
callbacks = [EarlyStopping(monitor='val_acc', patience=5,
verbose=1)]
```

7. Set network hyperparameters:

```
batch_size = 256
n_epochs = 300
```

8. Next, we can train our first model:

```
history = model.fit(X_train, y_train, batch_size=batch_size,
epochs=n_epochs, verbose=1, validation_data=(X_val, y_val),
callbacks=callbacks)
```

9. Now, let's add batch normalization to our network architecture:

```
model_bn = Sequential()

model_bn.add(Conv2D(32, kernel_size=(3, 3),
input_shape=input_shape, padding='same'))
model_bn.add(Activation('relu'))
model_bn.add(BatchNormalization())
```

```
model_bn.add(Conv2D(32, kernel_size=(3, 3), padding='same'))
model_bn.add(Activation('relu'))
model_bn.add(BatchNormalization())
model_bn.add(MaxPooling2D(pool_size=(2, 2), padding='same'))

model_bn.add(Dropout(0.25))

model_bn.add(Conv2D(64, kernel_size=(3, 3), padding='same'))
model_bn.add(Activation('relu'))
model_bn.add(BatchNormalization())
model_bn.add(Conv2D(64, kernel_size=(3, 3), padding='same'))
model_bn.add(Activation('relu'))
model_bn.add(BatchNormalization())
model_bn.add(MaxPooling2D(pool_size=(2, 2), padding='same'))

model_bn.add(Dropout(0.25))

model_bn.add(Conv2D(128, kernel_size=(3, 3), padding='same'))
model_bn.add(Activation('relu'))
model_bn.add(BatchNormalization())
model_bn.add(Conv2D(128, kernel_size=(3, 3), padding='same'))
model_bn.add(Activation('relu'))
model_bn.add(BatchNormalization())
model_bn.add(MaxPooling2D(pool_size=(2, 2), padding='same'))

model_bn.add(Dropout(0.25))

model_bn.add(Flatten())
model_bn.add(Dense(512, activation='relu'))
model_bn.add(BatchNormalization())
model_bn.add(Dropout(0.5))
model_bn.add(Dense(128, activation='relu'))
model_bn.add(Dense(n_classes, activation='softmax'))

model_bn.compile(loss='categorical_crossentropy', optimizer='adam,
metrics=['accuracy'])
model_bn.summary()
```

10. Now we are ready to train the model that includes batch normalization as well:

```
history_bn = model_bn.fit(X_train, y_train,
        batch_size=batch_size,
        epochs=n_epochs,
        verbose=1,
        validation_data=(X_val, y_val), callbacks=callbacks)
```

11. Let's plot the validation accuracy of both models to compare the performance:

```
val_acc_bn = history_bn.history['val_acc']
val_acc = history.history['val_acc']
plt.plot(range(len(val_acc)), val_acc, label='CNN model')
plt.plot(range(len(val_acc_bn)), val_acc_bn, label='CNN model with
BN')
plt.title('Validation accuracy on Cifar10 dataset')
plt.xlabel('epochs')
plt.ylabel('accuracy')
plt.legend()
plt.show()
```

The results of both models are as follows:

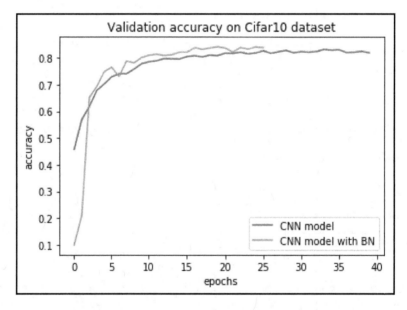

Figure 3.4: Comparing validation accuracy of a model with and without batch normalization

As we can see, the model with batch normalization takes the lead on validation accuracy after a couple of epochs and manages to stay ahead of the model without batch normalization, with a maximum validation accuracy of 84.16%, compared to a validation accuracy of 83.19% for the model without batch normalization. The model with batch normalization also converges faster (26 epochs vs 40 epochs). However, with 25 seconds per epoch, the model with batch normalization is slightly slower per epoch than the model without batch normalization (17 seconds).

Understanding padding and strides

Up until now, we've used the default strides of one for our networks. This indicates that the model convolves one input over each axis (step size of one). However, when a dataset contains less granular information on the pixel level, we can experiment with larger values as strides. By increasing the strides, the convolutional layer skips more input variables over each axis, and therefore the number of trainable parameters is reduced. This can speed up convergence without too much performance loss.

Another parameter that can be tuned is the padding. The padding defines how the borders of the input data (for example images) are handled. If no padding is added, only the border pixels (in the case of an image) will be included. So if you expect the borders to include valuable information, you can try to add padding to your data. This adds a border of dummy data that can be used while convolving over the data. A benefit of using padding is that the dimensions of the data are kept the same over each convolutional layer, which means that you can stack more convolutional layers on top of each other. In the following diagram, we can see an example of stride 1 with zero padding, and an example of stride 2 with padding:

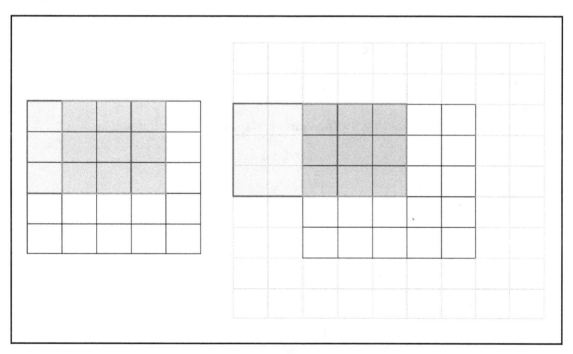

Figure 3.5: Left: an input image of 5 x 5 with stride 1 and zero padding; Right: an input image of 5 x 5 with stride 2 and same padding

There is no general rule for which value to choose for the padding and strides. It largely depends on the size and complexity of the data in combination with the potential pre-processing techniques used. Next, we will experiment with different settings for the strides and padding and compare the results of our models. The dataset we will use contains images of cats and dogs, and our task is to classify the animal.

How to do it...

1. Import all necessary libraries as follows:

```
import glob
import numpy as np
import cv2
from matplotlib import pyplot as plt
from sklearn.model_selection import train_test_split

from keras.utils import np_utils
from keras.models import Sequential
from keras.layers.core import Dense, Dropout, Activation, Flatten,
Lambda
from keras.optimizers import Adam
from keras.callbacks import EarlyStopping
from keras.layers import Conv2D, MaxPooling2D

SEED = 2017
```

2. Let's start with loading the filenames and outputting the training set sizes:

```
# Specify data directory and extract all file names for both
classes
DATA_DIR = 'Data/PetImages/'
cats = glob.glob(DATA_DIR + "Cat/*.jpg")
dogs = glob.glob(DATA_DIR + "Dog/*.jpg")

print('#Cats: {}, #Dogs: {}'.format(len(cats), len(dogs)))
# #Cats: 12500, #Dogs: 12500
```

3. To get a better understanding of the dataset, let's plot three examples of each class:

```
n_examples = 3
plt.figure(figsize=(15, 15))
i = 1
for _ in range(n_examples):
    image_cat = cats[np.random.randint(len(cats))]
```

```
    img_cat = cv2.imread(image_cat)
    img_cat = cv2.cvtColor(img_cat, cv2.COLOR_BGR2RGB)
    plt.subplot(3, 2, i)
    _ = plt.imshow(img_cat)
    i += 1
    image_dog = dogs[np.random.randint(len(dogs))]
    img_dog = cv2.imread(image_dog)
    img_dog = cv2.cvtColor(img_dog, cv2.COLOR_BGR2RGB)
    plt.subplot(3, 2, i)
    i += 1
    _ = plt.imshow(img_dog)
plt.show()
```

Figure 3.6: Example images of the labels cat and dog

4. Let's split the dataset in a training and validation set as follows:

```
dogs_train, dogs_val, cats_train, cats_val = train_test_split(dogs,
cats, test_size=0.2, random_state=SEED)
```

5. The training set is relatively large; we will be using a batch generator so that we don't have to load all images in memory:

```
def batchgen(cats, dogs, batch_size, img_size=50):
    # Create empty numpy arrays
    batch_images = np.zeros((batch_size, img_size, img_size, 3))
    batch_label = np.zeros(batch_size)

    # Custom batch generator
```

```
while 1:
    n = 0
    while n < batch_size:
        # Randomly pick a dog or cat image
        if np.random.randint(2) == 1:
            i = np.random.randint(len(dogs))
            img = cv2.imread(dogs[i])
            if img is None:
                break
            img = cv2.cvtColor(img, cv2.COLOR_BGR2RGB)
            # The images have different dimensions,
            # we resize all to 100x100
            img = cv2.resize(img, (img_size, img_size),
             interpolation = cv2.INTER_AREA)
            y = 1

        else:
            img = cv2.imread(cats[i])
            if img is None:
                break
            img = cv2.cvtColor(img, cv2.COLOR_BGR2RGB)
            img = cv2.resize(img, (img_size, img_size),
            interpolation = cv2.INTER_AREA)
            y = 0
        batch_images[n] = img
        batch_label[n] = y
        n+=1
    yield batch_images, batch_label
```

6. Next, we define a function that creates a model given parameters for the stride and padding:

```
def create_model(stride=1, padding='same', img_size=100):
    # Define architecture
    model = Sequential()
    model.add(Lambda(lambda x: (x / 255.) - 0.5,
    input_shape=(img_size, img_size, 3)))
    model.add(Conv2D(32, (3, 3), activation='relu',
    padding=padding, strides=stride))
    model.add(Conv2D(32, (3, 3), activation='relu',
    padding=padding, strides=stride))
    model.add(MaxPooling2D(pool_size=(2,2)))
    model.add(Dropout(0.5))
    model.add(Conv2D(64, (3, 3), activation='relu',
    padding=padding, strides=stride))
    model.add(Conv2D(64, (3, 3), activation='relu',
    padding=padding, strides=stride))
    model.add(Dropout(0.5))
```

```
model.add(Flatten())
model.add(Dense(64, activation='relu'))
model.add(Dropout(0.5))
model.add(Dense(1, activation='sigmoid'))
opt = Adam(0.001)
    model.compile(loss='binary_crossentropy', optimizer=opt,
    metrics=['binary_accuracy'])
return model
```

7. Now we can define a model for each setting, and we extract the number of trainable parameters:

```
img_size = 100

models = []
for stride in [1, 2]:
    for padding in ['same', 'valid']:
        model = create_model(stride, padding, img_size)
        pars = model.count_params()
        models.append(dict({'setting': '{}_{}'.format(stride,
                padding),
            'model': model,
            'parameters': pars
            }))
```

8. To output the scheme of a model, you can use the following:

```
models[0]['model'].summary()
```

9. To use early stopping, we define a callback as follows:

```
callbacks = [EarlyStopping(monitor='val_binary_accuracy',
patience=5)]
```

10. In the next step, we will train our models and store the results:

```
batch_size = 512
n_epochs = 500
validation_steps = round((len(dogs_val)+len(cats_val))/batch_size)
steps_per_epoch =
round((len(dogs_train)+len(cats_train))/batch_size)

train_generator = batchgen(dogs_train, cats_train, batch_size,
img_size)
val_generator = batchgen(dogs_val, cats_val, batch_size, img_size)

history = []
for i in range(len(models)):
```

```
    print(models[i])
    history.append(
        models[i]['model'].
        fit_generator(train_generator,
        steps_per_epoch=steps_per_epoch, epochs=n_epochs,
        validation_data=val_generator,
        validation_steps=validation_steps,
        callbacks=callbacks
                            )
    )
```

11. Let's visualize the results:

```
for i in range(len(models)):
    plt.plot(range(len(history[i].history['val_binary_accuracy'])),
history[i].history['val_binary_accuracy'],
label=models[i]['setting'])
    print('Max accuracy model {}: {}'.format(models[i]['setting'],
max(history[i].history['val_binary_accuracy'])))
plt.title('Accuracy on the validation set')
plt.xlabel('epochs')
plt.ylabel('accuracy')
plt.legend()
plt.show()
```

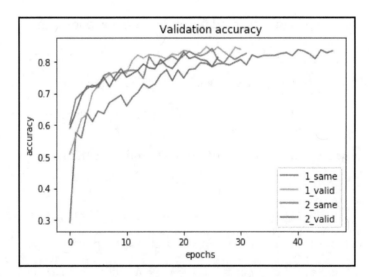

Figure 3.7: Performance comparison with different settings for padding and strides

By using a stride of 2, the number of trainable parameters are reduced significantly (from 10,305,697 to 102,561 when using padding). For this dataset, it shows that there is no performance loss by using a stride > 1. This is expected, because we use (resized) 100 x 100 x 3 images as input. Skipping a pixel in each direction shouldn't influence the performance too much.

Experimenting with different types of initialization

For CNNs, the initialization of the weights and biases can be extremely important. For very deep neural networks, some initialization techniques may lead to diminishing gradients caused by the magnitude of the gradient in the final layers. In the following recipe, we will show you how to use different initializations for a well-known network and demonstrate the difference in performance. By picking the right initialization, one can speed up convergence of a network. In the following recipe, we first initialize the weights and bias of the network with the popular Gaussian noise, with the mean equal to zero and a standard deviation of 0.01. Afterwards, we use Xavier initialization, both normal and uniform, and some other popular initialization distributions.

How to do it...

1. Import all necessary libraries as follows:

```
import glob
import numpy as np
import cv2
from matplotlib import pyplot as plt
from sklearn.model_selection import train_test_split

from keras.utils import np_utils
from keras import utils, losses, optimizers
from keras.models import Sequential
from keras.layers.core import Dense, Dropout, Activation, Flatten,
Lambda
from keras.callbacks import EarlyStopping, ModelCheckpoint
from keras.layers import Conv2D, MaxPooling2D

SEED = 2017
```

2. Let's start with loading the filenames and outputting the training set sizes:

```
# Specify data directory and extract all file names for both
classes
DATA_DIR = 'Data/PetImages/'
cats = glob.glob(DATA_DIR + "Cat/*.jpg")
dogs = glob.glob(DATA_DIR + "Dog/*.jpg")

print('#Cats: {}, #Dogs: {}'.format(len(cats), len(dogs)))
# #Cats: 12500, #Dogs: 12500
```

3. Next, we split the data in a training and validation set:

```
dogs_train, dogs_val, cats_train, cats_val =
train_test_split(dogs, cats, test_size=0.2, random_state=SEED)
```

4. The training set is relatively large; we will be using a batch generator so that we don't have to load all images in memory:

```
def batchgen(cats, dogs, batch_size, img_size=50):
    # Create empty numpy arrays
    batch_images = np.zeros((batch_size, img_size, img_size, 3))
    batch_label = np.zeros(batch_size)

    # Custom batch generator
    while 1:
        n = 0
        while n < batch_size:
            # Randomly pick a dog or cat image
            if np.random.randint(2) == 1:
                i = np.random.randint(len(dogs))
                img = cv2.imread(dogs[i])
                if img is None:
                    break
                img = cv2.cvtColor(img, cv2.COLOR_BGR2RGB)
                # The images have different dimensions, we
                #resize all to 100x100
                img = cv2.resize(img, (img_size, img_size),
                interpolation = cv2.INTER_AREA)
                y = 1

            else:
                i = np.random.randint(len(cats))
                img = cv2.imread(cats[i])
                if img is None:
                    break
                img = cv2.cvtColor(img, cv2.COLOR_BGR2RGB)
                img = cv2.resize(img, (img_size, img_size),
```

```
                    interpolation = cv2.INTER_AREA)
                y = 0
            batch_images[n] = img
            batch_label[n] = y
            n+=1
        yield batch_images, batch_label
```

5. Next, we define a function that creates a model, given parameters for the stride and padding:

```
def create_model(init_type='xavier', img_size=100):
    # Define architecture
    model = Sequential()
    model.add(Lambda(lambda x: (x / 255.) - 0.5,
    input_shape=(img_size, img_size, 3)))
    model.add(Conv2D(32, (3, 3), activation='relu',
    init=init_type))
    model.add(Conv2D(32, (3, 3), activation='relu',
    init=init_type))
    model.add(MaxPooling2D(pool_size=(2,2)))
    model.add(Dropout(0.5))
    model.add(Conv2D(64, (3, 3), activation='relu',
    init=init_type))
    model.add(Conv2D(64, (3, 3), activation='relu',
    init=init_type))

    model.add(Dropout(0.5))
    model.add(Flatten())
    model.add(Dense(64, activation='relu'))
    model.add(Dropout(0.5))
    model.add(Dense(1, activation='sigmoid'))

    sgd = optimizers.Adam()
    model.compile(loss='binary_crossentropy', optimizer=sgd,
        metrics=['binary_accuracy'])

    return model
```

6. Now we can define a model for each initialization type:

```
models = []
for init_type in ['random_uniform', 'glorot_normal',
'glorot_uniform', 'lecun_uniform', 'he_uniform']:
    model = create_model(init_type, img_size=50)
    models.append(dict({'setting': '{}'.format(init_type),
            'model': model
            }))
```

7. We want to use early stopping to prevent overfitting on the training data:

```
callbacks = [EarlyStopping(monitor='val_binary_accuracy',
  patience=3)]
```

8. In the next step, we will train our models and store the results:

```
batch_size = 512
n_epochs = 500
steps_per_epoch = 100
validation_steps = round((len(dogs_val)+len(cats_val))/batch_size)

train_generator = batchgen(dogs_train, cats_train, batch_size)
val_generator = batchgen(dogs_val, cats_val, batch_size)

history = []
for i in range(len(models)):
    print(models[i])
    history.append(
        models[i]['model'].
        fit_generator(train_generator,
        steps_per_epoch=steps_per_epoch, epochs=n_epochs,
        validation_data=val_generator,
        validation_steps=validation_steps, callbacks=callbacks)
    )
```

9. Let's visualize the results:

```
for i in range(len(models)):
    plt.plot(range(len(history[i].history['val_binary_accuracy'])),
history[i].history['val_binary_accuracy'],
label=models[i]['setting'])
    print('Max accuracy model {}: {}'.format(models[i]['setting'],
max(history[i].history['val_binary_accuracy'])))
plt.title('Accuracy on the validation set')
                    plt.xlabel('epochs')
plt.ylabel('accuracy')
plt.legend()
plt.show()
```

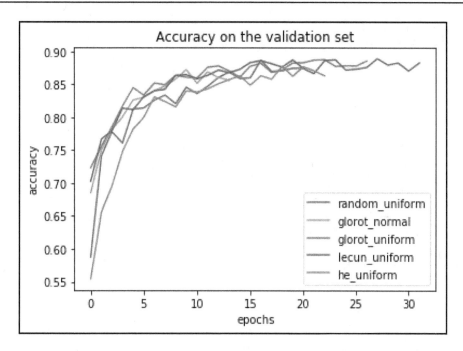

Figure 3.8: Performance comparison with different initialization settings for the weights

As you can see, the type of initialization of the weights can have an impact on the results. Testing all different initialization methods can be computer expensive, so is often not desired. For CNNs, the default settings of each framework often do a great job. For a 2D convolutional layer, the Glorot uniform distributed weights (also known as Xavier uniform initialization) are generally used as the default.

Implementing a convolutional autoencoder

In the previous chapter, we demonstrated how to implement an autoencoder for the `Street View House Numbers` dataset. We got some decent results, but the output could definitely be improved. In the following recipe, we will show how a convolutional autoencoder produces better outputs.

How to do it...

1. Let's start with importing the libraries as follows:

```
import numpy as np
import scipy.io

from matplotlib import pyplot as plt
from keras.utils import np_utils
from keras.models import Sequential, Input, Model
from keras.layers.core import Dense, Dropout, Activation, Reshape,
Flatten, Lambda
from keras.layers import Conv2D, MaxPooling2D, UpSampling2D
from keras.callbacks import EarlyStopping
```

2. Next, we load the dataset and extract the data we will use in this recipe:

```
mat = scipy.io.loadmat('Data/train_32x32.mat')
mat = mat['X']
b, h, d, n = mat.shape
```

3. Before feeding the data to our network, we pre-process the data:

```
#Convert all RGB-Images to greyscale
img_gray = np.zeros(shape =(n, b, h, 1))

def rgb2gray(rgb):
 return np.dot(rgb[...,:3], [0.299, 0.587, 0.114])

for i in range(n):
 #Convert to greyscale
 img = rgb2gray(mat[:,:,:,i])
 img = img.reshape(1, 32, 32, 1)
 img_gray[i,:] = img

# Normalize input
img_gray = img_gray/255.
```

4. We can now define our network architecture for the convolutional autencoder:

```
img_size = Input(shape=(b, h, 1))

x = Conv2D(16, (3, 3), activation='relu', padding='same')(img_size)
x = MaxPooling2D((2, 2), padding='same')(x)
x = Conv2D(8, (3, 3), activation='relu', padding='same')(x)
x = MaxPooling2D((2, 2), padding='same')(x)
x = Conv2D(8, (3, 3), activation='relu', padding='same')(x)
```

```
encoded = MaxPooling2D((2, 2), padding='same')(x)

x = Conv2D(8, (3, 3), activation='relu', padding='same')(encoded)
x = UpSampling2D((2, 2))(x)
x = Conv2D(8, (3, 3), activation='relu', padding='same')(x)
x = UpSampling2D((2, 2))(x)
x = Conv2D(16, (3, 3), activation='relu', padding='same')(x)
x = UpSampling2D((2, 2))(x)
decoded = Conv2D(1, (3, 3), activation='sigmoid',
padding='same')(x)

autoencoder = Model(img_size, decoded)
autoencoder.compile(optimizer='rmsprop',
loss='binary_crossentropy')#, metrics=['binary_accuracy'])

# Output summary of network
autoencoder.summary()
```

5. Next, we define the callback function for early stopping:

```
callbacks = EarlyStopping(monitor='val_loss', patience=5)
```

6. Let's define the hyperparameters and start training our network:

```
n_epochs = 1000
batch_size = 128

autoencoder.fit(
  img_gray, img_gray,
  epochs=n_epochs,
  batch_size=batch_size,
  shuffle=True, validation_split=0.2
     callbacks=callbacks
 )
```

7. Let's store the decoded images as follows:

```
pred = autoencoder.predict(img_gray)
```

8. Now, we can output some of the original images and corresponding decoded images:

```
n = 5
plt.figure(figsize=(15, 5))
for i in range(n):
 # display original
 ax = plt.subplot(2, n, i + 1)
 plt.imshow(mat[i].reshape(32, 32), cmap='gray')
```

```
ax = plt.subplot(2, n, i + 1 + n)
 plt.imshow(pred[i].reshape(32, 32), cmap='gray')
plt.show()
```

Our trained model outputs the following images:

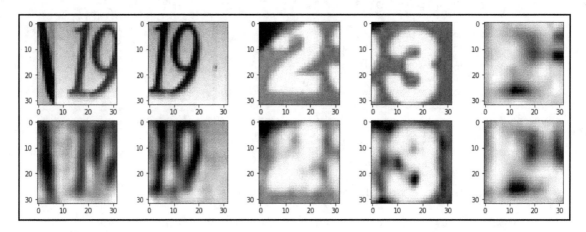

Figure 3.9: Examples of original and decoded images created with a convolutional autoencoder

Compared to the decoded images from the previous chapter, our output has improved significantly. In Chapter 6, *Generative Adversarial Networks*, we will introduce a different type of decoder-encoder network.

Applying a 1D CNN to text

So far, we've applied CNNs to image data. As stated in the introduction, CNNs can also be applied to other types of input data. In the following recipe, we will show how you can apply a CNN to textual data. More specifically, we will use the structure of CNNs to classify text. Unlike images, which are 2D, text has 1D input data. Therefore, we will be using 1D convolutional layers in our next recipe. The Keras framework makes it really easy to pre-process the input data.

How to do it...

1. Let's start with importing the libraries as follows:

```python
import numpy as np

from keras.preprocessing import sequence
from keras.models import Sequential
from keras.layers import Dense, Dropout, Activation
from keras.layers import Embedding
from keras.layers import Conv1D, GlobalMaxPooling1D
from keras.callbacks import EarlyStopping
from keras.datasets import imdb
```

2. We will be using the `imdb` dataset from keras; load the data with the following code:

```python
n_words = 1000
(X_train, y_train), (X_test, y_test) =
imdb.load_data(num_words=n_words)
print('Train seq: {}'.format(len(X_train)))
print('Test seq: {}'.format(len(X_train)))
```

3. Let's print an example output of the training and test data:

```python
print('Train example: \n{}'.format(X_train[0]))
print('\nTest example: \n{}'.format(X_test[0]))

# Note: the data is already preprocessed (words are mapped to
vectors)
```

4. By padding the sequences, we prepare our input for our network:

```python
# Pad sequences with max_len
max_len = 200
X_train = sequence.pad_sequences(X_train, maxlen=max_len)
X_test = sequence.pad_sequences(X_test, maxlen=max_len)
```

5. We are now ready to define our network architecture:

```
# Define network architecture and compile
model = Sequential()
model.add(Embedding(n_words, 50, input_length=max_len))
model.add(Dropout(0.5))
model.add(Conv1D(128, 3, padding='valid', activation='relu',
strides=1,))
model.add(GlobalMaxPooling1D())
model.add(Dense(250, activation='relu'))
model.add(Dropout(0.5))
model.add(Dense(1, activation='sigmoid'))

model.compile(loss='binary_crossentropy', optimizer='adam',
metrics=['accuracy'])
model.summary()
```

6. We define a callback function to prevent overfitting on the training data:

```
callbacks = [EarlyStopping(monitor='val_acc', patience=3)]
```

7. Let's define the hyperparameters and start training our network:

```
batch_size = 64
n_epochs = 100

model.fit(X_train, y_train, batch_size=batch_size, epochs=n_epochs,
validation_split=0.2, callbacks=callbacks)
```

8. Finally, we can check the performance of our trained network on the test set:

```
print('\nAccuracy on test set: {}'.format(model.evaluate(X_test,
y_test)[1]))

# Accuracy on test set: 0.873
```

The simple model used here is already able to classify the sentiment of text quite accurately, with an accuracy of 87.3% on the test set. In the next chapters, we will show you how to boost the performance of a text classifier further by combining a CNN with an RNN.

4
Recurrent Neural Networks

This chapter focuses on **recurrent neural networks** (**RNNs**). The following recipes are included in this chapter:

- Implementing a simple RNN
- Adding Long Short-Term Memory (LSTM)
- Using gated recurrent units (GRUs)
- Implementing bidirectional RNNs
- Character-level text generation

Introduction

In this chapter, we will introduce a new type of neural network. Before, we've only considered neural networks where the information flows through the network in one direction. Next, we will introduce recurrent neural networks. In these networks, data is processed the same way for every element in a sequence, and the output depends on the previous computations. This structure has proven to be very powerful for many applications, such as for **natural language processing** (**NLP**) and time series predictions. We will introduce the important building blocks that revolutionized how we process temporal or other forms of sequence data in neural networks.

A simple RNN unit is shown in *Figure 4.1*:

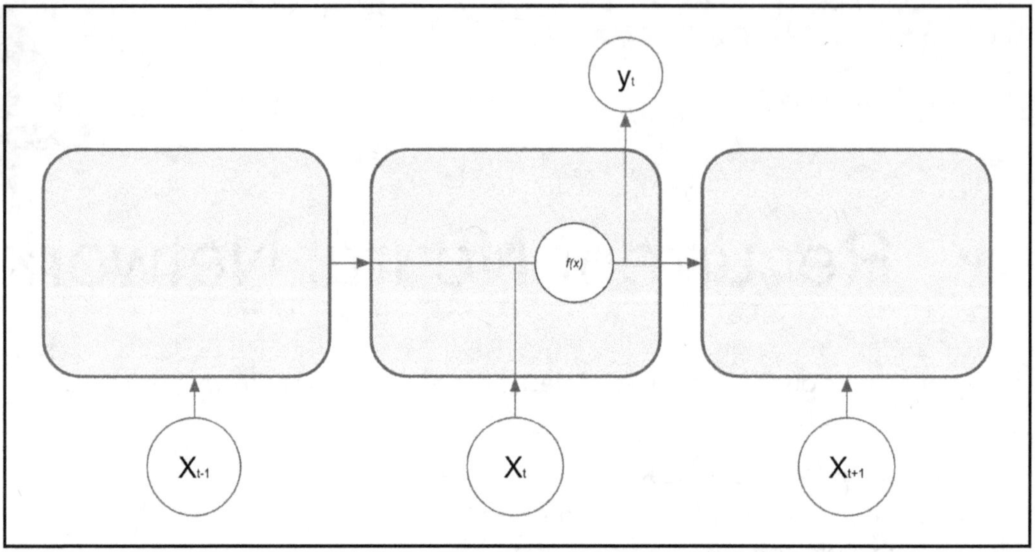

Figure 4.1: Example of the flow in an RNN unit

As we can see in the figure, the output of a RNN does not only depend on the current input X_t, but also on past inputs (X_{t-1}). Basically, this gives the network a type of memory. ;

There are multiple types of RNNs where the input and output dimension can differ. An RNN can have one input variable and multiple output variables (1-to-n, with $n > 1$), multiple input variables and one output variable (n-to-1, with $n > 1$), or multiple input and output variables (n-to-m, with $n,m > 1$). In this book, we will cover all variants.

Implementing a simple RNN

We start with implementing a simple form of a recurrent neural network to understand the basic idea of RNNs. In this example, we will feed the RNN four binary variables. These represent the weather types on a certain day. For example, [1, 0, 0, 0] stands for *sunny* and [1, 0, 1, 0] stands for *sunny and windy*. The target value is a double representing the percentage of rain on that day. For this problem, we can say that the quantity of rain on a certain day also depends on the values of the previous day. This makes this problem well suited for a 4-to-1 RNN model.

How to do it...

1. In this basic example, we will implement our simple RNN with NumPy:

```
import numpy as np
```

2. Let's start with creating the dummy dataset that we will be using:

```
X = []
X.append([1,0,0,0])
X.append([0,1,0,0])
X.append([0,0,1,0])
X.append([0,0,0,1])
X.append([0,0,0,1])
X.append([1,0,0,0])
X.append([0,1,0,0])
X.append([0,0,1,0])
X.append([0,0,0,1])

y = [0.20, 0.30, 0.40, 0.50, 0.05, 0.10, 0.20,
0.30, 0.40]
```

3. For this regression problem, we will be using a sigmoid activation function:

```
def sigmoid(x):
    return 1 / (1 + np.exp(-x))

def sigmoid_der(x):
    return 1.0 - x**2
```

4. Next, we initialize the layers and weights:

```
layers = []
# 4 input variables, 16 hidden units and 1 output variable
n_units = (4, 16, 1)
n_layers = len(n_units)

layers.append(np.ones(n_units[0]+1+n_units[1]))
for i in range(1, n_layers):
    layers.append(np.ones(n_units[i]))

weights = []
for i in range(n_layers-1):
    weights.append(np.zeros((layers[i].size,
    layers[i+1].size)))

weights_delta = [0,]*len(weights)
```

5. We are now ready to define the function for the forward pass:

```
def forwards(data):
    layers[0][:n_units[0]] = data
    layers[0][n_units[0]:-1] = layers[1]

    # Propagate the data forwards
    for i in range(1, n_layers):
        layers[i][...] = sigmoid(np.dot(layers[i-1],
        weights[i-1]))

    return layers[-1]
```

6. In the backwards pass, we will determine the errors and update the weights:

```
def backwards(target, learning_rate=0.1, momentum=0.1):
    deltas = []
    error = target - layers[-1]
    delta = error * sigmoid_der(layers[-1])
    deltas.append(delta)

    # Determine error in hidden layers
    for i in range(n_layers-2, 0, -1):
        delta = np.dot(deltas[0], weights[i].T) *
sigmoid_der(layers[i])
        deltas.insert(0, delta)

    # Update weights
    for i in range(len(weights)):
        layer = np.atleast_2d(layers[i])
        delta = np.atleast_2d(deltas[i])
        weights_delta_temp = np.dot(layer.T, delta)
        weights[i] += learning_rate*weights_delta_temp +
        momentum*weights_delta[i]
        weights_delta[i] = weights_delta_temp

    return (error**2).sum()
```

7. We are now ready to train our simple RNN:

```
n_epochs = 10000
for i in range(n_epochs):
    loss = 0
    for j in range(len(X)):
        forwards(X[j])
        backwards(y[j])
        loss += (y[j]-forwards(X[j]))**2
    if i%1000 == 0: print('epoch {} - loss:
```

```
{:04.4f}'.format(i, loss[0]))
```

8. Finally, let's inspect our results:

```
for i in range(len(X)):
    pred = forwards(X[i])
    loss = (y[i]-pred)**2
    print('X: {}; y: {:04.2f}; pred:
    {:04.2f}'.format(X[i], y[i], pred[0]))
```

The goal of this recipe is to get you familiar with RNNs and the internal structure. In our example, we've shown that the predicted value is not only dependent on the current input data, but also on previous value in a sequence.

Adding Long Short-Term Memory (LSTM)

One limitation of a simple RNN is that it only accounts for the direct inputs around the current input. In many applications, and specifically language, one needs to understand the context of the sentence in a larger part as well. This is why LSTM has played an important role in applying Deep Learning to unstructured data types such as text. An LSTM unit has an input, forget, and output gate, as is shown in *Figure 4.2*:

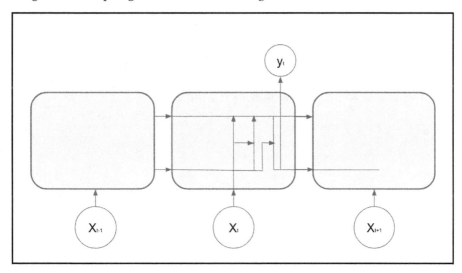

Figure 4.2: Example flow in an LSTM unit

In the following recipe, we will be classifying reviews from the IMDB dataset using the Keras framework.

How to do it...

1. Let's start with importing the libraries as follows:

```
import numpy as np

from keras.preprocessing import sequence
from keras.models import Sequential
from keras.layers import Dense, Dropout, Activation
from keras.layers import Embedding
from keras.layers import LSTM

from keras.datasets import imdb
```

2. We will be using the IMDB dataset from Keras; load the data with the following code:

```
n_words = 1000
(X_train, y_train), (X_test, y_test) =
imdb.load_data(num_words=n_words)
print('Train seq: {}'.format(len(X_train)))
print('Test seq: {}'.format(len(X_train)))
```

3. Let's print an example output of the training and test data:

```
print('Train example: \n{}'.format(X_train[0]))
print('\nTest example: \n{}'.format(X_test[0]))

# Note: the data is already preprocessed
#(words are mapped to vectors)
```

4. By padding the sequences, we prepare our input for our network:

```
# Pad sequences with max_len
max_len = 200
X_train = sequence.pad_sequences(X_train, maxlen=max_len)
X_test = sequence.pad_sequences(X_test, maxlen=max_len)
```

5. We are now ready to define our network architecture:

```
# Define network architecture and compile
model = Sequential()
model.add(Embedding(n_words, 50, input_length=max_len))
model.add(Dropout(0.2))
model.add(LSTM(100, dropout=0.2, recurrent_dropout=0.2))
model.add(Dense(250, activation='relu'))
model.add(Dropout(0.2))
model.add(Dense(1, activation='sigmoid'))

model.compile(loss='binary_crossentropy',
optimizer='adam', metrics=['accuracy'])
model.summary()
```

6. Let's define the hyperparameters and start training our network:

```
batch_size = 64
n_epochs = 10

model.fit(X_train, y_train, batch_size=batch_size,
epochs=n_epochs)
```

7. Finally, we can check the performance of our trained network on the test set:

```
print('\nAccuracy on test set: {}'.
format(model.evaluate(X_test, y_test)[1])

# Accuracy on test set: 0.82884
```

The test accuracy of our model is below the test accuracy of our 1D CNN network for text classification. In Chapter 8, *Natural Language Processing*, we will show how to combine CNNs and RNNs to create a more powerful text classification network.

Using gated recurrent units (GRUs)

Another type of unit often used in RNNs is **gated recurrent units** (**GRUs**). These units are actually simpler than LSTM units, because they only have two gates: update and reset. The update gate determines the memory and the reset gate combines the memory with the current input. The flow of data is made visual in the following figure:

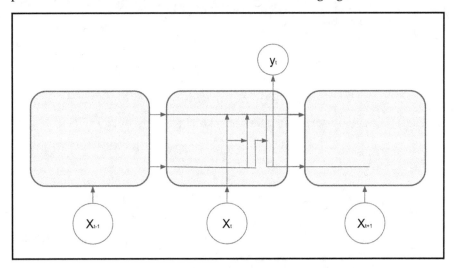

Figure 4.3: Example flow in a GRU unit

In this recipe, we will show how to incorporate a GRU into an RNN architecture to classify text with Keras.

How to do it...

1. Let's start with importing the libraries as follows:

```
import numpy as np
import pandas as pd

from keras.preprocessing import sequence
from keras.models import Sequential
from keras.layers import Dense, Dropout, Activation
from keras.layers import Embedding
from keras.layers import GRU
from keras.callbacks import EarlyStopping

from keras.datasets import imdbimport numpy as np
```

```
import pandas as pd

from keras.preprocessing import sequence
from keras.models import Sequential
from keras.layers import Dense, Dropout, Activation
from keras.layers import Embedding
from keras.layers import GRU
from keras.callbacks import EarlyStopping

from keras.datasets import imdb
```

2. We will be using the IMDb dataset that classifies the sentiment of text; load the data with the following code:

```
n_words = 1000
(X_train, y_train), (X_test, y_test) =
imdb.load_data(num_words=n_words)
print('Train seq: {}'.format(len(X_train)))
print('Test seq: {}'.format(len(X_train)))
```

3. By padding the sequences, we prepare our input for our network:

```
# Pad sequences with max_len
max_len = 200
X_train = sequence.pad_sequences(X_train, maxlen=max_len)
X_test = sequence.pad_sequences(X_test, maxlen=max_len)
```

4. We are now ready to define our network architecture:

```
# Define network architecture and compile
model = Sequential()
model.add(Embedding(n_words, 50, input_length=max_len))
model.add(Dropout(0.2))
model.add(GRU(100, dropout=0.2, recurrent_dropout=0.2))
model.add(Dense(250, activation='relu'))
model.add(Dropout(0.2))
model.add(Dense(1, activation='sigmoid'))

model.compile(loss='binary_crossentropy',
optimizer='adam', metrics=['accuracy'])
model.summary()
```

5. We use early stopping to prevent overfitting:

```
callbacks = [EarlyStopping(monitor='val_acc',
patience=3)]
```

6. Let's define the hyperparameters and start training our network:

```
batch_size = 512
n_epochs = 100

model.fit(X_train, y_train, batch_size=batch_size,
epochs=n_epochs, validation_split=0.2, callbacks=callbacks)
```

7. Finally, we can check the performance of our trained network on the test set:

```
print('\nAccuracy on test set: {}'.
format(model.evaluate(X_test, y_test)[1])

# Accuracy on test set: 0.83004
```

Implementing bidirectional RNNs

Until now, we've considered the information to flow in one direction through our network. However, sometimes it's beneficial to run the data through the network in both directions. We call such networks bidirectional RNNs. In the following example, we will implement the same LSTM network as we've implemented previously, but this time we will use a bidirectional RNN to classify the sentiment.

How to do it...

1. Let's start with importing the libraries as follows:

```
import numpy as np

from keras.preprocessing import sequence
from keras.models import Sequential
from keras.layers import Dense, Dropout,
Activation, Embedding, LSTM, Bidirectional
from keras.callbacks import EarlyStopping
from keras.datasets import imdb
```

2. We will be using the IMDB dataset from Keras; load the data with the following code:

```
n_words = 1000
(X_train, y_train), (X_test, y_test) =
imdb.load_data(num_words=n_words)
```

```
print('Train seq: {}'.format(len(X_train)))
print('Test seq: {}'.format(len(X_train)))
```

3. Let's print an example output of the training and test data:

```
print('Train example: \n{}'.format(X_train[0]))
print('\nTest example: \n{}'.format(X_test[0]))

# Note: the data is already preprocessed (words are mapped to
vectors)
```

4. By padding the sequences, we prepare our input for our network:

```
# Pad sequences with max_len
max_len = 200
X_train = sequence.pad_sequences
(X_train, maxlen=max_len)
X_test = sequence.pad_sequences
(X_test, maxlen=max_len)
```

5. We are now ready to define our network architecture:

```
# Define network architecture and compile
model = Sequential()
model.add(Embedding(n_words, 50, input_length=max_len))
model.add(Dropout(0.2))
model.add(Bidirectional(LSTM(100, dropout=0.2,
recurrent_dropout=0.2)))
model.add(Dense(250, activation='relu'))
model.add(Dropout(0.2))
model.add(Dense(1, activation='sigmoid'))

model.compile(loss='binary_crossentropy',
optimizer='adam', metrics=['accuracy'])
model.summary()
```

6. To prevent overfitting, we will be using early stopping:

```
callbacks = [EarlyStopping(monitor='val_acc', patience=3)]
```

7. Let's define the hyperparameters and start training our network:

```
batch_size = 1024
n_epochs = 100

model.fit(X_train, y_train, batch_size=batch_size, epochs=n_epochs,
validation_split=0.2, callbacks=callbacks)
```

8. Finally, we can check the performance of our trained network on the test set:

```
print('Accuracy on test set: {}'.format(model.evaluate(X_test,
y_test, batch_size=batch_size)[1]))

# Accuracy on test set: 0.8391600004386902
```

As we can see, the network is able to retrieve some additional information from parsing the data in both directions. This results in a slightly higher test accuracy of 83.91%.

Character-level text generation

RNNs are not only powerful to parse and classify text. RNNs can also be used to generate text. In it's simplest form, text is generated on character level. More specifically, the text is generated character per character. Before we can generate text, we need to train a decoder on full sentences. By including a GRU layer in our decoder, the model does not only depend on the previous input but does try to predict the next character based on the context around it. In the following recipe, we will demonstrate how to implement a character-level text generator with PyTorch.

How to do it...

1. Let's start with importing the libraries as follows:

```
import unidecode
import string
import random
import math

import torch
import torch.nn as nn
from torch.autograd import Variable
```

2. As input and output, we can use any character:

```
all_characters = string.printable
input_size = len(all_characters)
output_size = input_size
print(input_size)
```

3. We will be using a dataset with speeches from Obama:

```
filename = 'Data/obama.txt'
data = unidecode.unidecode(open(filename).read())
len_data = len(data)
```

4. We need to define the hyperparameters before moving on:

```
n_steps = 2000
batch_size = 512
hidden_size = 100
n_layers = 2
learning_rate = 0.01
len_text = 200
print_every = 50
```

5. Let's define a function that transforms characters to tensors:

```
def char_to_tensor(string):
    tensor = torch.zeros(len(string)).long()
    for c in range(len(string)):
        try:
            tensor[c] = all_characters.
            index(string[c])
        except:
            continue
    return tensor
```

6. Next, we define a batch generator:

```
def batch_gen(length_text, batch_size):
    X = torch.LongTensor(batch_size, length_text)
    y = torch.LongTensor(batch_size, length_text)
    for i in range(batch_size):
        start_index = random.randint
        (0, len_data - length_text)
        end_index = start_index + length_text + 1
        text = data[start_index:end_index]
        X[i] = char_to_tensor(text[:-1])
        y[i] = char_to_tensor(text[1:])
    X = Variable(X)
    y = Variable(y)
    X = X.cuda()
    y = y.cuda()
    return X, y
```

7. We are now ready to define our network architecture:

```
class create_model(nn.Module):
    def __init__(self, input_size, hidden_size,
    output_size, n_layers=1):
        super(create_model, self).__init__()
        self.input_size = input_size
        self.hidden_size = hidden_size
        self.output_size = output_size
        self.n_layers = n_layers

        self.encoder = nn.Embedding(input_size, hidden_size)
        self.rnn = nn.GRU(hidden_size, hidden_size, n_layers)
        self.decoder = nn.Linear(hidden_size, output_size)

    def forward(self, input, hidden):
        batch_size = input.size(0)
        encoded = self.encoder(input)
        output, hidden = self.rnn(encoded.view(1,
        batch_size, -1), hidden)
        output = self.decoder(output.view(batch_size, -1))
        return output, hidden

    def init_hidden(self, batch_size):
        return Variable(torch.zeros
        (self.n_layers, batch_size, self.hidden_size))
```

8. We continue by creating our model and defining the optimizer and loss function as follows:

```
decoder_model = create_model(
    input_size,
    hidden_size,
    output_size,
    n_layers=n_layers,
)

opt = torch.optim.Adam(decoder_model.parameters(),
lr=learning_rate)
loss = nn.CrossEntropyLoss()
decoder_model.cuda()
```

9. We also create a function that we can use to generate text during training:

```
def generate_text(decoder, start='The', predict_len=100):
    hidden = decoder.init_hidden(1).cuda()
    prime_input =
Variable(char_to_tensor(start).unsqueeze(0)).cuda()
```

```
predicted = start

for p in range(len(start) - 1):
    _, hidden = decoder(prime_input[:, p], hidden)
x = prime_input[:,-1]
for p in range(predict_len):
    output, hidden = decoder(x, hidden)
    output_dist = output.data.view(-1).div(0.8).exp()
    # Add some randomness
    top_i = torch.multinomial(output_dist, 1)[0]
    predicted_char = all_characters[top_i]
    predicted += predicted_char
    x = Variable(char_to_tensor(predicted_char).
  unsqueeze(0)).cuda()
return predicted
```

10. Finally, let's start training:

```
loss_avg = 0
for i in range(n_steps):
    X, y = batch_gen(len_text, batch_size)
    hidden = decoder_model.init_hidden(batch_size).cuda()
    decoder_model.zero_grad()
    loss_total = 0

    for c in range(len_text):
        output, hidden = decoder_model(X[:,c], hidden)
        loss_total += loss(output.view(batch_size, -1),
        y[:,c])

    loss_total.backward()
    opt.step()
    loss_value = loss_total.data[0] / len_text
    loss_avg += loss_value

    if i % print_every == 0:
        print('Epoch {}: loss {}'.format(i, loss_avg))
        print(generate_text(decoder_model,
        'The', 100), '\n')
```

In this chapter, we've introduced RNNs and some of the most popular techniques used in RNNs. We've also showed some applications of RNNs. In the following chapters, we will show you how to apply these networks to more advanced problems.

5
Reinforcement Learning

In this chapter, we will focus on reinforcement learning and we will cover the following topics:

- Implementing policy gradients
- Implementing a deep Q-learning algorithm

Introduction

So far, we've discussed supervised learning and unsupervised learning techniques. The third pillar of machine learning is **reinforcement learning** (**RL**). In reinforcement learning, the task isn't supervised nor unsupervised. Specifically, in RL, an agent has an end goal when receiving observations, but it doesn't receive feedback from the environment at every step. Instead, the agent gets positive or negative rewards only after a certain number of steps. This is interesting, because one could argue that, for some tasks, this is the same way humans learn. What makes this type of problem more complicated than normal supervised learning problems is that we don't explicitly now which action in one of the previous steps caused the desired reward. This is called the **credit assignment problem**.

Reinforcement learning is a hot topic nowadays because there has been a lot of progress in this field. Moreover, the problems solved by these algorithms are interesting and visually appealing. For example, with RL, a computer can teach itself to play games without explicitly specifying the steps it should undertake.

Reinforcement learning is a computation-expensive task. This means that we often need to run algorithms for a long time before we get valuable results.

Implementing policy gradients

In reinforcement learning, we cannot backpropagate the error in our network directly, because we don't have a truth set for each step. We only receive feedback now and then. This is why we need the **policy gradient** to propagate the rewards back to the network. The rules to determine the best action are called **policies**. The network for learning these policies is called **policy network**. This can be any type of network, for example, a simple, two-layer FNN or a CNN. The more complex the environment, the more you will benefit from a complex network. When using a policy gradient, we draw an action of the output distribution of our policy network. Because the reward is not always directly available, we treat the action as correct. Later we use the **discounted reward** as a scalar and backpropagate this to the network weights.

In the following recipe, we will teach an agent to play *Pong* from OpenAI by implementing a policy gradient in TensorFlow. *Pong* is a great game to start with, because it is simple (two actions, *up* or *down*, if we exclude *do nothing*), is easy to visualize, and has a straightforward reward (+1 if the agent wins the game and -1 if the agent loses the game). In this version of *Pong*, we play until one of the two players wins 21 games (this is called an **episode**). We want our agent to win a game of *Pong* with the highest score possible: 21 - 0.

Getting ready

Before start implementing the recipe, make sure the OpenAI Gym environment is installed. Follow the instructions on the website: `https://gym.openai.com/docs/`. When running Gym on a server you'll need to connect a fake display.

How to do it...

1. First, we import the necessary libraries, as follows:

```
import numpy as np
import gym
import tensorflow as tf
```

```
import matplotlib.pyplot as plt
```

2. Let's set up the Pong environment and plot a frame:

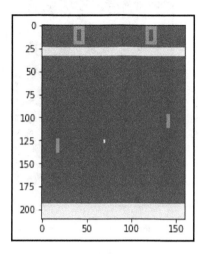

Figures 5.1: Frame of the Pong game by OpenAI

```
env = gym.make("Pong-v0") # environment info
observation = env.reset()

for i in range(22):
    # The ball is released after 20 frames
    if i > 20:
        plt.imshow(observation)
        plt.show()
    # Get the next observation
    observation, _, _, _ = env.step(1)
```

3. Before we implement the algorithm, we need a function that preprocesses the input data:

```
def preprocess_frame(frame):
    # remove top part of frame and some background
    frame = frame[35:195, 10:150]
    # grayscale frame and downsize by factor 2
    frame = frame[::2, ::2, 0]
    # set background to 0
    frame[frame == 144] = 0
    frame[frame == 109] = 0
    # set ball and paddles to 1
    frame[frame != 0] = 1
    return frame.astype(np.float).ravel()
```

4. Let's see what the preprocessed data looks like:

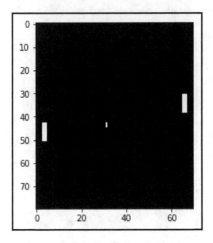

Figure 5.2: Preprocessed frame of Pong (reshaped to 2D)

```
obs_preprocessed = preprocess_frame(observation).
reshape(80, 70)
plt.imshow(obs_preprocessed, cmap='gray')
plt.show()
```

5. To extract temporal information from the game, we use the difference between two successive frames:

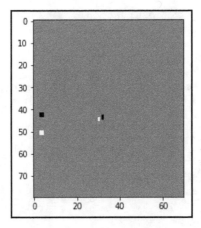

Figure 5.3: Difference between two successive frames of Pong (reshaped to 2D)

```
observation_next, _, _, _ = env.step(1)
diff = preprocess_frame(observation_next) -
preprocess_frame(observation)
plt.imshow(diff.reshape(80, 70), cmap='gray')
plt.show()
```

6. Now we can start implementing our three-layer model. Let's start by defining the weights:

```
input_dim = 80*70
hidden_L1 = 400
hidden_L2 = 200
actions = [1, 2, 3]
n_actions = len(actions)
model = {}
with tf.variable_scope('L1',reuse=False):
    init_W1 = tf.truncated_normal_initializer
    (mean=0, stddev=1./np.sqrt(input_dim),
    dtype=tf.float32)
    model['W1'] = tf.get_variable("W1",
    [input_dim, hidden_L1], initializer=init_W1)

with tf.variable_scope('L2',reuse=False):
    init_W2 = tf.truncated_normal_initializer
    (mean=0, stddev=1./np.sqrt(hidden_L1),
    dtype=tf.float32)
    model['W2'] = tf.get_variable("W2",
    [hidden_L1, n_actions], initializer=init_W2)
```

7. Next, we define the functions for our policies:

```
def policy_forward(x):
    x = tf.matmul(x, model['W1'])
    x = tf.nn.relu(x)
    x = tf.matmul(x, model['W2'])
    p = tf.nn.softmax(x)
    return p
```

8. For our algorithm, we need to define a function for the discounted reward:

```
def discounted_rewards(reward, gamma):
    discounted_function = lambda a, v:
    a*gamma + v;
    reward_reverse = tf.scan(discounted_function,
    tf.reverse(reward, [True, False]))
    discounted_reward = tf.reverse(reward_reverse,
    [True, False])
    return discounted_reward
```

9. Before proceeding, we need to define the hyperparamters:

```
learning_rate = 0.001
gamma = 0.99
batch_size = 10
```

10. We have to set our backwards update separately by defining placeholders:

```
# TensorFlow placeholders
episode_x = tf.placeholder(dtype=tf.float32,
shape=[None, input_dim])
episode_y = tf.placeholder(dtype=tf.float32,
shape=[None, n_actions])
episode_reward = tf.placeholder(dtype=tf.float32,
shape=[None, 1])

episode_discounted_reward = discounted_rewards
(episode_reward, gamma)
episode_mean, episode_variance=
tf.nn.moments(episode_discounted_reward,
[0], shift=None)

# Normalize discounted reward
episode_discounted_reward -= episode_mean
episode_discounted_reward /=
tf.sqrt(episode_variance + 1e-6)

# Optimizer settings
tf_aprob = policy_forward(episode_x)
loss = tf.nn.l2_loss(episode_y - tf_aprob)
optimizer = tf.train.AdamOptimizer(learning_rate)
gradients = optimizer.compute_gradients(loss,
var_list=tf.trainable_variables(),
grad_loss=episode_discounted_reward)
train_op = optimizer.apply_gradients(gradients)

# Initialize graph
sess = tf.InteractiveSession()
tf.global_variables_initializer().run()

# Settings to save the trained model
saver = tf.train.Saver(tf.global_variables())
save_path = 'checkpoints/pong_rl.ckpt'
```

11. Now, we can initialize the values and run our algorithm:

```
obs_prev = None
xs, ys, rs, = [], [], []
reward_sum = 0
episode_number = 0
reward_window = None
reward_best = -22
history = []

observation = env.reset()
while True:
# if True: env.render()
# uncomment if you want to see the agent
#play while training

    # Preprocess the observation,
    #set input to network to be difference image
    obs_cur = preprocess_frame(observation)
    obs_diff = obs_cur - obs_prev if obs_prev
    is not None else np.zeros(input_dim)
    obs_prev = obs_cur

    # Sample an action (policy)
    feed = {episode_x: np.reshape(obs_diff, (1,-1))}
    aprob = sess.run(tf_aprob, feed) ; aprob = aprob[0,:]
    action = np.random.choice(n_actions, p=aprob)
    label = np.zeros_like(aprob) ; label[action] = 1

    # Return action to environment and extract
    # next observation, reward, and status
    observation, reward, done, info =
    env.step(action+1)
    reward_sum += reward
    # record game history
    xs.append(obs_diff) ; ys.append(label) ;
    rs.append(reward)

    if done:
        history.append(reward_sum)
        reward_window = -21 if reward_window is
        None else np.mean(history[-100:])
        # Update the weights with the stored values
        # (update policies)
        feed = {episode_x: np.vstack(xs), episode_y:
        np.vstack(ys), episode_reward: np.vstack(rs), }
        _ = sess.run(train_op, feed)
        print('episode {:2d}: reward: {:2.0f}'.
```

```
        format(episode_number, reward_sum))
xs, ys, rs = [], [], []
episode_number += 1
observation = env.reset()
reward_sum = 0
# Save best model after every 10 episodes
if (episode_number % 10 == 0) & (reward_window >
reward_best):
    saver.save(sess, save_path,
    global_step=episode_number)
    reward_best = reward_window
    print("Save best model {:2d}:
    {:2.5f} (reward window)"
    .format(episode_number, reward_window))
```

12. When our algorithm reaches about 2500 episodes, we can stop training and plot the results:

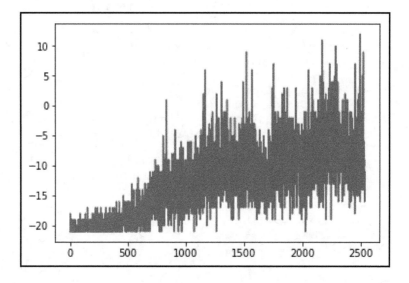

Figure 5.4: The scores against the number of trained episodes

```
plt.plot(history)
plt.show()
```

13. Finally, we want to see how our final model performs in OpenAI's Gym:

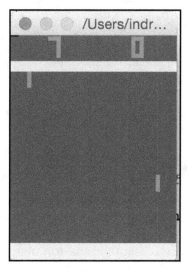

Figure 5.5: Our trained policy gradient agent in action

```
observation = env.reset()
while True:
    if True: env.render()

    # Preprocess the observation,
    #set input to network to be difference image
    obs_cur = preprocess_frame(observation)
    obs_diff = obs_cur - obs_prev if
    obs_prev is not None else np.zeros(input_dim)
    obs_prev = obs_cur

    # Sample an action (policy)
    feed = {tf_x: np.reshape(obs_diff, (1,-1))}
    aprob = sess.run(tf_aprob, feed) ; aprob = aprob[0,:]
    action = np.random.choice(n_actions, p=aprob)
    label = np.zeros_like(aprob) ; label[action] = 1

    # Return action to environment and extract
    #next observation, reward, and status
    observation, reward, done, info = env.step(action+1)
    if done: observation = env.reset()
```

As we can see, it takes quite a few training episodes before our implementation is able to win the episode more steadily. If you want to see how the agent performs while training, you can uncomment the first line of code within the `while` loop. This will render each observation while training.

One of the options to improve the preceding setup is to adjust the network architecture and fine-tune the hyperparameters. A more complex network architecture could help, but it will also increase the training time. Policy gradients are the most popular method for RL these days, because they are end-to-end and have shown better results when tuned correctly.

Implementing a deep Q-learning algorithm

Another popular method for reinforcement learning is Q-learning. In **Q-learning**, we don't focus on mapping an observation to a specific action, but we try to assign some value to the current state (of observations) and act based on that value. The states and actions can be seen as a **Markov decision process**, where the environment is stochastic. In a Markov process, the next state only depends on the current state and the following action. So, we assume that all previous states (and actions) are irrelevant.

The Q in Q-learning stands for quality; the function $Q(s, a)$ provides a quality score for action a in state s. The function can be of any type. In a simple form, it can be a lookup table. However, in a more complex environment, this won't work and that's where deep learning comes in place. In the following recipe, we will implement a deep Q-learning algorithm to play *Breakout* from OpenAI.

Getting ready

Before start implementing the recipe, make sure the OpenAI Gym environment is installed. Follow the instructions on the website: https://gym.openai.com/docs/. When running Gym on a server you'll need to connect a fake display.

How to do it...

1. Let's start with importing the necessary libraries, as follows:

```
import gym
import random
import numpy as np
import matplotlib.pyplot as plt
from collections import deque

from keras.models import Sequential
from keras.optimizers import Adam
from keras.layers import Dense, Flatten
from keras.layers.convolutional import Conv2D
from keras import backend as K
```

2. First, we will plot an example input image of the game:

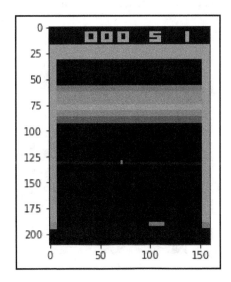

Figure 5.6: Example input image of Breakout by OpenAI

```
env = gym.make('BreakoutDeterministic-v4')
observation = env.reset()

for i in range(3):
    # The ball is released after 2 frames
    if i > 1:
        print(observation.shape)
        plt.imshow(observation)
```

```
        plt.show()
    # Get the next observation
    observation, _, _, _ = env.step(1)
```

3. Now, we can define a function that preprocesses the input data:

```
def preprocess_frame(frame):
    # remove top part of frame and some background
    frame = frame[35:195, 10:150]
    # grayscale frame and downsize by factor 2
    frame = frame[::2, ::2, 0]
    # set background to 0
    frame[frame == 144] = 0
    frame[frame == 109] = 0
    # set ball and paddles to 1
    frame[frame != 0] = 1
    return frame.astype(np.float).ravel()
```

4. Let's output the preceding preprocessed image to give us an idea of what our algorithm will process:

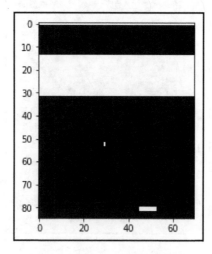

Figure 5.7: Preprocessed frame of Breakout

```
obs_preprocessed = preprocess_frame(observation)
plt.imshow(obs_preprocessed, cmap='gray')
plt.show()
```

5. For our deep Q-learning implementation, we need to define an agent that performs most of the tasks:

```
class DQLAgent:
    def __init__(self, cols, rows, n_actions, batch_size=32):
        self.state_size = (cols, rows, 4)
        self.n_actions = n_actions
        self.epsilon = 1.
        self.epsilon_start, self.epsilon_end = 1.0, 0.1
        self.exploration_steps = 1000000.
        self.epsilon_decay_step = (self.epsilon_start -
self.epsilon_end) / self.exploration_steps
        self.batch_size = batch_size
        self.discount_factor = 0.99
        self.memory = deque(maxlen=400000)
        self.model = self.build_model()
        self.target_model = self.build_model()
        self.optimizer = self.optimizer()
        self.avg_q_max, self.avg_loss = 0, 0

    def optimizer(self):
        a = K.placeholder(shape=(None,), dtype='int32')
        y = K.placeholder(shape=(None,), dtype='float32')

        py_x = self.model.output

        a_one_hot = K.one_hot(a, self.n_actions)
        q_value = K.sum(py_x * a_one_hot, axis=1)
        error = K.abs(y - q_value)

        quadratic_part = K.clip(error, 0.0, 1.0)
        linear_part = error - quadratic_part
        loss = K.mean(0.5 *
        K.square(quadratic_part) + linear_part)

        opt = Adam(lr=0.00025, epsilon=0.01)
        updates = opt.get_updates
        (self.model.trainable_weights, [], loss)
        train = K.function([self.model.input, a, y],
        [loss], updates=updates)

        return train

    def build_model(self):
```

```
        model = Sequential()
        model.add(Conv2D(32, (8, 8), strides=(4, 4),
        activation='relu', input_shape=self.state_size))
        model.add(Conv2D(64, (4, 4), strides=(2, 2),
        activation='relu'))
        model.add(Conv2D(64, (3, 3), strides=(1, 1),
        activation='relu'))
        model.add(Flatten())
        model.add(Dense(512, activation='relu'))
        model.add(Dense(self.n_actions))
        model.summary()
        return model

    def update_model(self):
        self.target_model.set_weights
        (self.model.get_weights())

    def action(self, history):
        history = np.float32(history / 255.0)
        if np.random.rand() <= self.epsilon:
            return random.randrange(self.n_actions)
        else:
            q_value = self.model.predict(history)
            return np.argmax(q_value[0])

    def replay(self, history, action, reward,
            next_history, dead):
        self.memory.append((history, action,
        reward, next_history, dead))

    def train(self):
        if len(self.memory) < self.batch_size:
            return
        if self.epsilon > self.epsilon_end:
            self.epsilon -= self.epsilon_decay_step

        mini_batch = random.sample(self.memory,
        self.batch_size)
        history = np.zeros((self.batch_size,
        self.state_size[0], self.state_size[1],
        self.state_size[2]))
        next_history = np.zeros((self.batch_size,
        self.state_size[0], self.state_size[1],
        self.state_size[2]))
        target = np.zeros((self.batch_size,))
        action, reward, dead = [], [], []

        for i in range(self.batch_size):
```

```
history[i] = np.float32
(mini_batch[i][0] / 255.)
next_history[i] = np.float32
(mini_batch[i][3] / 255.)
action.append(mini_batch[i][1])
reward.append(mini_batch[i][2])
dead.append(mini_batch[i][4])

target_value = self.target_model.
predict(next_history)

for i in range(self.batch_size):
    if dead[i]:
        target[i] = reward[i]
    else:
        target[i] = reward[i] +
        self.discount_factor * \
        np.amax(target_value[i])

loss = self.optimizer([history, action, target])
self.avg_loss += loss[0]
```

6. Next, we set the hyperparameters and some general settings and initialize our agent:

```
env = gym.make('BreakoutDeterministic-v4')

# General settings
n_warmup_steps = 50000
update_model_rate = 10000
cols, rows = 85, 70
n_states = 4

# Hyperparameters
batch_size = 32

# Initialization
agent = DQLAgent(cols, rows, n_actions=3)
scores, episodes = [], []
n_steps = 0
```

7. We are now ready to start training our model:

```
while True:
    done = False
    dead = False
    step, score, start_life = 0, 0, 5
    observation = env.reset()
```

```
        state = preprocess_frame(observation,
        cols, rows)
        history = np.stack((state, state,
        state, state), axis=2)
        history = np.reshape([history],
        (1, cols, rows, n_states))

        while not done:
# env.render()
            n_steps += 1
            step += 1
            # Get action
            action = agent.action(history)
            observation, reward, done, info =
            env.step(action+1)
            # Extract next state
            state_next = preprocess_frame
            (observation, cols, rows)
            state_next = np.reshape([state_next],
            (1, cols, rows, 1))
            history_next = np.append(state_next,
            history[:, :, :, :3], axis=3)

            agent.avg_q_max += np.amax(agent.model
            .predict(history)[0])
            reward = np.clip(reward, -1., 1.)

            agent.replay(history, action, reward,
            history_next, dead)
            agent.train()
            if n_steps % update_model_rate == 0:
                agent.update_model()
            score += reward

            if dead:
                dead = False
            else:
                history = history_next

            if done:
                print('episode {:2d}; score:
                {:2.0f}; q {:2f}; loss {:2f}; steps {}'
                    .format(n_steps, score,
                    agent.avg_q_max / float(step),
                    agent.avg_loss / float(step), step))

                agent.avg_q_max, agent.avg_loss = 0, 0
        # Save weights of model
```

```
if n_steps % 1000 == 0:
    agent.model.save_weights("weights/breakout_dql.h5")
```

8. When our algorithm scores well enough, we can stop training.

9. Let's see how our final model performs:

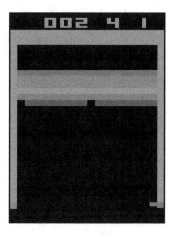

Figure 5.9: Our trained deep Q-learning agent in action

```
env = gym.make('BreakoutDeterministic-v4')
agent = DQLAgent(cols, rows, n_action=3)

for i in range(5):
    observation = env.reset()

    state = pre_processing(observation,
    cols, rows)
    history = np.stack((state, state,
    state, state), axis=2)
    history = np.reshape([history], (1, cols,
    rows, n_states))

    while not done:
        env.render()
        action = agent.get_action(history)
        observe, reward, done, info =
        env.step(action+1)
```

As with policy gradients, the network architecture of our DQL implementation can be made as complicated as we like. In more complex environments, more complex network architectures are the key to obtaining good results. Reinforcement learning is a fascinating field. In the following chapters, and especially in Chapter 11, *Game Playing Agents and Robotics*, we will show you how to apply reinforcement learning to other games and problems. Additionally, we will introduce some advanced techniques and techniques to speed up training, for example, by parallelization.

6
Generative Adversarial Networks

This chapter focuses on **Generative Adversarial Networks** (**GANs**). The following recipes are included in this chapter:

- Understanding GANs
- Implementing Deep Convolutional GANs (DCGANs)
- Upscaling the resolution of images with Super Resolution GANs (SRGANs)

Introduction

In this chapter, we will introduce GANs. Just as in autoencoder networks, GANs have a generator and a discriminator network. However, GANs are fundamentally different. They represent an unsupervised learning problem, where the two networks compete, and cooperate with each other at the same time. It is important that the generator and discriminator don't overpower each other. The idea behind GANs is to generate new examples based on training data. Applications can range from generating new handwritten MNIST images to generating music. GANs have received a lot of attention lately because the results of using them are fascinating.

Understanding GANs

To start implementing GANs, we need to. It is hard to determine the quality of examples produced by GANs. A lower loss value doesn't always represent better quality. Often, for images, the only way to determine the quality is by visually inspecting the generated examples. We can than determine whether the generated images are realistic enough, more or less like a simple Turing test. In the following recipe, we will introduce GANs by using the well-known MNIST dataset and the Keras framework.

How to do it...

1. We start by importing the necessary libraries, as follows:

```
import numpy as np
from keras.models import Sequential, Model
from keras.layers import Input, Dense, Activation, Flatten, Reshape
from keras.layers import Conv2D, Conv2DTranspose, UpSampling2D
from keras.layers import LeakyReLU, Dropout
from keras.layers import BatchNormalization
from keras.optimizers import Adam
from keras import initializers


from keras.datasets import mnist

import matplotlib.pyplot as plt
```

2. By using Keras, we can easily import both datasets with the following lines of code:

```
(X_train, y_train), (X_test, y_test) = mnist.load_data()

img_rows, img_cols = X_train.shape[1:]

X_train = X_train.reshape(-1, img_rows*img_cols,
1).astype(np.float32)/255.
```

3. For our GAN, we need to define three network architectures. Let's start with `discriminator_model`:

```
def discriminator_model(dropout=0.5):
    model = Sequential()
    model.add(Dense(1024, input_dim=784,
kernel_initializer=initializers.RandomNormal(stddev=0.02)))
    model.add(LeakyReLU(0.2))
    model.add(Dropout(dropout))
    model.add(Dense(512))
    model.add(LeakyReLU(0.2))
    model.add(Dropout(dropout))
    model.add(Dense(256))
    model.add(LeakyReLU(0.2))
    model.add(Dropout(dropout))
    model.add(Dense(1, activation='sigmoid'))
    model.compile(loss='binary_crossentropy', optimizer=adam)
    return model
```

4. Next, we define `generator_model`:

```
def generator_model():
    model = Sequential()
    model.add(Dense(256, input_dim=100,
kernel_initializer=initializers.RandomNormal(stddev=0.02)))
    model.add(LeakyReLU(0.2))
    model.add(Dense(512))
    model.add(LeakyReLU(0.2))
    model.add(Dense(1024))
    model.add(LeakyReLU(0.2))
    model.add(Dense(784, activation='tanh'))
    model.compile(loss='binary_crossentropy', optimizer=adam)
    return model
```

5. Finally, we can create our networks and the combined network:

```
discriminator = discriminator_model()
generator = generator_model()
discriminator.trainable = False
gan_input = Input(shape=(100,))
x = generator(gan_input)
gan_output = discriminator(x)
gan = Model(inputs=gan_input, outputs=gan_output)
gan.compile(loss='binary_crossentropy', optimizer='adam')
```

6. Before we train our GAN, we need to define a function to plot the generated images:

```
def plot_images(samples=16, step=0):
    images = generator.predict(noise)
    plt.figure(figsize=(5,5))
    for i in range(samples):
        plt.subplot(4, 4, i+1)
        image = images[i, :,]
        image = np.reshape(image, [img_rows, img_cols])
        plt.imshow(image, cmap='gray')
        plt.axis('off')
    plt.show()
```

7. We can now start training our GAN. While training our model, we will output the results:

```
batch_size = 32
n_steps = 100000
plot_every = 1000

noise_input = np.random.uniform(-1.0, 1.0, size=[16, 100])
for step in range(n_steps):
    noise = np.random.normal(0, 1, size=[batch_size, 100])
    batch = X_train[np.random.randint(0, X_train.shape[0],
    size=batch_size)].reshape(batch_size, 784)

    gen_output = generator.predict(noise)
    X = np.concatenate([batch, gen_output])

    y_D = np.zeros(2*batch_size)
    y_D[:batch_size] = 0.9

    discriminator.trainable = True
    loss_D = discriminator.train_on_batch(X, y_D)

    noise = np.random.normal(0, 1, size=[batch_size, 100])
    y_G = np.ones(batch_size)
    discriminator.trainable = False
    loss_G = gan.train_on_batch(noise, y_G)
    if step % plot_every == 0:
        plot_images(samples=noise_input.shape[0], step=(step+1))
```

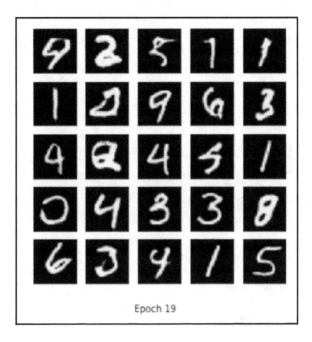

Epoch 19

Figure 6.1: Examples of generated images after 100,000 steps

Implementing Deep Convolutional GANs (DCGANs)

In the previous recipe, our network was able to generate realistic examples after a few epochs. The MNIST dataset has a low translation invariance, so it's easier for our network to generate these examples. In the early days of GANs, the networks were very unstable and small changes could mess up the output. In 2016, DCGANs were introduced. In DCGANs, both the discriminator and the generator are fully convolutional, and the output of DCGANs has proven to be more stable. In our next recipe, we will increase the complexity of our dataset by using the Fashion-MNIST dataset and demonstrate how to implement DCGANs in PyTorch.

How to do it...

1. We start by importing the necessary libraries, as follows:

```
import matplotlib.pyplot as plt
import itertools

import torch
import torch.nn as nn
import torch.nn.functional as F
import torch.optim as optim
from torch.autograd import Variable
from torch.utils.data.dataset import Dataset

import torchvision.datasets as dset
import torchvision.transforms as transforms
```

2. We then define our `discriminator` network in a function:

```
class discriminator(nn.Module):
    def __init__(self):
        super(discriminator, self).__init__()
        self.conv1 = nn.Conv2d(1, d, 4, 2, 1, bias=False)
        self.conv2 = nn.Conv2d(d, d*2, 4, 2, 1, bias=False)
        self.conv2_bn = nn.BatchNorm2d(*2)
        self.conv3 = nn.Conv2d(d*2, *4, 4, 2, 1, bias=False)
        self.conv3_bn = nn.BatchNorm2d(*4)
        self.conv4 = nn.Conv2d(d*4, d*8, 4, 2, 1, bias=False)
        self.conv4_bn = nn.BatchNorm2d(d*8)
        self.conv5 = nn.Conv2d(d*8, 3, 4, 1, 0, bias=False)

    def weight_init(self, mean, std):
        for m in self._modules:
            normal_init(self._modules[m], mean, std)

    def forward(self, input):
        x = F.leaky_relu(self.conv1(input), 0.2)
        x = F.leaky_relu(self.conv2_bn(self.conv2(x)), 0.2)
        x = F.leaky_relu(self.conv3_bn(self.conv3(x)), 0.2)
        x = F.leaky_relu(self.conv4_bn(self.conv4(x)), 0.2)
        x = F.sigmoid(self.conv5(x))
        return x
```

3. In the preceding function, we've used the `normal_init` function, which we will be using in the `generator` as well. We define it as follows:

```
def normal_init(m, mean, std):
    if isinstance(m, nn.ConvTranspose2d) or isinstance(m,
nn.Conv2d):
        m.weight.data.normal_(mean, std)
```

4. Next, we define `generator`:

```
class generator(nn.Module):
    def __init__(self):
        super(generator, self).__init__()
        self.deconv1 = nn.ConvTranspose2d(100, 1024, 4, 1, 0)
        self.deconv1_bn = nn.BatchNorm2d(1024)
        self.deconv2 = nn.ConvTranspose2d(1024, 512, 4, 2, 1)
        self.deconv2_bn = nn.BatchNorm2d(512)
        self.deconv3 = nn.ConvTranspose2d(512, 256, 4, 2, 1)
        self.deconv3_bn = nn.BatchNorm2d(256)
        self.deconv4 = nn.ConvTranspose2d(256, 128, 4, 2, 1)
        self.deconv4_bn = nn.BatchNorm2d(128)
        self.deconv5 = nn.ConvTranspose2d(128, 1, 4, 2, 1)

    def weight_init(self, mean, std):
        for m in self._modules:
            normal_init(self._modules[m], mean, std)

    def forward(self, input):
        x = F.relu(self.deconv1_bn(self.deconv1(input)))
        x = F.relu(self.deconv2_bn(self.deconv2(x)))
        x = F.relu(self.deconv3_bn(self.deconv3(x)))
        x = F.relu(self.deconv4_bn(self.deconv4(x)))
        x = F.tanh(self.deconv5(x))
        return x
```

5. To plot multiple random outputs during training, we create a function to plot the generated images:

```
def plot_output(epoch):
    z_ = torch.randn((5*5, 100)).view(-1, 100, 1, 1)
    z_ = Variable(z_.cuda(), volatile=True)

    G.eval()
    test_images = G(z_)
    G.train()

    size_figure_grid = 5
```

```
    fig, ax = plt.subplots(size_figure_grid, size_figure_grid,
figsize=(5, 5))
    for i, j in itertools.product(range(size_figure_grid),
range(size_figure_grid)):
        ax[i, j].get_xaxis().set_visible(False)
        ax[i, j].get_yaxis().set_visible(False)
```

6. In the following step, we will set the hyperparameters used during training. The hyperparameters have a big effect on the results of our GANs. The `generator` and `discriminator` shouldn't overpower each other. Batch size is an important hyperparameter for GANs. A general rule in deep learning is that a bigger batch size is better (up to a certain point). However, for GANs, a smaller batch size can also work better sometimes.

```
n_epochs = 24
batch_size = 32
learning_rate = 0.0002
```

7. For our model, we will use the Fashion-MNIST dataset and load it with the following code:

```
transform = transforms.Compose([transforms.Scale(64),
                                transforms.ToTensor(),
                                transforms.Normalize((0.5,),
(0.5,))])

train_dataset = fashion_mnist(root='./data',
                            train=True,
                            transform=transform,
                            download=True
                            )

train_loader = torch.utils.data.DataLoader(dataset=train_dataset,
                                        batch_size=batch_size,
                                        shuffle=True)
```

8. Let's create both networks by calling the defined functions, followed by initializing the weights:

```
G = generator(128)
D = discriminator(128)
G.weight_init(mean=0.0, std=0.02)
D.weight_init(mean=0.0, std=0.02)
```

9. Next, we need to make sure we use `cuda`:

```
G.cuda()
D.cuda()
```

10. For GANs, we can use the **Binary Cross Entropy (BCE)** loss:

```
BCE_loss = nn.BCELoss()
```

11. For both networks, we need to set the optimizers with the following settings:

```
beta_1 = 0.5
beta_2 = 0.999
G_optimizer = optim.Adam(G.parameters(), lr=learning_rate,
betas=(beta_1, beta_2))
D_optimizer = optim.Adam(D.parameters(), lr=learning_rate/2,
betas=(beta_1, beta_2))
```

12. Now we can start training our networks with the following code block:

```
for epoch in range(n_epochs):
    D_losses = []
    G_losses = []
    for x_, _ in train_loader:
        D.zero_grad()

        mini_batch = x_.size()[0]

        y_real_ = torch.ones(mini_batch)
        y_fake_ = torch.zeros(mini_batch)

        x_ = Variable(x_.cuda())
        y_real_ = Variable(y_real_.cuda())
        y_fake_ = Variable(y_fake_.cuda())
        D_result = D(x_).squeeze()
        D_real_loss = BCE_loss(D_result, y_real_)

        z_ = torch.randn((mini_batch, 100)).view(-1, 100, 1, 1)
        z_ = Variable(z_.cuda())
        G_result = G(z_)

        D_result = D(G_result).squeeze()
        D_fake_loss = BCE_loss(D_result, y_fake_)
        D_fake_score = D_result.data.mean()
        D_train_loss = D_real_loss + D_fake_loss

        D_train_loss.backward()
        D_optimizer.step()
```

```
        D_losses.append(D_train_loss.data[0])
        G.zero_grad()

        z_ = torch.randn((mini_batch, 100)).view(-1, 100, 1, 1)
        z_ = Variable(z_.cuda())

        G_result = G(z_)
        D_result = D(G_result).squeeze()
        G_train_loss = BCE_loss(D_result, y_real_)
        G_train_loss.backward()
        G_optimizer.step()
        G_losses.append(G_train_loss.data[0])

    print('Epoch %d - loss_d: %.3f, loss_g: %.3f' % ((epoch + 1),
torch.mean(torch.FloatTensor(D_losses)),
torch.mean(torch.FloatTensor(G_losses))))
    # Plot example output
    plot_output(epoch)
```

In the following figure, we can see the output after running our networks for 24 epochs:

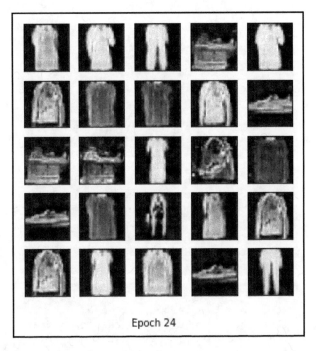

Epoch 24

Figure 6.2: Examples of generated images after 24 epochs

Upscaling the resolution of images with Super-Resolution GANs (SRGANs)

In Chapter 3, *Convolutional Neural Networks,* we demonstrated how a CNN can be used to autoencode an image to obtain a compression of the image. In the digital age, it's even more important to be able to scale up the resolution of an image to high quality. For example, a compressed version of an image can easily be shared via the internet. When the image arrives at the receiver, its quality will need to be increased, also known as **Super-Resolution imaging (SR)**. In the following recipe, we will show you how to increase the resolution of an image by training deep learning with the PyTorch framework.

How to do it...

1. First, we need to import all the necessary libraries:

```
import os
from os import listdir
from os.path import join
import numpy as np
import random
import matplotlib.pyplot as plt

import torchvision
from torchvision import transforms
import torchvision.datasets as datasets

import torch
import torch.nn as nn
import torch.nn.functional as F
import torch.optim as optim
from torch.autograd import Variable
```

2. In this recipe, we will be using the CelebA Faces dataset. We will import the data with a custom function in PyTorch:

```
class data_from_dir(data.Dataset):
    def __init__(self, image_dir, transform=None):
        super(DatasetFromFolder, self).__init__()
        self.image_dir = image_dir
        self.image_filenames = [ x for x in listdir(image_dir) if
        is_image_file(x)]
        self.transform = transform
```

```
def __getitem__(self, index):
    # Load Image
    image = Image.open(join(self.image_dir,
    self.image_filenames[index])).convert('RGB')
    image = self.transform(image)
    return image

def __len__(self):
    return len(self.image_filenames)
```

3. We will now define the hyperparameters that we will use for our model:

```
batch_size = 16
image_size = 125
image_channels = 3
n_conv_blocks = 2
up_sampling = 2
n_epochs = 100
learning_rate_G = 0.00001
learning_rate_D = 0.0000001
```

4. Before proceeding, we show an example image and a downsized version. The downscaled image will be used as input and the original image will be used as the target image. We've chosen to downscale the original images by a factor of two:

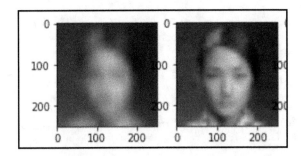

Figure 6.3: Example of a downscaled image and the original image (target, 250x250 pixels)

5. We can now define our `Discriminator` network. This network architecture is straightforward and based on well-known architectures for classification. The task of the discriminator is to classify the true output and generated output:

```
class discriminator_model(nn.Module)
    def __init__(self):
        super(discriminator_model, self).__init__()
        self.conv1 = nn.Conv2d(3, 64, 3, stride=1, padding=1)
```

```
self.conv2 = nn.Conv2d(64, 64, 3, stride=2, padding=1)
self.conv2_bn = nn.BatchNorm2d(64)
self.conv3 = nn.Conv2d(64, 128, 3, stride=1, padding=1)
self.conv3_bn = nn.BatchNorm2d(128)
self.conv4 = nn.Conv2d(128, 128, 3, stride=2, padding=1)
self.conv4_bn = nn.BatchNorm2d(128)
self.conv5 = nn.Conv2d(128, 256, 3, stride=1, padding=1)
self.conv5_bn = nn.BatchNorm2d(256)
self.conv6 = nn.Conv2d(256, 256, 3, stride=2, padding=1)
self.conv6_bn = nn.BatchNorm2d(256)
self.conv7 = nn.Conv2d(256, 512, 3, stride=1, padding=1)
self.conv7_bn = nn.BatchNorm2d(512)
self.conv8 = nn.Conv2d(512, 512, 3, stride=2, padding=1)
self.conv8_bn = nn.BatchNorm2d(512)
self.fc1 = nn.Linear(2048, 1024)
self.fc2 = nn.Linear(1024, 1)

def forward(self, x):
    x = F.elu(self.conv1(x))
    x = F.elu(self.conv2_bn(self.conv2(x)))
    x = F.elu(self.conv3_bn(self.conv3(x)))
    x = F.elu(self.conv4_bn(self.conv4(x)))
    x = F.elu(self.conv5_bn(self.conv5(x)))
    x = F.elu(self.conv6_bn(self.conv6(x)))
    x = F.elu(self.conv7_bn(self.conv7(x)))
    x = F.elu(self.conv8_bn(self.conv8(x)))
    x = x.view(x.size(0), -1)
    x = F.elu(self.fc1(x))
    x = F.sigmoid(self.fc2(x))
    return x
```

6. Before defining our generator architecture, we need to define two classes that we will use repeatedly. First is a convolution block that consists of batch normalization, a convolutional layer, and a dropout:

```
class conv_block(nn.Module):
    def __init__(self, in_channels, k, layers, p=0.2):
        super(conv_block, self).__init__()
        self.layers = layers

        for i in range(layers):
            self.add_module('batchnorm' + str(i+1),
            nn.BatchNorm2d(in_channels))
            self.add_module('conv' + str(i+1),
            nn.Conv2d(in_channels, k, 3, stride=1,
            padding=1))
            self.add_module('drop' + str(i+1),
            nn.Dropout2d(p=p))
```

```
                in_channels += k

    def forward(self, x):
        for i in range(self.layers):
            y = self.__getattr__('batchnorm' + str(i+1))(x.clone())
            y = F.elu(y)
            y = self.__getattr__('conv' + str(i+1))(y)
            y = self.__getattr__('drop' + str(i+1))(y)
            x = torch.cat((x,y), dim=1)
        return x
```

7. The other class is used for upsampling:

```
class upsample_block(nn.Module):
    def __init__(self, in_channels, out_channels):
        super(upsample_block, self).__init__()
        self.upsample1 = nn.Upsample(scale_factor=2,
        mode='nearest')
        self.conv1 = nn.Conv2d(in_channels, out_channels, 3,
    stride=1, padding=1)

    def forward(self, x):
        return F.elu(self.conv1(self.upsample1(x)))
```

8. Followed by the `Generator` model:

```
class generator_model(nn.Module):
    def __init__(self, n_conv_blocks, n_upsample_blocks):
        super(generator_model, self).__init__()
        self.n_dense_blocks = n_blocks
        self.upsample = upsample

        self.conv1 = nn.Conv2d(3, 64, 9, stride=1, padding=1)

        inchannels = 64
        for i in range(self.n_conv_blocks):
            self.add_module('conv_block' + str(i+1),
            conv_block(inchannels, 12, 4))
            inchannels += 12*4

        self.conv2 = nn.Conv2d(inchannels, 64, 3,
        stride=1, padding=1)
        self.conv2_bn = nn.BatchNorm2d(64)

        in_channels = 64
        out_channels = 256
        for i in range(self.n_upsample_blocks):
            self.add_module('upsample_block' + str(i+1),
```

```
            upsample_block(in_channels, out_channels))
            in_channels = out_channels
            out_channels = int(out_channels/2)

        self.conv3 = nn.Conv2d(in_channels, 3, 9,
        stride=1, padding=1)

    def forward(self, x):
        x = self.conv1(x)

        for i in range(self.n_dense_blocks):
            x = self.__getattr__('conv_block' + str(i+1))(x)

        x = F.elu(self.conv2_bn(self.conv2(x)))

        for i in range(self.upsample):
            x = self.__getattr__('upsample_blcok' + str(i+1))(x)

        return self.conv3(x)
```

9. We are now ready to create our datasets. First, we define the transformations we need:

```
normalize = transforms.Normalize(mean = [0.485, 0.456, 0.406],
                                 std = [0.229, 0.224, 0.225])

scale = transforms.Compose([transforms.ToPILImage(),
                            transforms.Scale(image_size),
                            transforms.ToTensor(),
                            transforms.Normalize
                            (mean = [0.485, 0.456, 0.406],
                            std = [0.229, 0.224, 0.225])
                            ])

transform =
transforms.Compose([transforms.Scale(image_size*n_upsampling),
                            transforms.ToTensor()])
```

10. Let's load the data and feed it into PyTorch's `DataLoader`:

```
dataset = data_from_dir('Data/CelebA/splits/train',
transform=transform)
dataloader = torch.utils.data.DataLoader(dataset,
batch_size=batch_size, shuffle=True)

netG = Generator(n_conv_blocks, n_upsampling)
netD = Discriminator()
```

11. As a loss function, we will use the `BCELoss` function:

```
adversarial_loss = nn.BCELoss()
```

12. We need to set the placeholders and activate the usage of CUDA:

```
target_real = Variable(torch.ones(batch_size, 1))
target_fake = Variable(torch.zeros(batch_size, 1))
target_real = target_real.cuda()
target_fake = target_fake.cuda()

inputs_G = torch.FloatTensor(batch_size, image_channels,
image_size, image_size)

netG.cuda()
netD.cuda()
feature_extractor =
FeatureExtractor(torchvision.models.vgg19(pretrained=True))
feature_extractor.cuda()

content_loss = nn.MSELoss()
adversarial_loss = nn.BCELoss()
content_loss.cuda()
adversarial_loss.cuda()
```

13. For both networks, we will use the `Adam` optimizer:

```
opt_G = optim.Adam(netG.parameters(), lr=learning_rate_G)
opt_D = optim.Adam(netD.parameters(), lr=learning_rate_D)
```

14. Finally, before training our networks, we define a function to plot the intermediate results:

```
def plot_output(inputs_G, inputs_D_real, inputs_D_fake):
    image_size = (250, 250)
    transform = transforms.Compose([transforms.Normalize
                        (mean = [-2.118, -2.036, -1.804],
                         std = [4.367, 4.464, 4.444]),
                        transforms.ToPILImage(),
        transforms.Scale(image_size)])
    figure, (lr_plot, hr_plot, fake_plot) = plt.subplots(1,3)
    i = random.randint(0, inputs_G.size(0) -1)

    lr_image = transform(inputs_G[i])
    hr_image = transform(inputs_D_real[i])
    fake_hr_image = transform(inputs_D_fake[i])
```

```
lr_image_ph = lr_plot.imshow(lr_image)
hr_image_ph = hr_plot.imshow(hr_image)
fake_hr_image_ph = fake_plot.imshow(fake_hr_image)

figure.canvas.draw()
plt.show()
```

15. We can now start training our network with the following code block:

```
inputs_G = torch.FloatTensor(batch_size, 3, image_size, image_size)

for epoch in range(n_epochs):
    for i, inputs in enumerate(dataloader):

        for j in range(batch_size):
            inputs_G[j] = scale(inputs[j])
            inputs[j] = normalize(inputs[j])

        inputs_D_real = Variable(inputs.cuda())
        inputs_D_fake = net_G(Variable(inputs_G).cuda())
        net_D.zero_grad()

        outputs = net_D(inputs_D_real)
        D_real = outputs.data.mean()

        loss_D_real = adversarial_loss(outputs, target_real)
        loss_D_real.backward()

        outputs = net_D(inputs_D_fake.detach())
        D_fake = outputs.data.mean()

        loss_D_fake = adversarial_criterion(outputs, target_fake)
        loss_D_fake.backward()

        opt_D.step()

        net_G.zero_grad()
        real_features =
        Variable(feature_extractor(inputs_D_real).data)
        fake_features = feature_extractor(inputs_D_fake)

        loss_G_content = content_loss(fake_features,
        real_features)
        loss_G_adversarial =
        adversarial_loss(net_D(inputs_D_fake).detach(),
        target_real)

        loss_G_total = 0.005*lossG_content +
```

```
0.001*lossG_adversarial
        loss_G_total.backward()
        opt_G.step()

    plot_output(inputs_G, inputs_D_real.cpu().data,
inputsD_fake.cpu().data)
```

In the following figure, we can see the output after running our networks for 100 epochs:

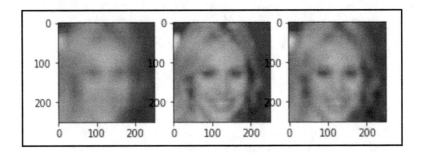

Figure 6.4: Example of a downscaled input, original image, and generated image

As you may have noticed, the generated image is not as sharp as the original image yet. Training a generator network to increase the resolution of an image is a heavy computational task. The dataset used in this recipe has a relatively low translation invariance. However, our model still needs to be fine-tuned further and trained for more epochs in order to achieve better results.

7
Computer Vision

In this chapter, we will implement deep neural networks related to processing data encoded as images, including video frames. These are the recipes we will cover:

- Augmenting images with computer vision techniques
- Classifying objects in images
- Localizing an object in images
- Segmenting classes in images with U-net
- Scene understanding (semantic segmentation)
- Finding facial key points
- Recognizing faces
- Transferring styles to images

Introduction

The focus of this chapter is on applications of deep learning in computer vision. Deep learning, especially **Convolutional Neural Networks** (**CNNs**), has revolutionized the field of computer vision. Most benchmarks were beaten by the introduction of deeper CNNs, and some surpassed human-level accuracy for the first time. In this chapter, we will show different kinds of applications within computer vision. Next to CNNs, we will also be using **recurrent neural networks** (**RNNs**) in some of these recipes.

Augmenting images with computer vision techniques

CNNs and computer vision are inseparable in deep learning. Before we dig deeper into the applications of deep learning for computer vision, we will introduce basic computer vision techniques that you can apply in your deep learning pipeline to make your model more robust. Augmentation can be used during training to increase the number of distinct examples and make your model more robust for slight variations. Moreover, it can be used during testing—**Test Time Augmentation (TTA)**. Not every augmentation is suitable for every problem. For example, flipping a traffic sign with an arrow to the left has a different meaning than the original. We will be implementing our augmentation function with OpenCV.

How to do it...

1. Let's first load all the necessary libraries:

```
import numpy as np
import cv2
import matplotlib.pyplot as plt
import glob
```

2. Next, we load some sample images that we will use and plot them:

```
DATA_DIR = 'Data/augmentation/'
images = glob.glob(DATA_DIR + '*')

plt.figure(figsize=(10, 10))
i = 1
for image in images:
    img = cv2.imread(image)
    img = cv2.cvtColor(img, cv2.COLOR_BGR2RGB)
    plt.subplot(3, 3, i)
    plt.imshow(img)
    i += 1
plt.show()
```

Figure 7.1: Example images that we will be using for augmentation

3. We start by defining a function to easily plot examples of our augmentations:

```
def plot_images(image, function, *args):
    plt.figure(figsize=(10, 10))
    n_examples = 3
    for i in range(n_examples):
        img = cv2.imread(image)
        img = cv2.cvtColor(img, cv2.COLOR_BGR2RGB)
        img = function(img, *args)
        plt.subplot(3, 3, i+1)
        plt.imshow(img)
    plt.show()
```

4. We define a function to randomly rotate an image and plot some examples:

```
def rotate_image(image, rotate=20):
    width, height, _ = image.shape
    random_rotation = np.random.uniform(low=-rotate, high=rotate)
    M = cv2.getRotationMatrix2D((width/2, height/2),
random_rotation, 1)
    return(cv2.warpAffine(image, M, (width, height)))

plot_images(images[2], rotate_image, 40)
```

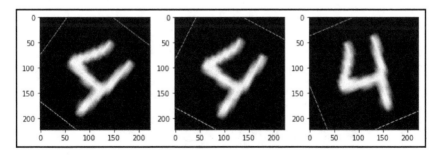

Figure 7.2: Examples of random rotations

5. Next, we define a function to adjust the brightness of an image:

```
def adjust_brightness(image, brightness=60):
    rand_brightness = np.random.uniform(low=-brightness,
high=brightness)
    return(cv2.add(image, rand_brightness))

plot_images(images[0], adjust_brightness, 85)
```

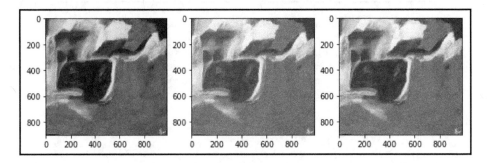

Figure 7.3: Examples of randomly adjusted brightness

6. The following function will randomly shift an image using the parameters provided:

```
def random_shifts(image, shift_max_x=100, shift_max_y=100):
    width, height, _ = image.shape
    shift_x = np.random.randint(shift_max_x)
    shift_y = np.random.randint(shift_max_y)
    M = np.float32([[1, 0, shift_x],[0, 1, shift_y]])
    return (cv2.warpAffine(image, M, (height, width)))

plot_images(images[1], random_shifts, 100, 20)
```

Figure 7.4: Examples of randomly shifted images

7. For some images, it is beneficial to scale up or down:

```
def scale_image(image, scale_range=[0.6, 1.4]):
    width, height, _ = image.shape
    scale_x = np.random.uniform(low=scale_range[0],
high=scale_range[1])
    scale_y = np.random.uniform(low=scale_range[0],
high=scale_range[1])
    scale_matrix = np.array([[scale_x, 0., (1. - scale_x) * width /
2.],
                             [0., scale_y, (1. - scale_y) * height
/ 2.]],
                            dtype=np.float32)
    return(cv2.warpAffine(image, scale_matrix, (width, height),
flags=cv2.INTER_LINEAR,
                borderMode=cv2.BORDER_REFLECT_101))

plot_images(images[2], scale_image, [0.7, 1.3])
```

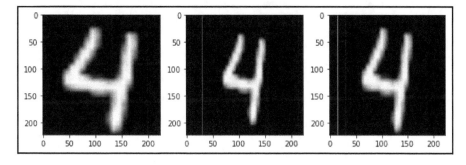

Figure 7.5: Examples of randomly scaled images

8. Our final augmentation is meant to randomly flip an image:

```
def random_flip(image, p_flip=0.5):
    rand = np.random.random()
    if rand < p_flip:
        image = cv2.flip(image, 1)
    return image

plot_images(images[2], random_flip)
```

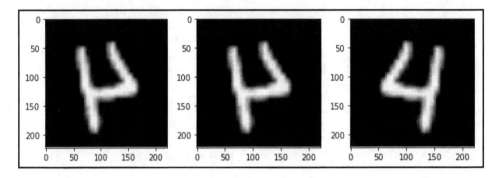

Figure 7.6: Examples of random flips

9. Let's apply all our augmentations together randomly and plot the results of 32 examples:

```
plt.figure(figsize=(15, 15))
image = images[1]
for i in range(32):
    img = cv2.imread(image)
    img = cv2.cvtColor(img, cv2.COLOR_BGR2RGB)
    img = transform_image(img)
    plt.subplot(8, 8, i+1)
    plt.axis('off')
    plt.imshow(img, interpolation="nearest")
plt.show()
```

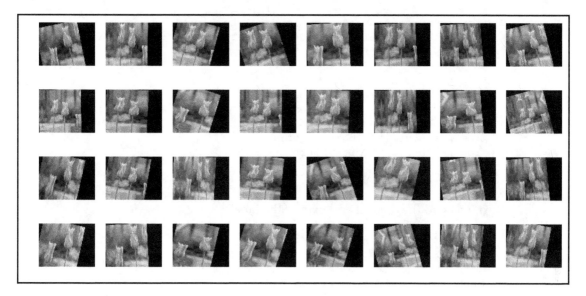

Figure 7.7: All augmentations randomly applied 32 times

 Most deep learning frameworks have their own implementations for image augmentations. For example, for PyTorch, take a look at `torchvision.transforms`. These transformations make it easy to add augmentations such as random cropping and flipping to your data. In Keras, you can use `ImageDataGenerator` for random augmentation.

Classifying objects in images

In this recipe, we will show you how to classify objects in images using a CNN. We will train the network from scratch to classify five different flower types in images. The images have different sizes. For this recipe, we will be using Keras.

How to do it...

1. Create a new Python file and import the necessary libraries:

```
import numpy as np
import glob
import cv2
import matplotlib.pyplot as plt
```

```
from sklearn.preprocessing import LabelBinarizer
from sklearn.model_selection import train_test_split
from sklearn.metrics import accuracy_score

import keras
from keras.models import Sequential, load_model
from keras.layers import Dense, Dropout, Activation, Flatten,
Conv2D, MaxPooling2D, Lambda, Cropping2D
from keras.utils import np_utils
from keras import optimizers

SEED = 2017
```

2. Next, we load the dataset and extract the labels:

```
# Specify data directory and extract all file names
DATA_DIR = '../Data/'
images = glob.glob(DATA_DIR + "flower_photos/*/*.jpg")
# Extract labels from file names
labels = [x.split('/')[3] for x in images]
```

3. Let's have a look at the data:

```
unique_labels = set(labels)
plt.figure(figsize=(15, 15))
i = 1
for label in unique_labels:
    image = images[labels.index(label)]
    img = cv2.imread(image)
    img = cv2.cvtColor(img, cv2.COLOR_BGR2RGB)
    plt.subplot(5, 5, i)
    plt.title("{0} ({1})".format(label, labels.count(label)))
    i += 1
    _ = plt.imshow(img)
plt.show()
```

Figure 7.8: Flower dataset examples per label and counts

4. Transform the labels into binary format:

```
encoder = LabelBinarizer()
encoder.fit(labels)
y = encoder.transform(labels).astype(float)
```

5. Split the dataset for training and testing:

```
X_train, X_val, y_train , y_val = train_test_split(images, y,
test_size=0.1, random_state=SEED)
```

6. Define a network architecture:

```
# Define architecture
model = Sequential()
model.add(Lambda(lambda x: (x / 255.) - 0.5, input_shape=(100, 100,
3)))
model.add(Conv2D(16, (5, 5), activation='relu', padding='same'))
model.add(MaxPooling2D(pool_size=(2,2)))
model.add(Dropout(0.5))
model.add(Conv2D(32, (5, 5), activation='relu', padding='same'))
model.add(MaxPooling2D(pool_size=(2,2)))
model.add(Dropout(0.5))
model.add(Conv2D(64, (3, 3), activation='relu', padding='same'))
model.add(MaxPooling2D(pool_size=(2,2)))
model.add(Dropout(0.5))
model.add(Flatten())
model.add(Dense(256, activation='relu'))
model.add(Dropout(0.5))
model.add(Dense(5, activation='softmax'))

# Define optimizer and compile
sgd = optimizers.SGD(lr=0.01, decay=1e-6, momentum=0.9,
nesterov=True)
model.compile(loss='categorical_crossentropy', optimizer=sgd,
metrics=['accuracy'])
```

7. Create a batch generator to loop through the data randomly:

```
img_rows = img_cols = 100
img_channels = 3

def batchgen(x, y, batch_size, transform=False):
    # Create empty numpy arrays
    images = np.zeros((batch_size, img_rows, img_cols, img_channels))
    class_id = np.zeros((batch_size, len(y[0])))

    while 1:
```

```
        for n in range(batch_size):
            i = np.random.randint(len(x))
            x_ = cv2.imread(x[i])
            x_ = cv2.cvtColor(x_, cv2.COLOR_BGR2RGB)
            # The images have different sizes, we transform all to 100x100
pixels
            x_ = cv2.resize(x_, (100, 100))
            images[n] = x_
            class_id[n] = y[i]
            yield images, class_id
```

8. Next, we can train the model:

```
batch_size = 256
n_epochs = 20
s_epoch = 100
val_size = 0.2
val_steps = 20

train_generator = batchgen(X_train, y_train, batch_size, True)
val_generator = batchgen(X_valid, y_valid, batch_size, False)

history = model.fit_generator(train_generator,
                              steps_per_epoch=s_epoch,
                              nb_epoch=n_epochs,
                              validation_data=val_generator,
                              validation_steps = val_steps
                    )
```

9. Let's plot the training results:

```
plt.plot(history.history['acc'])
plt.plot(history.history['val_acc'])
plt.title('model_accuracy')
plt.ylabel('accuracy')
plt.xlabel('epochs')
plt.legend(['train', 'validation'], loc='lower right')
plt.show()
```

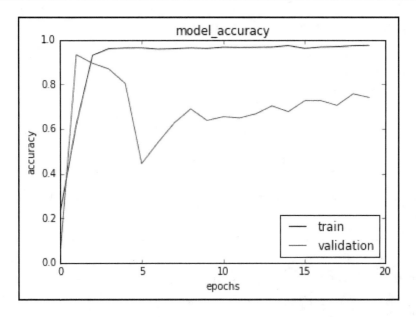

Figure 7.9: Training results on flower dataset

10. We can now check how our model performs on the unseen test set:

```
test_generator = batchgen(X_valid, y_valid, 1, False)
preds = model.predict_generator(test_generator, steps=len(X_valid))

y_valid_ = [np.argmax(x) for x in y_valid]
y_preds = [np.argmax(x) for x in preds]
accuracy_score(y_valid_, y_preds)
```

11. Finally, let's plot some of the predictions:

```
n_predictions = 5
plt.figure(figsize=(15, 15))
for i in range(n_predictions):
    plt.subplot(n_predictions, n_predictions, i+1)
    plt.title("{0} ({1})".format(list(set(labels))[np.argmax(preds[i])],
                                  list(set(labels))[np.argmax(y_valid[i])]))
    img = cv2.imread(X_valid[i])
    img = cv2.cvtColor(img, cv2.COLOR_BGR2RGB)
    plt.axis('off')
    plt.imshow(img)
    plt.tight_layout()
plt.show()
```

Figure 7-10: Predictions on the five test images and their true labels between brackets

In `Chapter 14`, *Pretrained Models*, we will show you how to leverage state-of-the art networks for object classification.

Localizing an object in images

Now that we can classify objects in images, the next step is to localize and classify (detect) objects in images. In the dataset we used in the previous recipe, the flowers (objects) were clearly visible, mostly centered, and they covered almost the complete image. However, often this is not the case and we'd want to detect one or multiple objects in an image. In the following recipe, we will show you how to detect an object in images using deep learning.

We will be using a dataset with annotated trucks. The images are taken by a camera mounted at the front of a car. We will be using TensorFlow to implement the object detector.

How to do it...

1. Let's import the libraries first:

```
import numpy as np
import pandas as pd
import glob
import cv2
import matplotlib.pyplot as plt

from sklearn.preprocessing import LabelBinarizer
from sklearn.model_selection import train_test_split
from sklearn.metrics import accuracy_score

from keras.models import Sequential, load_model
from keras.layers import Dense, Dropout, Activation, Flatten,
Conv2D, MaxPooling2D, Lambda, Cropping2D
from keras.utils import np_utils
from keras import backend as K
from keras.callbacks import EarlyStopping
from keras import optimizers
```

2. Load the dataset and plot the first rows of the CSV:

```
DATA_DIR = 'Data/object-detection-crowdai/'
labels = pd.read_csv(DATA_DIR + 'labels.csv',
usecols=[0,1,2,3,4,5])
# We will only localize Trucks
labels = labels[labels.Label == 'Truck']
# We only use images were one Truck is annotated
labels =
labels[~labels.Frame.isin(labels.Frame[labels.Frame.duplicated()].v
alues)]
labels.columns=['xmin', 'ymin', 'xmax', 'ymax', 'Frame', 'Label']
labels[30:50]
```

3. To understand the dataset, let's plot some example images and their accompanying bounding boxes:

```
image_list = ['1479498416965787036.jpg',
              '1479498541974858765.jpg']

plt.figure(figsize=(15,15))
i=1
for image in image_list:
    plt.subplot(len(image_list), len(image_list), i)
    img_info = labels[labels.Frame == image]
    img = cv2.imread(DATA_DIR + image)
    img = cv2.cvtColor(img, cv2.COLOR_BGR2RGB)
    print(img.shape)
    cv2.rectangle(img, (img_info.xmin,
img_info.ymin),(img_info.xmax, img_info.ymax), (255, 0 , 255), 4)
    print(img_info)
    plt.imshow(img)
    i+=1
plt.show()
```

Figure 7.11: Example images and their bounding boxes

4. Next, we output some statistics about the dataset:

```
X_train = labels.iloc[:1970]
X_val = labels.iloc[2000:]
print(X_train.shape)
print(X_val.shape)
```

5. The images included in this dataset are frames of a video, so we should be careful while splitting the data for training and validation (to prevent data leakage). Most images have overlap:

```
image_list = ['1479502622732414408.jpg',
              '1479502623247392322.jpg',
              '1479502623755460204.jpg',
              '1479502623247392322.jpg',
              '1479502625253159017.jpg']
n_images = len(image_list)

plt.figure(figsize=(15,15))
for i in range(n_images):
    plt.subplot(n_images, n_images, i+1)
    plt.title("{0}".format(image_list[i]))
    img = cv2.imread(DATA_DIR + 'object-detection-crowdai/'
    + image_list[i])
    img = cv2.cvtColor(img, cv2.COLOR_BGR2RGB)
    plt.axis('off')
    plt.imshow(img)
    plt.tight_layout()
plt.show()
```

Figure 7.12: Many images in the dataset show overlap

6. Therefore, we will make our training and validation split time-based:

```
X_train = labels.iloc[:1970] # We've picked this frame because the car
makes a right turn
X_val = labels.iloc[2000:]
print(X_train.shape)
print(X_val.shape)
```

7. We need to implement a custom function for the metric **Intersection Over Union** (**IOU**). We do this as follows:

```
def IOU_calc(y_true, y_pred, smooth=0.9):
    y_true_f = K.flatten(y_true)
    y_pred_f = K.flatten(y_pred)
    intersection = K.sum(y_true_f * y_pred_f)
    return 2*(intersection + smooth) / (K.sum(y_true_f) +
K.sum(y_pred_f) + smooth)
```

8. Now, let's define the architecture of our model:

```
img_rows = 200
img_cols = 200
img_channels = 3

model = Sequential()
model.add(Lambda(lambda x: (x / 255.) - 0.5, input_shape=(img_rows,
img_cols, img_channels)))
model.add(Conv2D(16, (5, 5), activation='relu', padding='same'))
model.add(MaxPooling2D(pool_size=(2,2)))
model.add(Conv2D(32, (5, 5), activation='relu', padding='same'))
model.add(MaxPooling2D(pool_size=(2,2)))
model.add(Conv2D(64, (3, 3), activation='relu', padding='same'))
model.add(MaxPooling2D(pool_size=(2,2)))
model.add(Flatten())
model.add(Dense(256, activation='relu'))
model.add(Dropout(0.5))
model.add(Dense(4, activation='sigmoid'))

# Define optimizer and compile
opt = optimizers.Adam(lr=1e-8)
model.compile(optimizer=opt, loss='mse', metrics=[IOU_calc])
model.summary()
```

9. To make sure the training data fits in memory, we can use a batch generator:

```
def batchgen(x, y, batch_size, transform=False):
    # Create empty numpy arrays
    images = np.zeros((batch_size, img_rows, img_cols,
img_channels))
    class_id = np.zeros((batch_size, 4))#len(y[0])))

    while 1:
        for n in range(batch_size):
            i = np.random.randint(len(x))
            x_ = x.Frame.iloc[i]
            x_ = cv2.imread(DATA_DIR + image)
```

```
x_ = cv2.cvtColor(img, cv2.COLOR_BGR2RGB)
x_min = (x.iloc[i].xmin * (img_cols/1920)) / img_cols
x_max = (x.iloc[i].xmax * (img_cols/1920)) / img_cols
y_min = (x.iloc[i].ymin * (img_rows/1200)) / img_rows
y_max = (x.iloc[i].ymax * (img_rows/1200)) / img_rows
y_ = (x_min, y_min, x_max, y_max)
x_ = cv2.resize(x_, (img_cols, img_rows))
images[n] = x_
class_id[n] = y_
yield images, class_id
```

10. To make sure our model doesn't overfit on the training data, we will be using `EarlyStopping`:

```
callbacks = [EarlyStopping(monitor='val_IOU_calc', patience=10,
verbose=0)]
```

11. We can now train our model and store the training results in history:

```
batch_size = 64
n_epochs = 1000
steps_per_epoch = 512
val_steps = len(X_val)

train_generator = batchgen(X_train, _, batch_size, True)
val_generator = batchgen(X_val, _, batch_size, False)

history = model.fit_generator(train_generator,
                              steps_per_epoch=steps_per_epoch,
                              epochs=n_epochs,
                              validation_data=val_generator,
                              validation_steps = val_steps,
                             callbacks=callbacks
                             )
```

Real-time detection frameworks

In some applications, the detection model we've implemented before is not sufficient. For these applications—where real-time perception is important in order to be able to actuate as quickly as possible—we need a model that is able to detect objects in near real time. The most popular real-time detection frameworks are **faster-RCNN, YOLO (You Only Look Once)**, and **SSD (Single-Shot Multibox Detector)**. Faster-RCNN has shown higher accuracy in benchmarks, but YOLO is able to infer predictions more quickly.

Segmenting classes in images with U-net

In the previous recipe, we focused on localizing an object by predicting a bounding box. However, in some cases, you'll want to know the exact location of an object and a box around the object is not sufficient. We also call this segmentation—putting a mask on an object. To predict the masks of objects, we will use the popular U-net model structure. The U-net model has proven to be state-of-the-art by winning multiple image segmentation competitions. A U-net model is a special type of encoder-decoder network with skip connections, convolutional blocks, and upscaling convolutions.

In the following recipe, we will show you how to segment objects in images. Specifically, we will be segmenting the background. To implement the U-net network architecture, we will use the Keras framework.

How to do it...

1. We start by importing all libraries, as follows:

```
import numpy as np
import cv2
import matplotlib.pyplot as plt
import glob

from keras.layers import Input, merge, Conv2D, MaxPooling2D,
UpSampling2D, Dropout, Cropping2D, merge
from keras.optimizers import Adam
from keras.callbacks import ModelCheckpoint, LearningRateScheduler
from keras import backend as K
from keras.models import Model
```

2. Then, we need to store all the training filenames:

```
import os
filenames = []
for path, subdirs, files in os.walk('Data/1obj'):
    for name in files:
        if 'src_color' in path:
            filenames.append(os.path.join(path, name))
print('# Training images: {}'.format(len(filenames)))
```

3. Let's plot some example training images and their masks:

```
n_examples = 3
for i in range(n_examples):
    plt.subplot(2, 2, 1)
    image = cv2.imread(filenames[i])
    image = cv2.cvtColor(image, cv2.COLOR_BGR2RGB)
    plt.imshow(image)

    plt.subplot(2, 2, 2)
    mask_file = filenames[i].replace('src_color', 'human_seg')
    mask = cv2.imread(glob.glob(mask_file[:-4]+'*')[0])
    ret, mask = cv2.threshold(mask, 0, 255, cv2.THRESH_BINARY_INV)
    mask = mask[:,:,0]
    plt.imshow((mask), cmap='gray')

    plt.show()
```

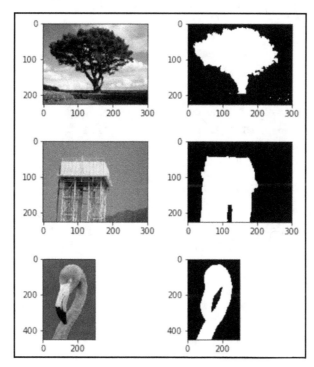

Figure 7.1A: Example training images and their masks

4. To determine the performance of our network and loss function, we will be using the `dice` coefficient. We need to implement these as functions to be able to compile them with our Keras model:

```
def dice_coef(y_true, y_pred, smooth=0.9):
    y_true_f = K.flatten(y_true)
    y_pred_f = K.flatten(y_pred)
    intersection = K.sum(y_true_f * y_pred_f)
    return (2. * intersection + smooth) / (K.sum(y_true_f) +
K.sum(y_pred_f) + smooth)


def dice_coef_loss(y_true, y_pred):
    return -dice_coef(y_true, y_pred)
```

5. Next, we define our U-net model's architecture:

```
img_rows = 240
img_cols = 240
img_channels = 3

inputs = Input((img_rows, img_cols, img_channels))

conv1 = Conv2D(64, 3, activation = 'relu', padding = 'same',
kernel_initializer = 'he_normal')(inputs)
conv1 = Conv2D(64, 3, activation = 'relu', padding = 'same',
kernel_initializer = 'he_normal')(conv1)
pool1 = MaxPooling2D(pool_size=(2, 2))(conv1)

conv2 = Conv2D(128, 3, activation = 'relu', padding = 'same',
kernel_initializer = 'he_normal')(pool1)
conv2 = Conv2D(128, 3, activation = 'relu', padding = 'same',
kernel_initializer = 'he_normal')(conv2)
pool2 = MaxPooling2D(pool_size=(2, 2))(conv2)

conv3 = Conv2D(256, 3, activation = 'relu', padding = 'same',
kernel_initializer = 'he_normal')(pool2)
conv3 = Conv2D(256, 3, activation = 'relu', padding = 'same',
kernel_initializer = 'he_normal')(conv3)
pool3 = MaxPooling2D(pool_size=(2, 2))(conv3)


conv4 = Conv2D(512, 3, activation = 'relu', padding = 'same',
kernel_initializer = 'he_normal')(pool3)
conv4 = Conv2D(512, 3, activation = 'relu', padding = 'same',
kernel_initializer = 'he_normal')(conv4)
drop4 = Dropout(0.5)(conv4)
```

```
pool4 = MaxPooling2D(pool_size=(2, 2))(drop4)

conv5 = Conv2D(1024, 3, activation = 'relu', padding = 'same',
kernel_initializer = 'he_normal')(pool4)
conv5 = Conv2D(1024, 3, activation = 'relu', padding = 'same',
kernel_initializer = 'he_normal')(conv5)
drop5 = Dropout(0.5)(conv5)

up6 = Conv2D(512, 2, activation = 'relu', padding = 'same',
kernel_initializer = 'he_normal')(UpSampling2D(size =
(2,2))(drop5))
merge6 = merge([drop4,up6], mode = 'concat', concat_axis = 3)
conv6 = Conv2D(512, 3, activation = 'relu', padding = 'same',
kernel_initializer = 'he_normal')(merge6)
conv6 = Conv2D(512, 3, activation = 'relu', padding = 'same',
kernel_initializer = 'he_normal')(conv6)

up7 = Conv2D(256, 2, activation = 'relu', padding = 'same',
kernel_initializer = 'he_normal')(UpSampling2D(size =
(2,2))(conv6))
merge7 = merge([conv3,up7], mode = 'concat', concat_axis = 3)
conv7 = Conv2D(256, 3, activation = 'relu', padding = 'same',
kernel_initializer = 'he_normal')(merge7)
conv7 = Conv2D(256, 3, activation = 'relu', padding = 'same',
kernel_initializer = 'he_normal')(conv7)

up8 = Conv2D(128, 2, activation = 'relu', padding = 'same',
kernel_initializer = 'he_normal')(UpSampling2D(size =
(2,2))(conv7))
merge8 = merge([conv2,up8], mode = 'concat', concat_axis = 3)
conv8 = Conv2D(128, 3, activation = 'relu', padding = 'same',
kernel_initializer = 'he_normal')(merge8)
conv8 = Conv2D(128, 3, activation = 'relu', padding = 'same',
kernel_initializer = 'he_normal')(conv8)

up9 = Conv2D(64, 2, activation = 'relu', padding = 'same',
kernel_initializer = 'he_normal')(UpSampling2D(size =
(2,2))(conv8))
merge9 = merge([conv1,up9], mode = 'concat', concat_axis = 3)
conv9 = Conv2D(64, 3, activation = 'relu', padding = 'same',
kernel_initializer = 'he_normal')(merge9)
conv9 = Conv2D(64, 3, activation = 'relu', padding = 'same',
kernel_initializer = 'he_normal')(conv9)
conv9 = Conv2D(2, 3, activation = 'relu', padding = 'same',
kernel_initializer = 'he_normal')(conv9)
conv10 = Conv2D(1, 1, activation = 'sigmoid')(conv9)

model = Model(input = inputs, output = conv10)
```

```
opt = Adam()
model.compile(optimizer = opt, loss=dice_coef_loss, metrics =
[dice_coef])
model.summary()
```

6. Let's load our training data:

```
X = np.ndarray((len(filenames), img_rows, img_cols , img_channels),
dtype=np.uint8)
y = np.ndarray((len(filenames), img_rows, img_cols , 1),
dtype=np.uint8)
i=0
for image in filenames:
    img = cv2.imread(image)
    img = cv2.cvtColor(img, cv2.COLOR_BGR2RGB)
    img = cv2.resize(img, (240,240))
    mask_file = image.replace('src_color', 'human_seg')
    label = cv2.imread(glob.glob(mask_file[:-4]+'*')[0], 0)
    ret, label = cv2.threshold(label, 0, 255,
cv2.THRESH_BINARY_INV)
    label = cv2.resize(img, (240, 240))
    label = label[:,:,0].reshape((240, 240, 1))
    img = np.array([img/255.])
    label = np.array([label])
    X[i] = img
    y[i] = label
    i+=1
```

7. Finally, we can start training our model, as follows:

```
n_epochs = 1
batch_size = 1
history = model.fit(X, y, batch_size=batch_size, epochs=10,
verbose=1, shuffle=True, validation_split=0.1)
```

Scene understanding (semantic segmentation)

In the previous recipe, we focused on segmenting one or two specific classes. However, in some cases, you'll want to segment all classes in an image to understand the complete scene. For example, for self-driving cars, it's important that all objects surrounding the car are segmented. In the following recipe, we will segment one class for performance reasons. However, with this network, it is straightforward to scale to multiple classes. The network architecture we will be using is called a fully convolutional network, because we use only convolutional layers in our model. We will be using the pretrained weights of VGG16 and the TensorFlow framework.

How to do it...

1. First, we start with loading the libraries, as follows:

```
import os
import glob
import tensorflow as tf
```

2. Because our task is slightly more complicated than outputting the predicted class, we need to define a function that extracts the values from different layers:

```
def extract_layers(vgg_layer3_out, vgg_layer4_out,
vgg_layer7_out, n_classes):
    decode_layer1_preskip0 =
tf.layers.conv2d_transpose(vgg_layer7_out,
512, (2, 2), (2, 2), name='decode_layer1_preskip0')
    decode_layer1_preskip1 = tf.layers.conv2d(vgg_layer4_out,
512, (1, 1), (1, 1), name='decode_layer1_preskip1')
    decode_layer1_out = tf.add(decode_layer1_preskip0,
decode_layer1_preskip1, name='decode_layer1_out')
    decode_layer2_preskip0 = tf.layers.conv2d_transpose
(decode_layer1_out, 256, (2, 2), (2, 2),
name='decode_layer2_preskip0')
    decode_layer2_preskip1 = tf.layers.conv2d
(vgg_layer3_out, 256, (1, 1), (1, 1),
name='decode_layer2_preskip1')
    decode_layer2_out = tf.add(decode_layer2_preskip0,
decode_layer2_preskip1, name='decode_layer2_out')
    decode_layer3_out = tf.layers.conv2d_transpose
(decode_layer2_out, 128, (2, 2), (2, 2), name='decode_layer3_out')
```

```
    decode_layer4_out = tf.layers.conv2d_transpose
(decode_layer3_out, 64, (2, 2), (2, 2),
name='decode_layer4_out')
    decode_layer5_out = tf.layers.conv2d_transpose
(decode_layer4_out, n_classes, (2, 2), (2, 2), name='fcn_out')
    return decode_layer5_out
```

3. To make efficient use of our memory, we will only load images with a batch generator function defined as follows:

```
def batch_generator(batch_size):
    image_paths = glob(os.path.join(data_path, 'image_2', '*.png'))
    label_paths = {
        re.sub(r'_(lane|road)_', '_', os.path.basename(path)): path
        for path in glob(os.path.join(data_path,
        'gt_image_2', '*_road_*.png'))}
    background_color = np.array([255, 0, 0])

    random.shuffle(image_paths)
    for batch_i in range(0, len(image_paths), batch_size):
        images = []
        gt_images = []
        for image_file in image_paths[batch_i:batch_i +
batch_size]:
            gt_image_file =
label_paths[os.path.basename(image_file)]

            image =
scipy.misc.imresize(scipy.misc.imread(image_file), image_shape)
            gt_image = scipy.misc.imresize(scipy.misc.imread
            (gt_image_file), image_shape)

            gt_bg = np.all(gt_image == background_color, axis=2)
            gt_bg = gt_bg.reshape(*gt_bg.shape, 1)
            gt_image = np.concatenate((gt_bg, np.invert(gt_bg)),
axis=2)

            images.append(image)
            gt_images.append(gt_image)

        yield np.array(images), np.array(gt_images)
```

4. Let's set our hyperparameters:

```
n_classes = 2
image_shape = (160, 576)
n_epochs = 23
batch_size = 16
```

5. Now, we start training our model:

```
with tf.Session() as sess:
    tf.saved_model.loader.load(sess, path, path)
    vgg_image_input =
sess.graph.get_tensor_by_name('image_input:0')
    vgg_keep_prob = sess.graph.get_tensor_by_name('keep_prob:0')
    vgg_layer3_out = sess.graph.get_tensor_by_name('layer3_out:0')
    vgg_layer4_out = sess.graph.get_tensor_by_name('layer4_out:0')
    vgg_layer7_out = sess.graph.get_tensor_by_name('layer7_out:0')
    temp = set(tf.global_variables())
    out_layer = layers(vgg_layer3_out, vgg_layer4_out,
    vgg_layer7_out, num_classes)
    softmax = tf.nn.softmax(out_layer, name='softmax')
    logits = tf.reshape(out_layer, (-1, num_classes),
name='logits')
    labels = tf.reshape(correct_label, (-1, num_classes))
    cross_entropy_loss =
tf.reduce_mean(tf.nn.softmax_cross_entropy_with_logits
    (logits=logits, labels=labels))
    train_op =
tf.train.AdamOptimizer(learning_rate).minimize(cross_entropy_loss)

    sess.run(tf.variables_initializer(set(tf.global_variables()) -
temp))
    for i in range(n_epochs):
        batches = batch_generator(batch_size)
        epoch_loss = 0
        epoch_size = 0
        for batch_input, batch_label in batches:
            _, loss = sess.run([train_op, cross_entropy_loss],
            feed_dict={input_image: batch_input,
correct_label: batch_label,
keep_prob: 0.5,
learning_rate: 1e-4})
            epoch_loss += loss * len(batch_input)
            epoch_size += len(batch_input)
        print("Loss at epoch {}: {}".format(i,
epoch_loss/epoch_size))
```

6. Finally, let's output the predicted segmentations:

```
for image_file in glob(os.path.join(data_path, 'image_2',
'*.png')):
    image = scipy.misc.imresize(scipy.misc.imread(image_file),
image_shape)

    pred_softmax = sess.run(
```

```
        [tf.nn.softmax(logits)],
        {keep_prob: 1.0, image_pl: [image]})
    pred_softmax = pred_softmax[0][:, 1].reshape(image_shape[0],
image_shape[1])
    segmentation = (pred_softmax > 0.5).reshape(image_shape[0],
image_shape[1], 1)
    mask = np.dot(segmentation, np.array([[0, 255, 0, 127]]))
    mask = scipy.misc.toimage(mask, mode="RGBA")
    street_im = scipy.misc.toimage(image)
    street_im.paste(mask, box=None, mask=mask)
```

In the following figure, we can see the output of our model:

Figure 7.2A: Example of a predicted segmented road

Finding facial key points

One of the applications that is most commonly used in traditional computer vision is detecting faces in images. This provides many solutions in different industries. The first step is to detect **facial keypoints** in an image (or frame). These facial keypoints, also known as facial landmarks, have proven to be unique and accurate for locating the faces in an image and the direction the face is pointing. More traditional computer vision techniques and machine learning techniques are still often used, such as HOG + Linear SVM. In the following recipe, we will show you how to use deep learning to do this. Specifically, we will implement a CNN for detecting facial keypoints. Afterward, we will show you how to use these keypoints for **head pose estimation**, **face morphing**, and **tracking** with OpenCV.

How to do it...

1. We start with importing all necessary libraries and setting the seed, as follows:

```
import pandas as pd
import numpy as np
import matplotlib.pyplot as plt

from sklearn.model_selection import train_test_split
import tensorflow as tf

SEED = 2017
```

2. Next, we load the dataset and output some numbers:

```
DIR = 'Data/faces/'
training_file = pd.read_csv(DIR + 'training.csv')

cols = training_file.columns[:-1]
training_file['Image'] = training_file['Image'].apply(lambda Image:
np.fromstring(Image, sep=' '))
training_file = training_file.dropna()
```

3. Before proceeding, we need to reshape and normalize the data:

```
img_cols = 96
img_rows = 96
img_channels = 1
n_labels = 30 # 15 times x, y pairs

X = np.vstack(training_file['Image'])
X = X.reshape(-1, img_cols, img_rows, 1)
y = training_file[cols].values

X = X / 255.
y = y / 96.

print(X.shape, y.shape)
```

4. We will split the training set randomly into a training and a validation set:

```
X_train, X_val, y_train, y_val = train_test_split(X, y,
test_size=0.2, random_state=SEED)
```

5. Let's plot five example images and mark the facial keypoints:

```
plt.figure(figsize=(15, 15))

n_examples = 5
for i in range(n_examples):
    plt.subplot(n_examples, n_examples, i+1)
    rand = np.random.randint(len(X_train))
    img = X_train[rand].reshape(img_cols, img_rows)
    plt.imshow(img, cmap='gray')
    kp = y_train[rand]
    plt.scatter(kp[0::2] * img_cols, kp[1::2] * img_rows)

plt.show()
```

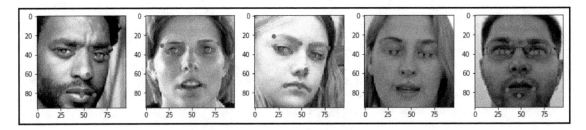

Figure 7.13: Random examples of a training set and labels

6. We can now define our network's architecture in a function so that we can reuse it for training and testing:

```
def model(data, dropout=1.0):
    conv = tf.nn.conv2d(data, conv1_weights, strides=[1, 1, 1, 1],
    padding='SAME')
    relu = tf.nn.relu(tf.nn.bias_add(conv, conv1_biases))
    pool = tf.nn.max_pool(relu, ksize=[1, 2, 2, 1],
    strides=[1, 2, 2, 1], padding='SAME')

    conv = tf.nn.conv2d(pool, conv2_weights, strides=[1, 1, 1, 1],
    padding='SAME')
    relu = tf.nn.relu(tf.nn.bias_add(conv, conv2_biases))
    pool = tf.nn.max_pool(relu, ksize=[1, 2, 2, 1], strides=
    [1, 2, 2, 1], padding='SAME')

    pool_shape = pool.get_shape().as_list()
    reshape = tf.reshape(pool, [pool_shape[0],
    pool_shape[1] * pool_shape[2] * pool_shape[3]])

    hidden1 = tf.nn.relu(tf.matmul(reshape, fc1_weights) +
```

```
fc1_biases)
    hidden1 = tf.nn.dropout(hidden1, dropout, seed=SEED)

    hidden2 = tf.nn.relu(tf.matmul(hidden1, fc2_weights) +
fc2_biases)
    hidden2 = tf.nn.dropout(hidden2, dropout, seed=SEED)
    output = tf.matmul(hidden2, fc3_weights) + fc3_biases

    return output
```

7. It's time to define the hyperparameters:

```
batch_size = 128
n_epochs = 500
learning_rate = 1e-4
print_every = 10
early_stopping_patience = 5
```

8. Before building our model, we need to set the placeholders:

```
inputs = tf.placeholder(tf.float32, shape=(batch_size,
img_cols, img_rows, img_channels))
targets = tf.placeholder(tf.float32, shape=(batch_size, n_labels))

evals = tf.placeholder(tf.float32, shape=(batch_size,
img_cols, img_rows, img_channels))

conv1_weights = tf.Variable(tf.truncated_normal([5, 5,
img_channels, 32], stddev=0.1,seed=SEED))
conv1_biases = tf.Variable(tf.zeros([32]))

conv2_weights = tf.Variable(tf.truncated_normal([5, 5, 32, 64],
stddev=0.1, seed=SEED))
conv2_biases = tf.Variable(tf.constant(0.1, shape=[64]))

fc1_weights = tf.Variable(tf.truncated_normal([img_cols //
4 * img_rows // 4 * 64, 512], stddev=0.1, seed=SEED))
fc1_biases = tf.Variable(tf.constant(0.1, shape=[512]))

fc2_weights = tf.Variable(tf.truncated_normal([512, 512],
stddev=0.1, seed=SEED))
fc2_biases = tf.Variable(tf.constant(0.1, shape=[512]))

fc3_weights = tf.Variable(tf.truncated_normal([512, n_labels],
stddev=0.1, seed=SEED))
fc3_biases = tf.Variable(tf.constant(0.1, shape=[n_labels]))
```

9. We can now initialize our model and start training including early stopping:

```
val_size = X_val.shape[0]

train_prediction = model(inputs, 0.5)
loss = tf.reduce_mean(tf.reduce_sum(tf.square(train_prediction -
targets), 1))
eval_prediction = model(evals)

train_step = tf.train.AdamOptimizer(learning_rate).minimize(loss)

init = tf.global_variables_initializer()
sess = tf.InteractiveSession()
sess.run(init)

history = []
patience_count = 0
for epoch in range(n_epochs):
    for step in range(int(len(X_train) / batch_size)):
        offset = step * batch_size
        batch_data = X_train[offset:(offset + batch_size), ...]
        batch_labels = y_train[offset:(offset + batch_size)]

        feed_dict = {inputs: batch_data, targets: batch_labels}
        _, loss_train = sess.run([train_step, loss],
feed_dict=feed_dict)
    predictions = np.ndarray(shape=(val_size, n_labels),
dtype=np.float32)
    for begin in range(0, val_size, batch_size):
        end = begin + batch_size
        if end <= val_size:
            predictions[begin:end, :] = sess.run(eval_prediction,
feed_dict={evals: X_val[begin:end, ...]})
        else:
            batch_predictions = sess.run(eval_prediction,
feed_dict={evals: X_val[-batch_size:, ...]})
            predictions[begin:, :] = batch_predictions[begin -
val_size:, :]
    loss_val = np.sum(np.power(predictions - y_val, 2)) /
(2 * predictions.shape[0])
    history.append(loss_val)
    if epoch % print_every == 0:
        print('Epoch {:04d}: train loss {:.8f};
validation loss {:.8f}'.format(epoch, loss_train, loss_val))
    if epoch > 0 and history[epoch-1] > history[epoch]:
        patience_count = 0
    else:
        patience_count += 1
```

```
if patience_count > early_stopping_patience:
    break
```

10. To validate, we can plot some example images with the predicted keypoints and the truth values:

```
plt.figure(figsize=(15, 15))

n_examples = 5
for i in range(n_examples):
    plt.subplot(n_examples, n_examples, i+1)
    rand = np.random.randint(len(X_val))
    img = X_val[rand].reshape(img_cols, img_rows)
    plt.imshow(img, cmap='gray')
    kp = y_val[rand]
    pred = predictions[rand]
    plt.scatter(kp[0::2] * img_cols, kp[1::2] * img_rows)
    plt.scatter(pred[0::2] * img_cols, pred[1::2] * img_rows)

plt.show()
```

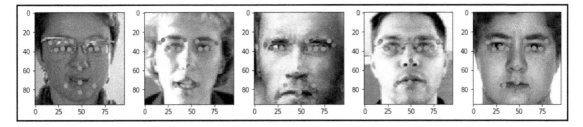

Figure 7.14: Examples of predicted and actual facial keypoints

Recognizing faces

In the previous recipe, we demonstrated how to detect facial keypoints with a neural network. In the following recipe, we will show how to recognize faces using a deep neural network. By training a classifier from scratch, we get a lot of flexibility.

How to do it...

1. As usual, let's start with importing the libraries and setting the seed:

```python
import glob
import re
import matplotlib.pyplot as plt
import numpy as np
import cv2
from sklearn.preprocessing import LabelBinarizer
from sklearn.model_selection import train_test_split
from sklearn.metrics import accuracy_score

from keras.models import Model
from keras.layers import Flatten, Dense, Input,
GlobalAveragePooling2D, GlobalMaxPooling2D, Activation
from keras.layers import Convolution2D, MaxPooling2D
from keras import optimizers
from keras import backend as K

seed = 2017
```

2. In the following step, we will load the data and output some example images to get an idea of the data:

```python
DATA_DIR = 'Data/lfw/'
images = glob.glob(DATA_DIR + '*/*.jpg')

plt.figure(figsize=(10, 10))

n_examples = 5
for i in range(5):
    rand = np.random.randint(len(images))
    image_name = re.search('Data/lfw\/(.+?)\/', images[rand],
re.IGNORECASE).group(1).replace('_', ' ')
    img = cv2.imread(images[rand])
    img = cv2.cvtColor(img, cv2.COLOR_BGR2RGB)
    plt.subplot(n_examples, n_examples, i+1)
    plt.title(image_name)
    plt.imshow(img)
plt.show()
```

Figure 7.15: Example images of faces

3. Some of the persons (labels) have multiple images; let's plot them to see if they look alike:

```
images_arnold = glob.glob(DATA_DIR +
'Arnold_Schwarzenegger/*.jpg')

plt.figure(figsize=(10, 10))

for i in range(n_examples):
    image_name = re.search('Data/lfw\/(.+?)\/', images_arnold[i],
re.IGNORECASE).group(1).replace('_', ' ')
    img = cv2.imread(images_arnold[i])
    img = cv2.cvtColor(img, cv2.COLOR_BGR2RGB)
    plt.subplot(n_examples, n_examples, i+1)
# plt.title(image_name)
    plt.imshow(img)
plt.show()
```

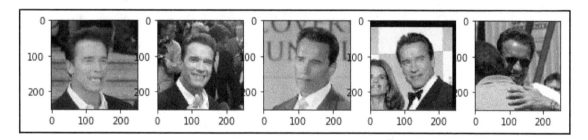

Figure 7.16: Example images of Arnold Schwarzenegger

What we see is that the images are quite different in terms of background and angle of the face. Also, in the fifth example, part of the face is covered and he is wearing glasses.

4. The images are neatly stored in separate folders per class (person), so we can extract the labels with a simple regular expression:

```
labels = np.asarray([re.search('Data/lfw\/(.+?)\/', image,
re.IGNORECASE).group(1) for image in np.asarray(images)])
```

5. Let's also output some statistics about our dataset:

```
print('Number of images: {}'.format(len(y)))
print('Number of unique labels: {}'.format(len(np.unique(labels))))
```

6. We're now ready to preprocess our labels:

```
encoder = LabelBinarizer()
encoder.fit(labels)
y = encoder.transform(labels).astype(float)
```

7. To validate our model, we will use a 20% split for our validation set:

```
X_train, X_val, y_train , y_val = train_test_split(X, y,
test_size=0.2, random_state=seed)
```

8. Next, we can define our model. We will take a network architecture inspired by the famous VGG16 network:

```
input_shape = (250, 250, 3)
img_input = Input(shape=input_shape)
inputs = img_input

# Block 1
x = Convolution2D(64, (3, 3), activation='relu', padding='same',
name='conv1_1')(img_input)
x = Convolution2D(64, (3, 3), activation='relu', padding='same',
name='conv1_2')(x)
x = MaxPooling2D((2, 2), strides=(2, 2), name='pool1')(x)

# Block 2
x = Convolution2D(128, (3, 3), activation='relu', padding='same',
name='conv2_1')(x)
x = Convolution2D(128, (3, 3), activation='relu', padding='same',
name='conv2_2')(x)
x = MaxPooling2D((2, 2), strides=(2, 2), name='pool2')(x)

# Block 3
x = Convolution2D(256, (3, 3), activation='relu', padding='same',
name='conv3_1')(x)
x = Convolution2D(256, (3, 3), activation='relu', padding='same',
```

```
                name='conv3_2')(x)
x = Convolution2D(256, (3, 3), activation='relu', padding='same',
                name='conv3_3')(x)
x = MaxPooling2D((2, 2), strides=(2, 2), name='pool3')(x)

# Block 4
x = Convolution2D(512, (3, 3), activation='relu', padding='same',
                name='conv4_1')(x)
x = Convolution2D(512, (3, 3), activation='relu', padding='same',
                name='conv4_2')(x)
x = Convolution2D(512, (3, 3), activation='relu', padding='same',
                name='conv4_3')(x)
x = MaxPooling2D((2, 2), strides=(2, 2), name='pool4')(x)

# Block 5
x = Convolution2D(512, (3, 3), activation='relu', padding='same',
                name='conv5_1')(x)
x = Convolution2D(512, (3, 3), activation='relu', padding='same',
                name='conv5_2')(x)
x = Convolution2D(512, (3, 3), activation='relu', padding='same',
                name='conv5_3')(x)
x = MaxPooling2D((2, 2), strides=(2, 2), name='pool5')(x)

x = Flatten(name='flatten')(x)
x = Dense(4096, name='fc6')(x)
x = Activation('relu', name='fc6/relu')(x)
x = Dense(4096, name='fc7')(x)
x = Activation('relu', name='fc7/relu')(x)
x = Dense(len(y[0]), name='fc8')(x)
x = Activation('relu', name='fc8/softmax')(x)

model = Model(inputs, x)

opt = optimizers.Adam()
model.compile(loss='categorical_crossentropy', optimizer=opt,
metrics=['accuracy'])
```

9. Currently, we have a rather limited training set. Therefore, we will be using image augmentation techniques to expand our dataset. We'll be using `random_shifts`, **random flipping**, and **random scaling**:

```
def random_shifts(image, shift_max_x=100, shift_max_y=100):
    width, height, _ = image.shape
    shift_x = np.random.randint(shift_max_x)
    shift_y = np.random.randint(shift_max_y)
    M = np.float32([[1, 0, shift_x],[0, 1, shift_y]])
    return (cv2.warpAffine(image, M, (height, width)))
```

```
def random_flip(image, p_flip=0.5):
    rand = np.random.random()
    if rand < p_flip:
        image = cv2.flip(image, 1)
    return image

def scale_image(image, scale_range=[0.6, 1.4]):
    width, height, _ = image.shape
    scale_x = np.random.uniform(low=scale_range[0],
    high=scale_range[1])
    scale_y = np.random.uniform(low=scale_range[0],
    high=scale_range[1])
    scale_matrix = np.array([[scale_x, 0., (1. - scale_x) *
    width / 2.], [0., scale_y, (1. - scale_y) * height / 2.]],
    dtype=np.float32)
    return(cv2.warpAffine(image, scale_matrix, (width, height),
    flags=cv2.INTER_LINEAR,
    borderMode=cv2.BORDER_REFLECT_101))
```

10. We don't want to load all the images in memory, so we will implement a batch generator that uses our image augmentation functions:

```
img_rows = img_cols = 250
img_channels = 3

def batchgen(x, y, batch_size, transform=False):
    # Create empty numpy arrays
    images = np.zeros((batch_size, img_rows, img_cols, img_channels))
    class_id = np.zeros((batch_size, len(y[0])))

    while 1:
        for n in range(batch_size):
            i = np.random.randint(len(x))
            x_ = cv2.imread(x[i])
            x_ = cv2.cvtColor(x_, cv2.COLOR_BGR2RGB)
            if transform:
                x_ = random_shifts(x_, 10, 10)
                x_ = random_flip(x_)
                x_ = scale_image(x_, [0.8, 1,2])
            images[n] = x_
            class_id[n] = y[i]
        yield images, class_id
```

11. For our model, we will define the following hyperparamters:

```
batch_size = 32
n_epochs = 1000
s_epoch =
val_steps = (len(X_val)/batch_size)
```

12. Let's start training our model:

```
train_generator = batchgen(X_train, y_train, batch_size, True)
val_generator = batchgen(X_val, y_val, batch_size, False)

history = model.fit_generator(train_generator,
                              steps_per_epoch=s_epoch,
                              epochs=n_epochs,
                              validation_data=val_generator,
                              validation_steps = val_steps,
                              verbose=1
                             )
```

13. Now, let's see how our model performs and plot some results:

```
test_generator = batchgen(X_val, y_val, batch_size, False)
preds = model.predict_generator(test_generator, steps=1)

y_val_ = [np.argmax(x) for x in y_val]
y_preds = [np.argmax(x) for x in preds]

accuracy_score(y_val_, y_preds)
```

Figure 7.17: Example predictions on the test set

If we want to add new faces to our model, we can use **fine-tuning** to adjust the weights of our trained model. More specifically, we will use a slightly smaller learning rate when training on the new examples. In Chapter 14, *Pretrained Models*, we will demonstrate how to use fine-tuning for the model trained in this recipe.

Transferring styles to images

In the last couple of years, transferring styles from one image to another has had an enormous boost thanks to deep learning. Many people have experimented with transferring a certain style, often from a well-known painter, to a photo. The resulting images are often interesting to see because they show a mix between the painter's style and the original image. In the following recipe, we will show you how to use pretrained weights from VGG16 to transfer the style of one image to another.

How to do it...

1. We start with importing all the necessary libraries as follows:

```
from keras.preprocessing.image import load_img, img_to_array
from scipy.misc import imsave
import numpy as np
from scipy.optimize import fmin_l_bfgs_b
import time
import argparse

from keras.applications import vgg16
from keras import backend as K
```

2. Next, we load the two images that we will use for style transfer and plot them:

```
base_image_path = 'Data/golden_gate.jpg'
style_reference_image_path = 'Data/starry_night.jpg'
result_prefix = 'result_'

width, height = load_img(base_image_path).size
img_rows = 400
img_cols = 600
img_channels = 3

plt.figure(figsize=(15, 15))
plt.subplot(2, 2, 1)
img = load_img(base_image_path)
```

```
plt.imshow(img)
plt.subplot(2, 2, 2)
img = load_img(style_reference_image_path)
plt.imshow(img)
plt.show()
```

Figure 7.18: Input images for style transfer (left: original image, right: style reference image)

3. We define two functions that can preprocess and process images:

```
def preprocess_image(image_path):
    img = load_img(image_path, target_size=(img_rows, img_cols))
    img = img_to_array(img)
    img = np.expand_dims(img, axis=0)
    img = trained_model.preprocess_input(img)
    return img

def deprocess_image(x):
    x = x.reshape((img_rows, img_cols, img_channels))
    x[:, :, 0] += 103.939
    x[:, :, 1] += 116.779
    x[:, :, 2] += 123.68
    x = x[:, :, ::-1]
    x = np.clip(x, 0, 255).astype('uint8')
    return x
```

4. We now define the placeholders we need for training:

```
base_image = K.variable(preprocess_image(base_image_path))
style_reference_image = K.variable(preprocess_image
(style_reference_image_path))
combination_image = K.placeholder((1, img_rows, img_cols, 3))
input_tensor = K.concatenate([base_image,
style_reference_image, combination_image], axis=0)
```

5. Let's import the VGG16 model and create a `dict` for the model's architecture:

```
model = vgg16.VGG16(input_tensor=input_tensor, weights='imagenet',
include_top=False)
model_dict = dict([(layer.name, layer.output)
for layer in model.layers])
```

6. For our style transfer, we need three different loss functions:

```
def gram_matrix(x):
    features = K.batch_flatten(K.permute_dimensions(x, (2, 0, 1)))
    gram = K.dot(features, K.transpose(features))
    return gram

def style_loss(style, combination):
    assert K.ndim(style) == 3
    assert K.ndim(combination) == 3
    S = gram_matrix(style)
    C = gram_matrix(combination)
    channels = 3
    size = img_nrows * img_ncols
    return K.sum(K.square(S - C)) /
    (4. * (channels ** 2) * (size ** 2))

def content_loss(base, combination):
    return K.sum(K.square(combination - base))

def total_variation_loss(x):
    a = K.square(x[:, :img_nrows - 1, :img_ncols - 1, :] -
x[:, 1:, :img_ncols - 1, :])
    b = K.square(x[:, :img_nrows - 1, :img_ncols - 1, :] -
x[:, :img_nrows - 1, 1:, :])
    return K.sum(K.pow(a + b, 1.25))
```

7. It's time to define the hyperparameters:

```
total_variation_weight = 1.0
style_weight = 1.0
content_weight = 0.25
iterations = 10
```

8. Next, we need to create placeholder functions to determine the losses during training:

```
loss = K.variable(0.)
layer_features = model_dict['block5_conv2']
base_image_features = layer_features[0, :, :, :]
combination_features = layer_features[2, :, :, :]
loss += content_weight * content_loss(base_image_features,
combination_features)

feature_layers = ['block1_conv1', 'block2_conv1',
'block3_conv1', 'block4_conv1', 'block5_conv1']
for layer_name in feature_layers:
    layer_features = model_dict[layer_name]
    style_reference_features = layer_features[1, :, :, :]
    combination_features = layer_features[2, :, :, :]
    sl = style_loss(style_reference_features, combination_features)
    loss += (style_weight / len(feature_layers)) * sl
loss += total_variation_weight *
total_variation_loss(combination_image)

grads = K.gradients(loss, combination_image)

outputs = [loss]
if isinstance(grads, (list, tuple)):
    outputs += grads
else:
    outputs.append(grads)

f_outputs = K.function([combination_image], outputs)
```

9. We also need to define functions to evaluate the losses:

```
def eval_loss_and_grads(x):
    x = x.reshape((1, img_nrows, img_ncols, 3))
    outs = f_outputs([x])
    loss_value = outs[0]
    if len(outs[1:]) == 1:
        grad_values = outs[1].flatten().astype('float64')
    else:
        grad_values =
np.array(outs[1:]).flatten().astype('float64')
    return loss_value, grad_values


class Evaluator(object):

    def __init__(self):
        self.loss_value = None
        self.grads_values = None

    def loss(self, x):
        assert self.loss_value is None
        loss_value, grad_values = eval_loss_and_grads(x)
        self.loss_value = loss_value
        self.grad_values = grad_values
        return self.loss_value

    def grads(self, x):
        assert self.loss_value is not None
        grad_values = np.copy(self.grad_values)
        self.loss_value = None
        self.grad_values = None
        return grad_values

evaluator = Evaluator()
```

10. Let's start the style transfer and plot the results for each iteration:

```
x = preprocess_image(base_image_path)

for i in range(iterations):
    print(i)
    x, min_val, info = fmin_l_bfgs_b(evaluator.loss, x.flatten(),
fprime=evaluator.grads, maxfun=20)

    print('Current loss value:', min_val)

    img = deprocess_image(x.copy())
    fname = result_prefix + '_at_iteration_%d.png' % i
    plt.imshow(img)
    plt.show()
```

Figure 7.19: Example of transferring styles after 10 iterations

8
Natural Language Processing

This chapter contains recipes related to textual data processing. This includes recipes related to textual feature representation and processing, word embeddings, and text data storage:

- Analyzing sentiment
- Translating sentences
- Summarizing text

Introduction

Another field revolutionized by deep learning is **Natural Language Processing** (**NLP**). This revolution is mainly caused by the introduction of RNNs, but CNNs have also proven to be valuable when processing text. Deep learning is used in many different NLP applications, from analyzing sentiment in Twitter feeds to summarizing text. In this chapter, we will show you how to apply deep learning to solve these problems.

Analyzing sentiment

In an age where more and more data is generated, and especially where every individual can post his or her opinion on the internet, the value of automatically analyzing these posts with high accuracy on a large scale is important for businesses and politics. In Chapter 4, *Recurrent and Recursive Neural Networks*, we've already shown how to apply RNNs with LSTM units to classify short sentences, such as movie reviews. In the following recipe, we will increase the complexity by classifying the sentiments of Twitter messages. We do this by predicting both binary classes and fine-grained classes.

How to do it...

1. We start by importing all the libraries as follows:

```
from nltk.tokenize import word_tokenize
from nltk.stem import WordNetLemmatizer
import numpy as np
import random
import pickle
from collections import Counter

import tensorflow as tf
```

2. Next, we process the English sentences with the nltk package. We start by defining the functions we need for preprocessing:

```
lemmatizer = WordNetLemmatizer()
pos = '../Data/positive.txt'
neg = '../Data/negative.txt'
def create_lexicon(pos, neg):
    lexicon = []
    for fi in [pos, neg]:
        with open(fi, 'r') as f:
            contents = f.readlines()
            for l in contents[:10000000]:
                all_words = word_tokenize(l.lower())
                lexicon += list(all_words)
    lexicon = [lemmatizer.lemmatize(i) for i in lexicon]
    w_counts = Counter(lexicon)
    l2 =[]
    for w in w_counts:
        if 1000 > w_counts[w] > 50:
            l2.append(w)
    return l2
def sample_handling(sample,lexicon,classification):
    featureset = []
    with open(sample,'r') as f:
        contents = f.readlines()
        for l in contents[:10000000]:
            current_words = word_tokenize(l.lower())
            current_words = [lemmatizer.lemmatize(i) for i in
            current_words]
            features = np.zeros(len(lexicon))
            for word in current_words:
                if word.lower() in lexicon:
                    index_value = lexicon.index(word.lower())
```

```
            features[index_value] += 1
        features = list(features)
        featureset.append([features,classification])
    return featureset
```

3. Next, we process the data as follows:

```
lexicon = create_lexicon(pos,neg)
features = []
features += sample_handling(pos, lexicon,[1,0])
features += sample_handling(neg, lexicon,[0,1])
random.shuffle(features)
features = np.array(features)

testing_size = int(0.1*len(features))

X_train = list(features[:,0][:-testing_size])
y_train = list(features[:,1][:-testing_size])
X_test = list(features[:,0][-testing_size:])
y_test = list(features[:,1][-testing_size:])
```

4. Before we implement the model, we need to set the hyperparameters:

```
n_epochs = 10
batch_size = 128
h1 = 500
h2 = 500
n_classes = 2
```

5. Next, we define the input placeholders and the initializators for the weights and biases:

```
x_input = tf.placeholder('float')
y_input = tf.placeholder('float')

hidden_1 = {'weight':tf.Variable(tf.random_normal([len(X_train[0]),
h1])),
                'bias':tf.Variable(tf.random_normal([h1]))}

hidden_2 = {'weight':tf.Variable(tf.random_normal([h1, h2])),
                'bias':tf.Variable(tf.random_normal([h2]))}
output_layer = {'weight':tf.Variable(tf.random_normal([h2,
            n_classes])),
                'bias':tf.Variable(tf.random_normal([n_classes])),}
```

6. Define the network architecture, loss, and optimizer as follows:

```
l1 = tf.add(tf.matmul(x_input, hidden_1['weight']),
hidden_1['bias'])
l1 = tf.nn.relu(l1)
l2 = tf.add(tf.matmul(l1, hidden_2'weight']), hidden_2['bias'])
l2 = tf.nn.relu(l2)
output = tf.matmul(l2, output_layer['weight']) +
output_layer['bias']

loss =
tf.reduce_mean(tf.nn.softmax_cross_entropy_with_logits(logits=outpu
t, labels=y_input))
opt = tf.train.AdamOptimizer().minimize(loss)
```

7. Finally, we can start training our model:

```
with tf.Session() as sess:
 sess.run(tf.global_variables_initializer())

 for epoch in range(n_epochs):
 epoch_loss = 0
 i = 0
 while i < len(X_train):
 start = i
 end = i + batch_size
 batch_x = np.array(X_train[start:end])
 batch_y = np.array(y_train[start:end])

 _, batch_loss = sess.run([opt, loss], feed_dict={x_input: batch_x,
y_input: batch_y})
 epoch_loss += batch_loss
 i += batch_size

 print('Epoch {}: loss {}'.format(epoch, epoch_loss))
```

Translating sentences

Another application of deep learning in text has got its boost in performance and popularity thanks to a couple of large search engines. Translating sentences is a hard task because each language has its own rules, exceptions, and expressions. What we tend to forget is that the translation of words often largely depends on the context around it. Some believe that solving a language thoroughly can be a huge milestone for achieving general AI, because intelligence and language are well connected and small nuances in language can be crucial to understanding.

In our next recipe, we will demonstrate how to use a sequence-to-sequence model to translate sentences from English to French. We will be using the CNTK framework.

How to do it...

1. Let's start with loading the libraries:

```
import numpy as np
import os

from cntk import Trainer, Axis
from cntk.io import MinibatchSource, CTFDeserializer, StreamDef,
StreamDefs, INFINITELY_REPEAT
from cntk.learners import momentum_sgd, fsadagrad,
momentum_as_time_constant_schedule, learning_rate_schedule,
UnitType
from cntk import input, cross_entropy_with_softmax,
classification_error, sequence,
                element_select, alias, hardmax, placeholder,
combine, parameter, times, plus
from cntk.ops.functions import CloneMethod, load_model, Function
from cntk.initializer import glorot_uniform
from cntk.logging import log_number_of_parameters, ProgressPrinter
from cntk.logging.graph import plot
from cntk.layers import *
from cntk.layers.sequence import *
from cntk.layers.models.attention import *
from cntk.layers.typing import *
```

2. First, we need to load the dataset used. It contains English and French sentences:

```
data_eng = '../Data/translations/small_vocab_en'
data_fr = '../Data/translations/small_vocab_fr'

with open(data_eng, 'r', encoding='utf-8') as f:
    sentences_eng = f.read()
with open(data_fr, 'r', encoding='utf-8') as f:
    sentences_fr = f.read()
```

3. Let's output some statistics about the dataset:

```
word_counts = [len(sentence.split()) for sentence in sentences_eng]
print('Number of unique words in English: {}'.format(len({word: None for
word in sentences_eng.lower().split()})))
print('Number of sentences: {}'.format(len(sentences_eng)))
```

```
print('Average number of words in a sentence:
{}'.format(np.average(word_counts)))

n_examples = 5
for i in range(n_examples):
    print('\nExample {}'.format(i))
    print(sentences_eng.split('\n')[i])
    print(sentences_fr.split('\n')[i])
```

4. We need to create lookup tables for both languages: one table for vocabulary to integer and one for integer to vocabulary. We do this by defining a function, `create_lookup_tables`:

```
def create_lookup_tables(text):
    vocab = set(text.split())
    vocab_to_int = {'<S>': 0, '<E>': 1, '<UNK>': 2, '<PAD>': 3 }

    for i, v in enumerate(vocab, len(vocab_to_int)):
        vocab_to_int[v] = i

    int_to_vocab = {i: v for v, i in vocab_to_int.items()}

    return vocab_to_int, int_to_vocab

vocab_to_int_eng, int_to_vocab_eng =
create_lookup_tables(sentences_eng.lower())
vocab_to_int_fr, int_to_vocab_fr =
create_lookup_tables(sentences_fr.lower())
```

5. Now that we have all the lookup tables ready, we can start transforming the input (English sentences) and target (French sentences) data:

```
def text_to_ids(source_text, target_text, source_vocab_to_int,
target_vocab_to_int):
    source_id_text = [[source_vocab_to_int[word] for word in
    sentence.split()] for sentence in source_text.split('\n')]
    target_id_text = [[target_vocab_to_int[word] for word in
    sentence.split()]+[target_vocab_to_int['<E>']] for sentence
    in target_text.split('\n')]
    return source_id_text, target_id_text

X, y = text_to_ids(sentences_eng.lower(), sentences_fr.lower(),
vocab_to_int_eng, vocab_to_int_fr)
```

6. Before defining our model, we need to define the hyperparameters:

```
input_vocab_dim = 128
label_vocab_dim = 128
hidden_dim = 256
n_layers = 2
attention_dim = 128
attention_span = 12
embedding_dim = 200
n_epochs = 20
learning_rate = 0.001
batch_size = 64
```

7. For our model, we define a function. Within the `create_model` function, we include the `Embedding`, `Stabilizer`, `LSTM` layers, and `AttentionModel`:

```
def create_model(n_layers):
    embed = Embedding(embedding_dim, name='embed')
    LastRecurrence = C.layers.Recurrence
    encode = C.layers.Sequential([
        embed,
        C.layers.Stabilizer(),
        C.layers.For(range(num_layers-1), lambda:
            C.layers.Recurrence(C.layers.LSTM(hidden_dim))),
        LastRecurrence(C.layers.LSTM(hidden_dim),
        return_full_state=True),
        (C.layers.Label('encoded_h'), C.layers.Label('encoded_c')),
    ])
    with default_options(enable_self_stabilization=True):
        stab_in = Stabilizer()
        rec_blocks = [LSTM(hidden_dim) for i in range(n_layers)]
        stab_out = Stabilizer()
        out = Dense(label_vocab_dim, name='out')
        attention_model = AttentionModel(attention_dim, None, None,
        name='attention_model')

        @Function
        def decode(history, input):
            encoded_input = encode(input)
            r = history
            r = embed(r)
            r = stab_in(r)
            for i in range(n_layers):
                rec_block = rec_blocks[i]
                @Function
                def lstm_with_attention(dh, dc, x):
                    h_att =
```

```
                   attention_model(encoded_input.outputs[0], dh)
                            x = splice(x, h_att)
                            return rec_block(dh, dc, x)
                    r = Recurrence(lstm_with_attention)(r)
               r = stab_out(r)
               r = out(r)
               r = Label('out')(r)
               return r

        return decode
```

8. Let's define the loss function:

```
    def create_loss_function(model):
        @Function
        @Signature(input = InputSequence[Tensor[input_vocab_dim]],
    labels = LabelSequence[Tensor[label_vocab_dim]])
        def loss (input, labels):
            postprocessed_labels = sequence.slice(labels, 1, 0)
            z = model(input, postprocessed_labels)
            ce = cross_entropy_with_softmax(z, postprocessed_labels)
            errs = classification_error (z, postprocessed_labels)
            return (ce, errs)
        return loss
```

9. Finally, let's start training:

```
    model = create_model(n_layers)
    loss = create_loss_function(model)
    learner = fsadagrad(model.parameters,
                    lr = learning_rate,
                    momentum =
    momentum_as_time_constant_schedule(1100),
                    gradient_clipping_threshold_per_sample=2.3,
                    gradient_clipping_with_truncation=True)
    trainer = Trainer(None, loss, learner)

    total_samples = 0
    n_batches = len(X)//batch_size

    for epoch in range(n_epochs):
        for i in range(n_batches):
            batch_input = train_reader.next_minibatch(minibatch_size)
    trainer.train_minibatch(batch_input[train_reader.streams.features],
    batch_input[train_reader.streams.labels])
```

Summarizing text

Reading comprehension (RC) is the ability to read text, process it, and understand its meaning. There are two types of summarization: extractive and abstractive. **Extractive summarization** identifies important text and throws away the rest, leaving the passage shorter. Depending on the implementation, it can sound weird and disjointed since text is plucked from different paragraphs. **Abstractive summarization** is a lot more difficult and it requires the model to understand the text and language in more depth. In the following recipe, we will implement a text summarization algorithm with the TensorFlow framework.

How to do it...

1. We start by loading all the necessary libraries, as follows:

```
import numpy as np
import tensorflow as tf
```

2. First, we load the text data:

```
article_filename =
'Data/summary/"Data/sumdata/train/train.article.txt'
title_filename = 'Data/summary/"Data/sumdata/train/train.title.txt'

with open(article_filename) as article_file:
 articles = article_file.readlines()
with open(title_filename) as title_file:
 titles = title_file.readlines()
```

3. To make our data readable for our model, we need to define a function that creates lookup tables for integers to vocabulary and vice versa:

```
def create_lookup_tables(text):
    vocab = set(text.split())
    vocab_to_int = {'<S>': 0, '<E>': 1, '<UNK>': 2, '<PAD>': 3 }

    for i, v in enumerate(vocab, len(vocab_to_int)):
        vocab_to_int[v] = i

    int_to_vocab = {i: v for v, i in vocab_to_int.items()}

    return vocab_to_int, int_to_vocab

vocab_to_int_article, int_to_vocab_article =
create_lookup_tables(articles.lower())
```

```
vocab_to_int_title, int_to_vocab_title =
create_lookup_tables(titles.lower())
```

4. Next, we transform the input data (articles) and the target data (titles):

```
def text_to_ids(source_text, target_text, source_vocab_to_int,
target_vocab_to_int):
source_id_text = [[source_vocab_to_int[word] for word in
sentence.split()] for sentence in source_text.split('\n')]
    target_id_text = [[target_vocab_to_int[word] for word in
sentence.split()]+[target_vocab_to_int['<E>']] for sentence in
target_text.split('\n')]
    return source_id_text, target_id_text

X, y = text_to_ids(articles.lower(), titles.lower(),
vocab_to_int_articles, vocab_to_int_titles)
```

5. Before we define our model, we set the hyperparameters:

```
learning_rate = 0.001
hidden_units = 400
embedding_size = 200
n_layers = 1
dropout = 0.5
n_iters = 40
```

6. We will use a bidirectional model, so we define a forward and backward embedding and apply a dropout wrapper:

```
encoder_forward_cell = tf.contrib.rnn.GRUCell(state_size)
encoder_backward_cell = tf.contrib.rnn.GRUCell(state_size)
decoder_cell = tf.contrib.rnn.GRUCell(state_size)

encoder_forward_cell =
tf.contrib.rnn.DropoutWrapper(encoder_forward_cell,
output_keep_prob = (1-dropout))
encoder_backward_cell =
tf.contrib.rnn.DropoutWrapper(encoder_backward_cell,
output_keep_prob = (1-dropout))
decoder_cell = tf.contrib.rnn.DropoutWrapper(decoder_cell,
output_keep_prob = (1-dropout))
```

7. Next, we stack all the elements together:

```
with tf.variable_scope("seq2seq", dtype=dtype):
    with tf.variable_scope("encoder"):

        encoder_embedding = tf.get_variable("embedding",
```

```
[source_vocab_size, embedding_size],initializer=embedding_init)
        encoder_inputs_embedding =
tf.nn.embedding_lookup(encoder_embedding, self.encoder_inputs)
        encoder_outputs, encoder_states =
tf.nn.bidirectional_dynamic_rnn(encoder_forward_cell,
encoder_backward_cell, encoder_inputs_embedding,
sequence_length=self.encoder_len, dtype=dtype)

    with tf.variable_scope("init_state"):
        init_state = fc_layer(
            tf.concat(encoder_states, 1), state_size)
        # the shape of bidirectional_dynamic_rnn is weird
        # None for batch_size
        self.init_state = init_state
        self.init_state.set_shape([self.batch_size, state_size])
        self.att_states = tf.concat(encoder_outputs, 2)
        self.att_states.set_shape([self.batch_size, None,
state_size*2])

    with tf.variable_scope("attention"):
        attention = tf.contrib.seq2seq.BahdanauAttention(
            state_size, self.att_states, self.encoder_len)
        decoder_cell = tf.contrib.seq2seq.DynamicAttentionWrapper(
            decoder_cell, attention, state_size * 2)
        wrapper_state =
tf.contrib.seq2seq.DynamicAttentionWrapperState(
            self.init_state, self.prev_att)

    with tf.variable_scope("decoder") as scope:

        decoder_emb = tf.get_variable("embedding",
[target_vocab_size, embedding_size],initializer=emb_init)

        decoder_cell =
tf.contrib.rnn.OutputProjectionWrapper(decoder_cell,
target_vocab_size)

        decoder_inputs_emb = tf.nn.embedding_lookup(decoder_emb,
self.decoder_inputs)

        helper =
tf.contrib.seq2seq.TrainingHelper(decoder_inputs_emb,
self.decoder_len)
        decoder = tf.contrib.seq2seq.BasicDecoder(decoder_cell,
helper, wrapper_state)

        outputs, final_state =
tf.contrib.seq2seq.dynamic_decode(decoder)
```

```
            outputs_logits = outputs[0]
            self.outputs = outputs_logits

            weights = tf.sequence_mask(self.decoder_len,
    dtype=tf.float32)

            loss_t = tf.contrib.seq2seq.sequence_loss(outputs_logits,
    self.decoder_targets, weights, average_across_timesteps=False,
    average_across_batch=False)
            self.loss = tf.reduce_sum(loss_t) / self.batch_size

            params = tf.trainable_variables()
            opt = tf.train.AdadeltaOptimizer(self.learning_rate,
            epsilon=1e-6)
            gradients = tf.gradients(self.loss, params)
            clipped_gradients, norm = tf.clip_by_global_norm(gradients,
            max_gradient)
            self.updates = opt.apply_gradients(zip(clipped_gradients,
            params), global_step=self.global_step)
```

8. Before we start training, we need a function that retrieves the correct batches:

```
def get_batches(int_text, batch_size, seq_length):
    n_batches = int(len(int_text) / (batch_size * seq_length))
    inputs = np.array(int_text[: n_batches * batch_size *
seq_length])
    outputs = np.array(int_text[1: n_batches * batch_size *
seq_length + 1])

    x = np.split(inputs.reshape(batch_size, -1), n_batches, 1)
    y = np.split(outputs.reshape(batch_size, -1), n_batches, 1)

    return np.array(list(zip(x, y)))
```

9. We are now ready to start training:

```
with tf.Session() as sess:
    model = create_model(sess, False)
    loss = 0.0
    current_step = sess.run(model.global_step)

    while current_step <= n_iters:
        rand = np.random.random_sample()
        bucket_id = min([i for i in range(len(train_buckets_scale))
                    if train_buckets_scale[i] > rand])

        encoder_inputs, decoder_inputs, encoder_len, decoder_len =
        model.get_batches(train_set, bucket_id)
```

```
step_loss, _ = model.step(sess, encoder_inputs,
decoder_inputs, encoder_len, decoder_len, False,
train_writer)
loss += step_loss * batch_size / np.sum(decoder_len)
current_step += 1
```

As we have demonstrated in this chapter, you can achieve great results with relatively small datasets. However, understanding languages is a complicated task, and to understand all the small ins-and-outs of a language, one should train their models on terabytes of training data. For subtasks such as translating from one language to another in a certain area (for example, tourist talk), a relatively small training set and stacked RNN model can work well.

9

Speech Recognition and Video Analysis

This chapter reports recipes relating to stream data processing. This includes audio, video, frame sequences, and data coming from IoT sensors.

- Implementing a speech recognition pipeline from scratch
- Identifying speakers with voice recognition
- Understanding videos with deep learning

Introduction

In this chapter, we will focus on data that is less static but streaming. Specifically, it is data where the temporal element plays a crucial role in the distribution of the data, such as speech and video. When processing such data, the distribution of the input data can often change rapidly over time. For example, in sensor data, we can have small peaks during rush hour and there can be a lot of changes in a video of a sports game. Another challenge with types of data is the size of the dataset for training. The datasets used for video classification are often larger than 100 GB. This means computing power is essential.

Implementing a speech recognition pipeline from scratch

Speech recognition, also known as **Automatic Speech Recognition** (**ASR**) and **speech-to-text** (**STT/S2T**), has a long history. More traditional AI approaches have been used in the industry for a long time; however, with recent interest in deep learning speech, recognition is getting a new boost in performance. Many major tech companies of the world have an interest in speech recognition because of the different applications for which it can be used, for example, **Voice Search** by Google, **Siri** by Apple, and **Alexa** by Amazon.

Many companies use pre-trained speech recognition software. However, in the following recipe, we will demonstrate how to implement and train a speech recognition pipeline from scratch. The accuracy of this newly trained model will be lower than the ones used in the industry. The main reason is that the quality and volume of the training data play a crucial role in accuracy. Interestingly enough, there is a lot of training data (thousands of hours of open source data) available for use. In addition, many (online) videos have subtitles that can be used for training.

We'll be using a dataset that contains spoken numbers from zero to nine by different people. The files are in `.wav` format and the labels and speakers are included in the filenames. To implement our speech recognition model, we will use the Keras framework.

How to do it...

1. We start by importing `keras` and other libraries, as follows:

```
import glob
import numpy as np
import random
import librosa
from sklearn.model_selection import train_test_split

import keras
from keras.layers import LSTM, Dense, Dropout, Flatten
from keras.models import Sequential
from keras.optimizers import Adam
from keras.callbacks import EarlyStopping, ModelCheckpoint
```

2. First, we set the location of the training files, and for reproducibility, we also set a SEED:

```
SEED = 2017
DATA_DIR = 'Data/spoken_numbers_pcm/'
```

3. The training files are located in a directory, and we will be using a batch generator to retrieve them. First, we split the training files into a training and a validation set:

```
files = glob.glob(DATA_DIR + "*.wav")
X_train, X_val = train_test_split(files, test_size=0.2,
random_state=SEED)

print('# Training examples: {}'.format(len(X_train)))
print('# Validation examples: {}'.format(len(X_val)))
```

4. Before proceeding to the batch generator, we need to define some settings:

```
n_features = 20
max_length = 80
n_classes = 10
```

5. This ensures that the used .wav files are all standardized to the same length.

6. Our batch generator should return a batch of preprocessed .wav files and their labels:

```
def batch_generator(data, batch_size=16):
    while 1:
        random.shuffle(data)
        X, y = [], []
        for i in range(batch_size):
            wav = data[i]
            wave, sr = librosa.load(wav, mono=True)
            label = one_hot_encode(int(wav.split('/')[-1][0]),
                    n_classes)
            y.append(label)
            mfcc = librosa.feature.mfcc(wave, sr)
            mfcc = np.pad(mfcc, ((0,0), (0, max_length-
            len(mfcc[0]))), mode='constant', constant_values=0)
            X.append(np.array(mfcc))
        yield np.array(X), np.array(y)
```

7. In our batch generator, we've used a `dense_to_one_hot` function to `one_hot_encode` the labels. This function can be defined as follows:

```
def one_hot_encode(labels_dense, n_classes=10):
    return np.eye(n_classes)[labels_dense]
```

8. Now, let's extract an example of the training set to determine the final shapes:

```
X_example, y_example = next(batch_generator(X_train,
batch_size=1))
print('Shape of training example: {}'.format(X_example.shape))
print('Shape of training example label:
{}'.format(y_example.shape))
```

9. Next, we define the hyperparameters before defining our network architecture:

```
learning_rate = 0.001
batch_size = 64
n_epochs = 50
dropout = 0.5

input_shape = X_example.shape[1:]
steps_per_epoch = 50
```

10. The network architecture we will use is quite straightforward. We will stack an LSTM layer on top of a dense layer, as follows:

```
model = Sequential() model.add(LSTM(256, return_sequences=True,
input_shape=input_shape, dropout=dropout))
model.add(Flatten()) model.add(Dense(128, activation='relu'))
model.add(Dropout(dropout))
model.add(Dense(n_classes, activation='softmax'))
```

11. As a loss function, we use softmax cross entropy and we compile the model:

```
opt = Adam(lr=learning_rate)
model.compile(loss='categorical_crossentropy', optimizer=opt,
metrics=['accuracy']) model.summary()
```

To check the progress during training, we will be measuring the accuracy.

12. We are ready to start training and we will store the results in `history`:

```
history = model.fit_generator(
    generator=batch_generator(X_train, batch_size),
    steps_per_epoch=steps_per_epoch,
    epochs=n_epochs,
    verbose=1,
    validation_data=batch_generator(X_val, 32),
    validation_steps=5
)
```

The high validation accuracy obtained with this relatively simple model shows the power of deep learning. However, we must note that the task is relatively straightforward. Upon increasing the number of labels, the amount of training data necessary to obtain good results grows significantly as well. Also, different accents, background noise, and other factors play an important role in real-world applications.

Identifying speakers with voice recognition

Next to speech recognition, there is more we can do with sound fragments. While speech recognition focuses on converting speech (spoken words) to digital data, we can also use sound fragments to identify the person who is speaking. This is also known as voice recognition. Every individual has different characteristics when speaking, caused by differences in anatomy and behavioral patterns. Speaker verification and speaker identification are getting more attention in this digital age. For example, a home digital assistant can automatically detect which person is speaking.

In the following recipe, we'll be using the same data as in the previous recipe, where we implemented a speech recognition pipeline. However, this time, we will be classifying the speakers of the spoken numbers.

How to do it...

1. In this recipe, we start by importing all libraries:

```
import glob
import numpy as np
import random
import librosa
from sklearn.model_selection import train_test_split
```

```
from sklearn.preprocessing import LabelBinarizer

import keras
from keras.layers import LSTM, Dense, Dropout, Flatten
from keras.models import Sequential
from keras.optimizers import Adam
from keras.callbacks import EarlyStopping, ModelCheckpoint
```

2. Let's set `SEED` and the location of the `.wav` files:

```
SEED = 2017
DATA_DIR = 'Data/spoken_numbers_pcm/'
```

3. Let's split the `.wav` files in a training set and a validation set with scikit-learn's `train_test_split` function:

```
files = glob.glob(DATA_DIR + "*.wav")
X_train, X_val = train_test_split(files, test_size=0.2,
random_state=SEED)

print('# Training examples: {}'.format(len(X_train)))
print('# Validation examples: {}'.format(len(X_val)))
```

4. To extract and print all unique `labels`, we use the following code:

```
labels = []
for i in range(len(X_train)):
    label = X_train[i].split('/')[-1].split('_')[1]
    if label not in labels:
        labels.append(label)
print(labels)
```

5. We can now define our `one_hot_encode` function as follows:

```
label_binarizer = LabelBinarizer()
label_binarizer.fit(list(set(labels)))

def one_hot_encode(x): return label_binarizer.transform(x)
```

6. Before we can feed the data to our network, some preprocessing needs to be done. We use the following settings:

```
n_features = 20
max_length = 80
n_classes = len(labels)
```

7. We can now define our batch generator. The generator includes all preprocessing tasks, such as reading a `.wav` file and transforming it into usable input:

```
def batch_generator(data, batch_size=16):
    while 1:
        random.shuffle(data)
        X, y = [], []
        for i in range(batch_size):
            wav = data[i]
            wave, sr = librosa.load(wav, mono=True)
            label = wav.split('/')[-1].split('_')[1]
            y.append(one_hot_encode(label))
            mfcc = librosa.feature.mfcc(wave, sr)
            mfcc = np.pad(mfcc, ((0,0), (0, max_length-
            len(mfcc[0]))), mode='constant', constant_values=0)
            X.append(np.array(mfcc))
        yield np.array(X), np.array(y)
```

Please note the difference in our batch generator compared to the previous recipe.

8. Let's define the hyperparameters before defining our network architecture:

```
learning_rate = 0.001
batch_size = 64
n_epochs = 50
dropout = 0.5

input_shape = (n_features, max_length)
steps_per_epoch = 50
```

9. The network architecture we will use is quite straightforward. We will stack an LSTM layer on top of a dense layer, as follows:

```
model = Sequential()
model.add(LSTM(256, return_sequences=True,
input_shape=input_shape,
    dropout=dropout))
model.add(Flatten())
model.add(Dense(128, activation='relu'))
model.add(Dropout(dropout))
model.add(Dense(n_classes, activation='softmax'))
```

10. Next, we set the loss function, compile the model, and output a summary of our model:

```
opt = Adam(lr=learning_rate)
model.compile(loss='categorical_crossentropy', optimizer=opt,
metrics=['accuracy'])
model.summary()
```

11. To prevent overfitting, we will be using early stopping and automatically store the model that has the highest validation accuracy:

```
callbacks =
[ModelCheckpoint('checkpoints/voice_recognition_best_model_{epoch:0
2d}.hdf5', save_best_only=True),
                EarlyStopping(monitor='val_acc', patience=2)]
```

12. We are ready to start training and we will store the results in `history`:

```
history = model.fit_generator(
    generator=batch_generator(X_train, batch_size),
    steps_per_epoch=steps_per_epoch,
    epochs=n_epochs,
    verbose=1,
    validation_data=batch_generator(X_val, 32),
    validation_steps=5,
    callbacks=callbacks
)
```

In the following figure, the **training accuracy** and **validation accuracy** are plotted against the epochs:

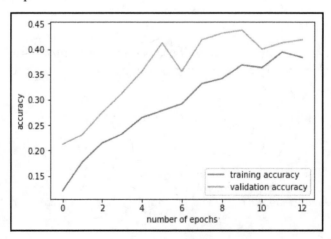

Figure 9.1: Training and validation accuracy

Understanding videos with deep learning

In Chapter 7, *Computer Vision*, we showed how to detect and segment objects in single images. The objects in these images were fixed. However, if we add a temporal dimension to our input, objects can move within a certain scene. Understanding what is happening throughout multiple frames (a video) is a much harder task. In this recipe, we want to demonstrate how to get started when tackling videos. We will focus on combining a CNN and an RNN. The CNN is used to extract features for single frames; these features are combined and used as input for an RNN. This is also known as **stacking**, where we build (stack) a second model on top of another model.

For this recipe, we will be using a dataset that contains 13,321 short videos. These videos are distributed over a total of 101 different classes. Because of the complexity of this task, we don't want to train our models from scratch. Therefore, we will be using the pretrained weights of the InceptionV3 model provided within Keras.

How to do it...

1. We start by importing all the necessary libraries, as follows:

```
from keras.applications.inception_v3 import InceptionV3
from keras.preprocessing.image import ImageDataGenerator
from keras.models import Sequential, Model
from keras.layeSequential import Dense, GlobalAveragePooling2D
from keras.optimizers import Adam
from keras.callbacks import EarlyStopping, ModelCheckpoint
```

2. After importing, we can set the hyperparameters:

```
batch_size = 32
n_epochs = 50
steps_per_epoch = 100
```

3. Because of the size of the dataset, it's important to use a batch generator. Before creating the generators, we will define Keras's ImageDataGenerator for preprocessing purposes:

```
train_datagen = ImageDataGenerator(
        rescale=1./255,
        shear_range=0.2,
        horizontal_flip=True,
        rotation_range=10.,
        width_shift_range=0.2,
```

```
        height_shift_range=0.2)

    val_datagen = ImageDataGenerator(rescale=1./255)
```

4. We have chosen to apply small image augmentation techniques for our training set. To make our model robust, we can decide to apply more aggressive image augmentation.

5. We can now create the generator for training and validation, as follows:

```
classes = np.loadtxt('Data/videos/classes.txt')
 train_generator = train_datagen.flow_from_directory(
 'Data/videos/train/',
 target_size=(299, 299),
 batch_size=batch_size,
 classes=classes,
 class_mode='categorical')
 validation_generator = val_datagen.flow_from_directory(
 'Data/videos/test/',
 target_size=(299, 299),
 batch_size=batch_size,
 classes=classes,
 class_mode='categorical')
```

6. We first load the `InceptionV3` model:

```
inception_model = InceptionV3(include_top=False)
```

7. Next, we define the layers we want to add to this model, as follows:

```
x = inception_model.output
x = GlobalAveragePooling2D()(x)
x = Dense(1024, activation='relu')(x)
predictions = Dense(len(classes), activation='softmax')(x)
model = Model(inputs=inception_model.input, outputs=predictions)
```

8. However, we only want to train these last two layers and keep the other weights fixed:

```
for layer in model.layers[:-2]:
 layer.trainable = False
```

9. Now let's compile our model with the `Adam` optimizer and output the summary:

```
model.compile(optimizer=Adam(), loss='categorical_crossentropy',
metrics=['accuracy'])
```

10. Let's start training our CNN model:

```
model.fit_generator(
    train_generator,
    steps_per_epoch=steps_per_epoch,
    validation_data=validation_generator,
    validation_steps=10,
    epochs=n_epochs)
```

11. Our model is now trained. However, we want to extract the features; we don't want the information from our final layer (the classification) but from the max-pooling layer. We do this as follows:

```
model.layers.pop()
model.layers.pop()
model.outputs = [model.layers[-1].output]
model.output_layers = [model.layers[-1]]
model.layers[-1].outbound_nodes = []
```

12. Next, we loop through the video frames to extract these features per frame and save them to a file:

```
for video in data:
    path = 'Data/videos/' + str(video)
    frames = get_frame(video)
    sequence = []
    for image in frames:
        features = model.predict(image)
        sequence.append(features)
    np.savetxt(path, sequence)
```

13. We can now define the LSTM model that we want to apply to these features:

```
model_lstm = Sequential()
model_lstm.add(LSTM(1024, return_sequences=True,
input_shape=input_shape, dropout=dropout))
model_lstm.add(Flatten())
model_lstm.add(Dense(512, activation='relu'))
model_lstm.add(Dropout(dropout))
model_lstm.add(Dense(self.nb_classes, activation='softmax'))
```

14. Make sure the data split used for validation for this second layer model is the same as the first layer split (otherwise, you will have data leakage):

```
batch_size_lstm = 32
n_epochs_lstm = 40
```

15. Finally, let's start training our second layer model:

```
model_lstm.fit(X_train,
               y_train,
               batch_size=batch_size_lstm,
               validation_data=(X_val, y_val),
               verbose=1,
               epochs=n_epochs_lstm)
```

State-of-the-art models have proven to achieve well above 90% accuracy on these videos. However, our main goal in this recipe is to provide a stepping stone for those interested in classifying videos.

Instead of using an `LSTM` as a second layer model, one can also use a shallow neural network. Other options include blending the results of frames within a video or using a 3D convolution network.

10
Time Series and Structured Data

This chapter provides recipes related to number crunching. This includes sequences and time series, binary encoding, and floating-point representation.

- Predicting stock prices with neural networks
- Predicting bike sharing demand
- Using a shallow neural network for binary classification

Introduction

In the previous chapters, we've mainly focused on the fields where deep learning stands out compared to other machine learning algorithms. However, for more structured datasets, deep learning can be of added value as well, especially when data has a temporal relationship. In this chapter, we will mainly focus on applying deep learning to predict time series and trends.

Predicting stock prices with neural networks

When machine learning became popular, immediately there was a lot of attention given to predicting stock prices. Many different algorithms have been applied to predict stock prices, from more traditional algorithms such as random forests to the more recent extreme gradient boosting. While the latter might still outperform deep learning approaches in most cases, it can still be of valuable to use in a neural network approach. This can, for example, be used in an ensemble of networks or for multi-layer stacking. In the following recipe, we will predict stock prices with the Keras framework.

How to do it...

1. We start by importing all the libraries, as follows:

```
import matplotlib.pyplot as plt
import numpy as np
import pandas as pd
from sklearn.preprocessing import MinMaxScaler

from keras.layers.core import Dense,
Activation, Dropout
from keras.layers.recurrent import LSTM
from keras.models import Sequential
```

2. Let's load the data and print the first rows:

```
data = pd.read_csv('Data/stock-data-2000-2017.csv')
# Reorder the columns for convenience
data = data[['Open', 'High', 'Low', 'Volume',
'Close']]
data.head()
```

The following figure shows the output of the preceding code:

	Open	High	Low	Volume	Close
0	3352.149902	3376.919922	3233.189941	1437770000	3355.560059
1	3326.889893	3383.399902	3229.010010	1874430000	3240.540039
2	3152.330078	3258.239990	3103.530029	2340450000	3168.489990
3	3241.260010	3249.110107	3071.250000	2128660000	3074.679932
4	3054.550049	3316.969971	3054.550049	2070750000	3316.770020

Figure 10.1: First five entries of the stock dataset

3. Before we move on, we need to set the hyperparameters:

```
sequence_length = 21 # 20 preceeding inputs
n_features = len(data.columns)
val_ratio = 0.1
n_epochs = 300
batch_size = 512
```

4. The data needs to be preprocessed before we can feed it to an RNN. Every input should include the data of 20 proceding (`sequence_length - 1`) inputs. This means, one row of data (including the label) should be of the shape `sequence_length` by `n_features`:

```
data = data.as_matrix()
data_processed = []
for index in range(len(data) - sequence_length):
    data_processed.append(data[index :
    index + sequence_length])
data_processed = np.array(data_processed)
```

5. When modeling time series data, we should be extremely careful with splitting the data for training and validation. The split should resemble the training data and test data split. In this case, we should split the training data for training and validation as time-based:

```
val_split = round((1-val_ratio) *
data_processed.shape[0])
train = data_processed[: int(val_split), :]
val = data_processed[int(val_split) :, :]

print('Training data: {}'.format(train.shape))
print('Validation data: {}'.format(val.shape))
```

6. As we can see in *Figure 10-1*, the values used as input are quite large. Moreover, one of the variables, `Volume`, has significantly larger values than the other variables. Therefore, it's important that we normalize the data with scikit-learn's `MinMaxScaler`, as follows:

```
train_samples, train_nx, train_ny = train.shape
val_samples, val_nx, val_ny = val.shape

train = train.reshape((train_samples, train_nx * train_ny))
val = val.reshape((val_samples, val_nx * val_ny))

preprocessor = MinMaxScaler().fit(train)
train = preprocessor.transform(train)
```

```
val = preprocessor.transform(val)

train = train.reshape((train_samples,
train_nx, train_ny))
val = val.reshape((val_samples,
val_nx, val_ny))
```

7. Next, we need to make sure that the labels are correctly extracted. From our 21 x 5 matrix, we need the last value as a label. As input data, we will use the first 20 rows only (using the input variables of the 21st row would be cheating):

```
X_train = train[:, : -1]
y_train = train[:, -1][: ,-1]
X_val = val[:, : -1]
y_val = val[:, -1][ : ,-1]

X_train = np.reshape(X_train, (X_train.shape[0],
X_train.shape[1], n_features))
X_val = np.reshape(X_val, (X_val.shape[0],
X_val.shape[1], n_features))
```

8. We can now define our model architecture. We will stack two LSTM cells and an output layer with a dropout in between. We'll be using `adam` as the optimizer and `mse` as the loss function:

```
model = Sequential()
model.add(LSTM(input_shape=(X_train.shape[1:]), units = 128,
return_sequences=True))
model.add(Dropout(0.5))
model.add(LSTM(128, return_sequences=False))
model.add(Dropout(0.25))
model.add(Dense(units=1))
model.add(Activation("linear"))

model.compile(loss="mse", optimizer="adam")
```

9. Let's start training our model and store the training results in `history`:

```
history = model.fit(
    X_train,
    y_train,
    batch_size=batch_size,
    epochs=n_epochs,
    verbose=2)
```

As you can see, we didn't use a validation split while training. If we do want to use a validation set during training, we should split the training set time-based and use a fixed validation set.

10. Instead, we'll be validating our results after training. In addition, we store the differences between the labels and the predictions, as follows:

```
preds_val = model.predict(X_val)
diff = []
for i in range(len(y_val)):
    pred = preds_val[i][0]
    diff.append(y_val[i] - pred)
```

11. Because we've normalized all input variables and the label, our predictions will also be normalized. That's why we need an inverse transformation to get the actual values:

```
real_min = preprocessor.data_min_[104]
real_max = preprocessor.data_max_[104]
print(preprocessor.data_min_[104])
print(preprocessor.data_max_[104])

preds_real = preds_val *
(real_max - real_min) + real_min
y_val_real = y_val *
(real_max - real_min) + real_min
```

12. Finally, we can plot the actual stock prices and the predicted prices, as follows:

```
plt.plot(preds_real, label='Predictions')
plt.plot(y_val_real, label='Actual values')
plt.xlabel('test')
plt.legend(loc=0)
plt.show()
```

In the following figure, we've plotted the actual stock prices and our predictions. As you can see the predictions do follow the actual prices quite closely but overestimate the price in most of the steps:

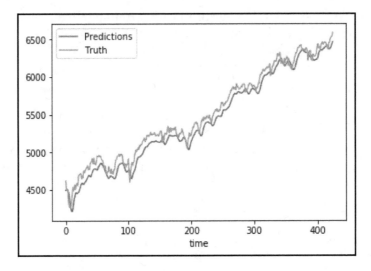

Figure 10-2: Actual stock prices and predictions on the validation set

Predicting bike sharing demand

In the previous dataset, the features were strongly correlated with the labels. However, in some time series, we have features that might be less correlated or not correlated with the labels at all. The main idea behind machine learning is that the algorithm tries to figure out by itself which features are valuable and which are not. Especially in deep learning, we want to keep the feature engineering limited. In the following recipe, we will be predicting the demand for bike sharing rentals. The data includes some interesting features, such as weather type, holiday, temperature, and season.

How to do it...

1. First, we import all libraries:

```
from sklearn import preprocessing
import pandas as pd
import numpy as np
from math import pi, sin, cos
from datetime import datetime

from keras.models import Sequential
from keras.layers import Dense, Activation, Dropout
from keras.optimizers import Adam
from keras.callbacks import EarlyStopping
```

2. The training and test data is stored in two separate .csv files:

```
train = pd.read_csv('Data/bike-sharing/train.csv')
test = pd.read_csv('Data/bike-sharing/test.csv')
data = pd.concat([train, test])
test_split = train.shape[0]
```

3. Let's output the first five rows to have a look at the data:

```
data.head()
```

In the following figure, we can see that the datetime feature cannot be parsed correctly by a neural network:

	atemp	casual	count	datetime	holiday	humidity	registered	season	temp	weather	windspeed	workingday
0	14.395	3.0	16.0	2011-01-01 00:00:00	0	81	13.0	1	9.84	1	0.0	0
1	13.635	8.0	40.0	2011-01-01 01:00:00	0	80	32.0	1	9.02	1	0.0	0
2	13.635	5.0	32.0	2011-01-01 02:00:00	0	80	27.0	1	9.02	1	0.0	0
3	14.395	3.0	13.0	2011-01-01 03:00:00	0	75	10.0	1	9.84	1	0.0	0
4	14.395	0.0	1.0	2011-01-01 04:00:00	0	75	1.0	1	9.84	1	0.0	0

Figure 10-3: First five entries of training data

4. We preprocess this variable as follows:

```
data['hour'] = data.apply(lambda x:
datetime.strptime(x['datetime'],
'%Y-%m-%d %H:%M:%S').hour, axis=1)
data['weekday'] = data.apply(lambda x:
datetime.strptime(x['datetime'],
'%Y-%m-%d %H:%M:%S').weekday(), axis=1)
data['month'] = data.apply(lambda x:
datetime.strptime(x['datetime'],
'%Y-%m-%d %H:%M:%S').month, axis=1)
data['year'] = data.apply(lambda x:
datetime.strptime(x['datetime'],
'%Y-%m-%d %H:%M:%S').year, axis=1)
```

5. Even though we want to keep the amount of feature engineering limited, we might want to make sure that our model understands that, after the end of the week, a new week starts. More specifically, these time variables are circular. We can add this information with the following code:

```
data['hour_sin'] = data.apply(lambda x:
sin(x['hour'] / 24.0 * 2 * pi), axis=1)
data['hour_cos'] = data.apply(lambda x:
cos(x['hour'] / 24.0 * 2 * pi), axis=1)
data['weekday_sin'] = data.apply(lambda x:
sin(x['weekday'] / 7.0 * 2 * pi), axis=1)
data['weekday_cos'] = data.apply(lambda x:
cos(x['weekday'] / 7.0 * 2 * pi), axis=1)
data['month_sin'] = data.apply(lambda x:
sin(((x['month'] - 5) % 12) / 12.0 * 2 * pi), axis=1)
data['month_cos'] = data.apply(lambda x:
cos(((x['month'] - 5) % 12) / 12.0 * 2 * pi), axis=1)
data['season_sin'] = data.apply(lambda x:
sin(((x['season'] - 3) % 4) / 4.0 * 2 * pi), axis=1)
data['season_cos'] = data.apply(lambda x:
cos(((x['season'] - 3) % 4) / 4.0 * 2 * pi), axis=1)
```

6. After preprocessing, we can split the training and test data again:

```
X_train = data[:test_split].drop(['datetime',
'casual', 'registered', 'count'], inplace=False, axis=1)
X_test = data[test_split:].drop(['datetime',
'casual', 'registered', 'count'], inplace=False, axis=1)
y_train = data['count'][:test_split]
y_test = data['count'][test_split:]
```

7. Before feeding the data, we should normalize the inputs:

```
scaler = preprocessing.StandardScaler()
X_train = scaler.fit_transform(X_train)
X_test = scaler.transform(X_test)
```

The split in training and test data for this problem can be considered as unorthodox. The entries in the training set are the first 19 days of each month and the entries in the test set are from day 20 to the end of the month. If we want to validate our results correctly, we should also split our validation set in the same way. For example, use days 14 to 19 as a validation set.

8. We can now define our model architecture and optimizer and compile our model:

```
model = Sequential()
model.add(Dense(200, input_dim=X_train.shape[1]))
model.add(Activation('relu'))
model.add(Dropout(0.1))
model.add(Dense(200))
model.add(Activation('relu'))
model.add(Dropout(0.1))
model.add(Dense(1))

opt = Adam()
model.compile(loss='mean_squared_logarithmic_error',
 optimizer=opt)
```

9. We'll be using the following hyperparameters:

```
n_epochs = 1000
batch_size = 128
```

10. Let's start training with early stopping:

```
callbacks = [EarlyStopping(monitor='val_loss',
patience=5)]
history = model.fit(X_train, y_train, shuffle=True,
epochs=n_epochs, batch_size=batch_size,
validation_split=0.1, verbose=1, callbacks=callbacks)
```

In this recipe, we used a standard feed-forward neural network architecture. The temporal nature of this data has been captured by the features and not by the model.

Using a shallow neural network for binary classification

Throughout this book, we've focused on giving ready-to-use examples for real-world problems. For some relatively simple tasks, a simple neural network can provide a good-enough solution to a problem. In this recipe, we'll demonstrate how straightforward it can be to implement a shallow neural network for binary classification in Keras.

How to do it...

1. Start with importing all libraries as follows:

```
import numpy as np
import pandas as pd
from sklearn.preprocessing import LabelEncoder

from keras.models import Sequential
from keras.layers import Dense
from keras.callbacks import EarlyStopping
```

2. Next, we load the dataset:

```
dataframe = pandas.read_csv("Data/sonar.all-data",
header=None)
data = dataframe.values
```

3. Let's split the labels from the features:

```
X = data[:,0:60].astype(float)
y = data[:,60]
```

4. Currently, the labels are strings. We need to binarize them for our network:

```
encoder = LabelEncoder()
encoder.fit(y)
y = encoder.transform(y)
```

5. Let's define a simple network with one hidden layer:

```
model = Sequential()
model.add(Dense(32, input_dim=60, activation='relu'))
model.add(Dense(1, activation='sigmoid'))
model.compile(loss='binary_crossentropy',
optimizer='adam', metrics=['accuracy'])
```

6. We want to use early stopping to prevent overfitting by defining a callback:

```
callbacks = [EarlyStopping(monitor='val_acc', patience=20)]
```

7. Next, we define the hyperparameters and start training:

```
n_epochs = 1000
batch_size = 2
model.fit(X, y, epochs=n_epochs, batch_size=batch_size,
validation_split=0.1, callbacks=callbacks)
```

Within fewer than 100 epochs, you should have obtained a validation accuracy that is greater than 90%.

 In this recipe, we have demonstrated that it's not always necessary to implement deep networks to get good results. In some cases, a smaller and less complex network can work just as well or even better. When the data is structured nicely and the task is straightforward, it can be valuable to keep it simple.

11
Game Playing Agents and Robotics

This chapter focuses on state-of-the-art deep learning research applications applied in complex environments. This includes recipes related to game playing agents in a complex environment (simulations) and autonomous vehicles.

- Learning to drive a car with end-to-end learning
- Learning to play games with deep reinforcement learning
- Genetic Algorithm (GA) to optimize hyperparameters

Introduction

As is discussed in this book, deep learning also had a major influence on robotics and game playing agents. Other machine learning algorithms already demonstrated how to beat human players in less complex environments. However, deep learning models were able to achieve above human performance in more complex environments. Driving a car has always been seen as a complex task that could only be done by humans and maybe in the distant future by robots as well. Recent advancements in AI and sensor technologies made it clear that autonomous vehicles are not a distant future dream anymore.

Learning to drive a car with end-to-end learning

What is fascinating about deep learning is that we don't need to focus on feature engineering. Ideally, the network learns by itself what is important and what is not. An excellent example of such as case is behavioral cloning: a human demonstrates a certain task—this is the training data and an agent (deep learning model) tries to copy that behavior without specifying steps. In the case of autonomous vehicles in a protected environment with only a single agent, the agent should learn to drive on the road. We will demonstrate how to implement a deep learning model that teaches an agent to drive a car around a track.

Getting started

For this recipe, we will be using **Udacity's Self-Driving Car Simulator**. This simulator is based on Unity and the instructions to install this simulator can be found on the following GitHub page: `https://github.com/udacity/self-driving-car-sim`.

How to do it...

1. First, we import all libraries as follows:

```
import pandas as pd
import numpy as np
import cv2
import math

from keras.models import Sequential
from keras.layers.core import Dense, Dropout, Activation, Lambda
from keras.layers import Input, ELU
from keras.optimizers import SGD, Adam, RMSprop
from keras.utils import np_utils
from keras.layers import Conv2D, MaxPooling2D, Flatten
from keras import initializers
from keras.callbacks import ModelCheckpoint
```

2. Next, we load the training data as follows:

```
data_path = 'Data/SDC/training.csv'
data = pd.read_csv(data_path, header=None, skiprows=[0],
names=['center', 'left', 'right', 'steering', 'throttle', 'brake',
'speed'])
```

3. We need to define some image parameters before proceeding:

```
img_cols = 64
img_rows = 64
img_channels = 3
```

4. For data augmentation, we define the following function:

```
def augment_image(image):
    image = cv2.cvtColor(image,cv2.COLOR_RGB2HSV)
    random_bright = .25 + np.random.uniform()
    image[:,:,2] = image[:,:,2] * random_bright
    image = cv2.cvtColor(image,cv2.COLOR_HSV2RGB)
    return(image)
```

5. Next, we define a function to preprocess the incoming images:

```
def preprocess_image(data):
    # Randomly pick left, center or right
    # camera image
    rand = np.random.randint(3)
    if (rand == 0):
        path_file = data['left'][0].strip()
        shift_ang = .25
    if (rand == 1):
        path_file = data['center'][0].strip()
        shift_ang = 0.
    if (rand == 2):
        path_file = data['right'][0].strip()
        shift_ang = -.25
    y = data['steering'][0] + shift_ang

    # Read image
    image = cv2.imread(path_file)
    image = cv2.cvtColor(image, cv2.COLOR_BGR2RGB)

    # Crop image
    shape = image.shape
    image = image[math.floor(shape[0]/4):
    shape[0]-20, 0:shape[1]]
```

```
# Resize image
image = cv2.resize(image, (img_cols, img_rows),
interpolation=cv2.INTER_AREA)

# Augment image
image = augment_image(image)
image = np.array(image)

if np.random.choice([True, False]):
    image = cv2.flip(image,1)
    y = -y
return(image, y)
```

6. Our total training set is quite large, so we use a batch generator to load the images on the fly:

```
def batch_gen(data, batch_size):
    # Create empty numpy arrays
    batch_images = np.zeros((batch_size, img_rows,
    img_cols, img_channels))
    batch_steering = np.zeros(batch_size)

    small_steering_threshold = 0.8

    # Custom batch generator
    while 1:
        for n in range(batch_size):
            i = np.random.randint(len(data))
            data_sub = data.iloc[[i]].reset_index()
            # Only keep training data with small
            #steering angles with probablitiy
            keep = False
            while keep == False:
                x, y = preprocess_image(data_sub)
                pr_unif = np.random
                if abs(y) < .01:
                    next;
                if abs(y) < .10:
                    small_steering_rand = np.random.uniform()
                    if small_steering_rand >
                    small_steering_threshold:
                        keep = True
                else:
                    keep = True

            batch_images[n] = x
            batch_steering[n] = y
        yield batch_images, batch_steering
```

7. Let's define our model architecture:

```
input_shape = (img_rows, img_cols, img_channels)
model = Sequential()
model.add(Lambda(lambda x: x/255.-0.5,
input_shape=input_shape))
model.add(Conv2D(3, (1, 1), padding='valid',
kernel_initializer='he_normal'))
model.add(ELU())
model.add(Conv2D(32, (3, 3), padding='valid',
kernel_initializer='he_normal'))
model.add(ELU())
model.add(Conv2D(32, (3, 3), padding='valid',
kernel_initializer='he_normal'))
model.add(ELU())
model.add(MaxPooling2D(pool_size=(2, 2)))
model.add(Dropout(0.5))
model.add(Conv2D(64, (3, 3), padding='valid',
kernel_initializer='he_normal'))
model.add(ELU())
model.add(Conv2D(64, (3, 3), padding='valid',
kernel_initializer='he_normal'))
model.add(ELU())
model.add(MaxPooling2D(pool_size=(2, 2)))
model.add(Dropout(0.5))
model.add(Conv2D(128, (3, 3), padding='valid',
kernel_initializer='he_normal'))
model.add(ELU())
model.add(Conv2D(128, (3, 3), padding='valid',
kernel_initializer='he_normal'))
model.add(ELU())
model.add(MaxPooling2D(pool_size=(2, 2)))
model.add(Dropout(0.5))
model.add(Flatten())
model.add(Dense(512, kernel_initializer='he_normal',
activation='relu'))
model.add(ELU())
model.add(Dropout(0.5))
model.add(Dense(64, kernel_initializer='he_normal'))
model.add(ELU())
model.add(Dropout(0.5))
model.add(Dense(16, kernel_initializer='he_normal'))
model.add(ELU())
model.add(Dropout(0.5))
model.add(Dense(1, kernel_initializer='he_normal'))

opt = Adam(lr=1e-4, beta_1=0.9, beta_2=0.999,
epsilon=1e-08, decay=0.0)
```

```
model.compile(optimizer=opt, loss='mse')
model.summary()
```

8. To store our trained model, we use a callback function:

```
callbacks = [ModelCheckpoint('checkpoints/sdc.h5',
save_best_only=False)]
```

9. Next, we create the generator for training and validation:

```
train_generator = batchgen(data, batch_size)
val_generator = batchgen(data, batch_size)
```

10. Before we start training, we need to set some hyperparameters:

```
n_epochs = 8
batch_size = 64
steps_per_epoch = 500
validation_steps = 50
```

11. Finally, we can start training:

```
history = model.fit_generator(train_generator,
steps_per_epoch=steps_per_epoch, epochs=n_epochs,
validation_data=val_generator,
validation_steps=validation_steps, callbacks=callbacks)
```

In this recipe, we've trained an agent to drive around a track without specifying any rules. The agent copies the behavior of the training data and learns to steer. Therefore, this is also called end-to-end learning.

Learning to play games with deep reinforcement learning

In this recipe, we will demonstrate how to leverage deep learning models to play games. In our example, we show how to apply a **Deep-Q Network** for playing breakout with the Keras framework.

How to do it...

1. Let's start with importing the necessary libraries, as follows:

```
import gym
import random
import numpy as np
import matplotlib.pyplot as plt
from collections import deque

from keras.models import Sequential
from keras.optimizers import Adam
from keras.layers import Dense, Flatten
from keras.layers.convolutional import Conv2D
from keras import backend as K
```

2. First, we will plot an example input image of the game:

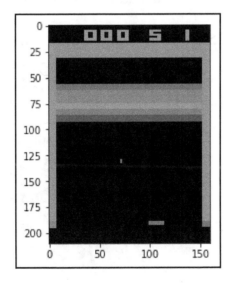

Figure 11.1: Example input image of Breakout by OpenAI

```
env = gym.make('BreakoutDeterministic-v4')
observation = env.reset()

for i in range(3):
    # The ball is released after 2 frames
    if i > 1:
        print(observation.shape)
        plt.imshow(observation)
```

```
        plt.show()
      # Get the next observation
      observation, _, _, _ = env.step(1)
```

3. Now, we can define a function that preprocesses the input data:

```
def preprocess_frame(frame):
    # remove top part of frame and some background
    frame = frame[35:195, 10:150]
    # grayscale frame and downsize by factor 2
    frame = frame[::2, ::2, 0]
    # set background to 0
    frame[frame == 144] = 0
    frame[frame == 109] = 0
    # set ball and paddles to 1
    frame[frame != 0] = 1
    return frame.astype(np.float).ravel()
```

4. Let's output the preceding preprocessed image to give us an idea of what our algorithm will process:

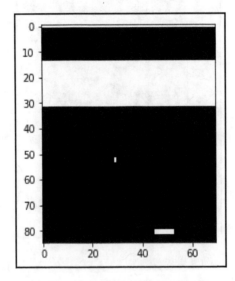

Figure 11.2: Preprocessed frame of Breakout

```
obs_preprocessed = preprocess_frame(observation)
plt.imshow(obs_preprocessed, cmap='gray')
plt.show()
```

5. For our deep Q-learning implementation, we need to define an agent that performs most of the tasks:

```
class DQLAgent:
    def __init__(self, cols, rows, n_actions,
    batch_size=32):
        self.state_size = (cols, rows, 4)
        self.n_actions = n_actions
        self.epsilon = 1.
        self.epsilon_start, self.epsilon_end = 1.0, 0.1
        self.exploration_steps = 1000000.
        self.epsilon_decay_step = (self.epsilon_start -
        self.epsilon_end) / self.exploration_steps
        self.batch_size = batch_size
        self.discount_factor = 0.99
        self.memory = deque(maxlen=400000)
        self.model = self.build_model()
        self.target_model = self.build_model()
        self.optimizer = self.optimizer()
        self.avg_q_max, self.avg_loss = 0, 0

    def optimizer(self):
        a = K.placeholder(shape=(None,), dtype='int32')
        y = K.placeholder(shape=(None,), dtype='float32')

        py_x = self.model.output

        a_one_hot = K.one_hot(a, self.n_actions)
        q_value = K.sum(py_x * a_one_hot, axis=1)
        error = K.abs(y - q_value)

        quadratic_part = K.clip(error, 0.0, 1.0)
        linear_part = error - quadratic_part
        loss = K.mean(0.5 *
        K.square(quadratic_part) + linear_part)

        opt = Adam(lr=0.00025, epsilon=0.01)
        updates = opt.get_updates
        (self.model.trainable_weights, [], loss)
        train = K.function([self.model.input, a, y],
        [loss], updates=updates)

        return train

    def build_model(self):
        model = Sequential()
        model.add(Conv2D(32, (8, 8), strides=(4, 4),
        activation='relu', input_shape=self.state_size))
```

```python
        model.add(Conv2D(64, (4, 4), strides=(2, 2),
        activation='relu'))
        model.add(Conv2D(64, (3, 3), strides=(1, 1),
        activation='relu'))
        model.add(Flatten())
        model.add(Dense(512, activation='relu'))
        model.add(Dense(self.n_actions))
        model.summary()
        return model

    def update_model(self):
        self.target_model.set_weights
        (self.model.get_weights())

    def action(self, history):
        history = np.float32(history / 255.0)
        if np.random.rand() <= self.epsilon:
            return random.randrange(self.n_actions)
        else:
            q_value = self.model.predict(history)
            return np.argmax(q_value[0])

    def replay(self, history, action, reward,
            next_history, dead):
        self.memory.append((history, action,
        reward, next_history, dead))

    def train(self):
        if len(self.memory) < self.batch_size:
            return
        if self.epsilon > self.epsilon_end:
            self.epsilon -= self.epsilon_decay_step

        mini_batch = random.sample(self.memory,
        self.batch_size)
        history = np.zeros((self.batch_size,
        self.state_size[0], self.state_size[1],
        self.state_size[2]))
        next_history = np.zeros((self.batch_size,
        self.state_size[0], self.state_size[1],
        self.state_size[2]))
        target = np.zeros((self.batch_size,))
        action, reward, dead = [], [], []

        for i in range(self.batch_size):
            history[i] = np.float32
            (mini_batch[i][0] / 255.)
            next_history[i] = np.float32
```

```
    (mini_batch[i][3] / 255.)
    action.append(mini_batch[i][1])
    reward.append(mini_batch[i][2])
    dead.append(mini_batch[i][4])

target_value = self.target_model.
predict(next_history)

for i in range(self.batch_size):
    if dead[i]:
        target[i] = reward[i]
    else:
        target[i] = reward[i] +
        self.discount_factor * \
        np.amax(target_value[i])

loss = self.optimizer([history, action,
target])
self.avg_loss += loss[0]
```

6. Next, we set the hyperparameters and some general settings and initialize our
   agent:

```
env = gym.make('BreakoutDeterministic-v4')

# General settings
n_warmup_steps = 50000
update_model_rate = 10000
cols, rows = 85, 70
n_states = 4

# Hyperparameters
batch_size = 32

# Initialization
agent = DQLAgent(cols, rows, n_actions=3)
scores, episodes = [], []
n_steps = 0
```

7. We are now ready to start training our model:

```
while True:
    done = False
    dead = False
    step, score, start_life = 0, 0, 5
    observation = env.reset()
```

```
            state = preprocess_frame(observation,
            cols, rows)
            history = np.stack((state, state,
            state, state), axis=2)
            history = np.reshape([history],
            (1, cols, rows, n_states))

            while not done:
    # env.render()
                n_steps += 1
                step += 1
                # Get action
                action = agent.action(history)
                observation, reward, done, info =
                env.step(action+1)
                # Extract next state
                state_next = preprocess_frame
                (observation, cols, rows)
                state_next = np.reshape([state_next],
                (1, cols, rows, 1))
                history_next = np.append(state_next,
                history[:, :, :, :3], axis=3)

                agent.avg_q_max += np.amax(agent.model
                .predict(history)[0])
                reward = np.clip(reward, -1., 1.)

                agent.replay(history, action, reward,
                history_next, dead)
                agent.train()
                if n_steps % update_model_rate == 0:
                    agent.update_model()
                score += reward

                if dead:
                    dead = False
                else:
                    history = history_next

                if done:
                    print('episode {:2d}; score:
                    {:2.0f}; q {:2f}; loss {:2f}; steps {}'
                        .format(n_steps, score,
                        agent.avg_q_max / float(step),
                        agent.avg_loss / float(step), step))

                    agent.avg_q_max, agent.avg_loss = 0, 0
        # Save weights of model
```

```
if n_steps % 1000 == 0:
    agent.model.save_weights
    ("weights/breakout_dql.h5")
```

8. When we want to evaluate our algorithm, we can stop training.

9. Let's see how our final model performs:

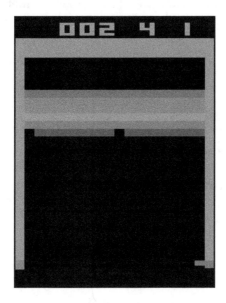

Figure 11.3: Our trained deep Q-learning agent in action

```
env = gym.make('BreakoutDeterministic-v4')
agent = DQLAgent(cols, rows, n_action=3)

for i in range(5):
    observation = env.reset()

    state = pre_processing(observation,
    cols, rows)
    history = np.stack((state, state,
    state, state), axis=2)
    history = np.reshape([history], (1, cols,
    rows, n_states))

    while not done:
        env.render()
        action = agent.get_action(history)
        observe, reward, done, info =
        env.step(action+1)
```

Genetic Algorithm (GA) to optimize hyperparameters

In all previous recipes, we've only considered static network architectures. More specifically, while training our network or agents the network didn't change. What we've also seen is that the network architecture and the hyperparameters can have a big affect on the results. However, often we don't know if a network will perform well or not in advance so we need to test it thoroughly. There are different ways to optimize these hyperparameters. In Chapter 12, *Hyperparameter Selection, Tuning, and Neural Network Learning*, we demonstrate how to apply a grid search (with brute force) to find optimal hyperparameters. However, sometimes the hyperparameter space is enormous and using brute force will take too much time.

Evolutionary Algorithms (EA) have proven to be powerful. One of the most impressive outcomes is life. The **optimization algorithms** used in evolution have been and are studied thoroughly. One of these is a Genetic Algorithm. This algorithm is inspired by life, it uses evolution, fitness, crossover, and mutation. The theory behind these algorithms is beyond the scope of this book. However, we do want to briefly introduce a Genetic Algorithm to optimize hyperparameters in the following recipe.

How to do it..

1. We start by importing all libraries as follows:

```
from functools import reduce
from operator import add
import random

from keras.datasets import mnist
from keras.models import Sequential
from keras.layers import Dense, Dropout
from keras.utils.np_utils import to_categorical
from keras.callbacks import EarlyStopping,
ModelCheckpoint
```

2. After importing the libraries, we set some of the hyperparameters:

```
n_classes = 10
batch_size = 128
n_epochs = 1000
```

3. Next, we load and preprocess the training data:

```
(X_train, y_train), (X_val, y_val) = mnist.load_data()
X_train = X_train.reshape(60000, 28, 28, 1)
X_val = X_val.reshape(10000, 28, 28, 1)
X_train = X_train.astype('float32')
X_val = X_val.astype('float32')
X_val /= 255
X_val /= 255

y_train = to_categorical(y_train, n_classes)
y_val = to_categorical(y_val, n_classes)
```

4. Next, we define a function that creates and compiles a model. Some of the settings of our network are not set, but can be set as parameter. These include the dropout percentage, the learning rate, and the number of hidden units in our final fully connected layer:

```
def create_model(parameters, n_classes, input_shape):
    print(parameters)
    dropout = parameters['dropout']
    learning_rate = parameters['learning_rate']
    hidden_inputs = parameters['hidden_inputs']

    model = Sequential()
    model.add(Conv2D(32, (3, 3), padding='same',
input_shape=input_shape))
    model.add(Activation('relu'))
    model.add(Conv2D(32, (3, 3)))
    model.add(Activation('relu'))
    model.add(MaxPooling2D(pool_size=(2, 2)))
    model.add(Dropout(dropout))

    model.add(Conv2D(64, (3, 3), padding='same'))
    model.add(Activation('relu'))
    model.add(Conv2D(64, (3, 3)))
    model.add(Activation('relu'))
    model.add(MaxPooling2D(pool_size=(2, 2)))
    model.add(Dropout(dropout))

    model.add(Flatten())
    model.add(Dense(hidden_inputs))
    model.add(Activation('relu'))
    model.add(Dropout(dropout))
    model.add(Dense(n_classes))
    model.add(Activation('softmax'))
    opt = Adam(learning_rate)
```

```
      model.compile(loss='categorical_crossentropy',
      optimizer=opt, metrics=['accuracy'])

      return model
```

5. We need a class `Network` that we can use to create a network with random parameters and train the network. Moreover, it should be able to retrieve the accuracy of the network:

```
class Network():
    def __init__(self, parameter_space=None):
        self.accuracy = 0.
        self.parameter_space = parameter_space
        self.network_parameters = {}

    def set_random_parameters(self):
        for parameter in self.parameter_space:
            self.network_parameters[parameter] =
random.choice(self.parameter_space[parameter])

    def create_network(self, network):
        self.network_parameters = network

    def train(self):
        model = create_model(self.network_parameters,
        n_classes, input_shape)
        history = model.fit(X_train, y_train,
        batch_size=batch_size, epochs=n_epochs,
        verbose=0, validation_data=(X_val, y_val),
        callbacks=callbacks)
        self.accuracy = max(history.history['val_acc'])
```

6. Next, we will be defining a class that does the heavy lifting. Our class GA should be able to create a random population and evolve–including breeding and mutating a network. Also, it should be able to retrieve some statistics of the networks in the population:

```
class Genetic_Algorithm():
    def __init__(self, parameter_space, retain=0.3,
random_select=0.1, mutate_prob=0.25):
        self.mutate_prob = mutate_prob
        self.random_select = random_select
        self.retain = retain
        self.parameter_space = parameter_space

    def create_population(self, count):
        population = []
```

```
        for _ in range(0, count):
            network = Network(self.parameter_space)
            network.set_random_parameters()
            population.append(network)
        return population

    def get_fitness(network):
        return network.accuracy

    def get_grade(self, population):
        total = reduce(add, (self.fitness(network)
        for network in population))
        return float(total) / len(population)

    def breed(self, mother, father):
        children = []
        for _ in range(2):
            child = {}
            for param in self.parameter_space:
                child[param] = random.choice(
                    [mother.network[param],
                    father.network[param]]
                )
            network = Network(self.nn_param_choices)
            network.create_set(child)
            if self.mutate_chance > random.random():
                network = self.mutate(network)
            children.append(network)
        return children

    def mutate(self, network):
        mutation = random.choice(list
        (self.parameter_space.keys()))
        network.network[mutation] =
        random.choice(self.parameter_space[mutation])
        return network

    def evolve(self, pop):
        graded = [(self.fitness(network),
        network) for network in pop]
        graded = [x[1] for x in sorted(graded,
        key=lambda x: x[0], reverse=True)]
        retain_length = int(len(graded)*self.retain)

        parents = graded[:retain_length]

        for individual in graded[retain_length:]:
            if self.random_select > random.random():
```

```
                    parents.append(individual)

        parents_length = len(parents)
        desired_length = len(pop) - parents_length
        children = []

        while len(children) < desired_length:

            male = random.randint(0,
            parents_length-1)
            female = random.randint(0,
            parents_length-1)

            if male != female:
                male = parents[male]
                female = parents[female]

                children_new = self.breed(male,
                 female)

                for child_new in children_new:
                    if len(children) < desired_length:
                        children.append(child_new)

        parents.extend(children)

        return parents
```

7. Our last function will retrieve the average accuracy across a population:

```
def get_population_accuracy(population):
    total_accuracy = 0
    for network in population:
        total_accuracy += network.get_accuracy

    return total_accuracy / len(population)
```

8. We can now set the remaining hyperparameters that we want to explore:

```
n_generations = 10
population_size = 20

parameter_space = {
    'dropout': [0.25, 0.5, 0.75],
    'hidden_inputs': [256, 512, 1024],
    'learning_rate': [0.1, 0.01, 0.001, 0.0001]
}
```

9. Next, we create our `Genetic_Algorithm` and create a population:

```
GA = Genetic_Algorithm(parameter_space)
population = GA.create_population(population_size)
```

10. Let's start training our `Genetic_Algorithm`:

```
for i in range(n_generations):
    print('Generation {}'.format(i))

    for network in population:
        network.train()

    average_accuracy = get_population_accuracy(population)
    print('Average accuracy: {:.2f}'.
    format(average_accuracy))

    # Evolve
    if i < n_generations - 1:
        s = GA.evolve(networks)
```

In this recipe, we focused on optimizing the hyperparameters. However, Genetic Algorithms can also be used to evolve complete network architectures. For example, the number of layers and the layer type.

12
Hyperparameter Selection, Tuning, and Neural Network Learning

This chapter provides a collection of recipes on the many aspects involved in the learning process of a neural network. The overall objective of the recipes is to provide very neat and specific tricks to boost networks' performances.

- Visualizing training with TensorBoard and Keras
- Working with batches and mini-batches
- Using grid search for parameter tuning
- Learning rates and learning rate schedulers
- Comparing optimizers
- Determining the depth of the network
- Adding dropouts to prevent overfitting
- Making a model more robust with data augmentation

Introduction

Optimizing and tuning a deep learning architecture can be challenging. Sometimes, small changes in hyperparameters can have a big impact on training, resulting in worse performance. On the other hand, overfitting the training data is a well-known problem in machine learning. In this chapter, we'll demonstrate how to combat both. Also, we'll demonstrate the solutions and steps for hyperparameter tuning.

Visualizing training with TensorBoard and Keras

Analyzing training results (during or after training) is much more convenient if we can visualize the metrics. A great tool for this is TensorBoard. Originally developed for TensorFlow, it can also be used with other frameworks such as Keras and PyTorch. TensorBoard gives us the ability to follow loss, metrics, weights, outputs, and more. In the following recipe, we'll show you how to use TensorBoard with Keras and leverage it to visualize training data interactively.

How to do it...

1. First, we import all the libraries in Python, as follows:

```
from keras.datasets import cifar10
from keras.preprocessing.image import ImageDataGenerator
from keras.models import Sequential
from keras.layers import Dense, Dropout, Activation, Flatten
from keras.layers import Conv2D, MaxPooling2D
from keras.optimizers import Adam
from keras.callbacks import EarlyStopping, TensorBoard,
ModelCheckpoint
from keras.utils import to_categorical
```

2. Let's load the `cifar10` dataset for this example and pre-process the training and validation data:

```
(X_train, y_train), (X_val, y_val) = cifar10.load_data()

X_train = X_train.astype('float32')
X_train /=255.
X_val = X_val.astype('float32')
```

```
X_val /=255.

n_classes = 10
y_train = to_categorical(y_train, n_classes)
y_val = to_categorical(y_val, n_classes)
```

3. Next, we define the the network architecture:

```
model = Sequential()
model.add(Conv2D(32, (3, 3), padding='same',
input_shape=X_train.shape[1:]))
model.add(Activation('relu'))
model.add(Conv2D(32, (3, 3)))
model.add(Activation('relu'))
model.add(MaxPooling2D(pool_size=(2, 2)))
model.add(Dropout(0.25))

model.add(Conv2D(64, (3, 3), padding='same'))
model.add(Activation('relu'))
model.add(Conv2D(64, (3, 3)))
model.add(Activation('relu'))
model.add(MaxPooling2D(pool_size=(2, 2)))
model.add(Dropout(0.25))

model.add(Flatten())
model.add(Dense(512))
model.add(Activation('relu'))
model.add(Dropout(0.5))
model.add(Dense(n_classes))
model.add(Activation('softmax'))
```

4. We will be using the `Adam` optimizer with default settings:

```
opt = Adam()
model.compile(loss='categorical_crossentropy', optimizer=opt,
metrics=['accuracy'])
```

5. Next, we add data augmentation to our dataset with Keras's `ImageDataGenerator`:

```
data_gen = ImageDataGenerator(
    rotation_range=15,
    width_shift_range=0.15,
    height_shift_range=0.15,
    horizontal_flip=True,
    vertical_flip=False)

data_gen.fit(X_train)
```

6. In our `callbacks`, we will add `TensorBoard` as follows:

```
callbacks = [EarlyStopping(monitor='val_acc', patience=5,
verbose=2), ModelCheckpoint('checkpoints/weights.
{epoch:02d}.hdf5', save_best_only=True),
TensorBoard('~/notebooks/logs',
write_graph=True, write_grads=True, write_images=True,
embeddings_freq=0, embeddings_layer_names=None,
embeddings_metadata=None)]
```

7. Next, we go to a new terminal window. If you're logged in to a server, make sure you start a new connection to your server and use a different port for SSH-tunneling, for example, when using GCP (replace `instance-zone` and `instance-name` with your own namings):

```
gcloud compute ssh --ssh-flag="-L 6006:localhost:6006"  --zone
"instance-zone" "instance-name"
```

8. After logging in, you can start the `tensorBoard` connection, as follows:

```
tensorboard --logdir='~/notebooks/logs'
```

The terminal will output the location where you can connect with TensorBoard, for example, `http://instance-name:6006`. In our case, because we've enabled SSH-tunneling, we can go to our local browser and use the address `http://localhost:6006/` to access the dashboard. TensorBoard won't be showing any data yet.

9. Now, back in the Python environment, we can start training our model:

```
model.fit_generator(data_gen.flow(X_train, y_train,
batch_size=batch_size),
                    steps_per_epoch=X_train.shape[0] // batch_size,
                    epochs=n_epochs,
                    validation_data=(X_val, y_val),
                    callbacks=callbacks
                    )
```

After starting to train our model, we should see data coming into our TensorBoard dashboard. This is the output we get after 10 epochs:

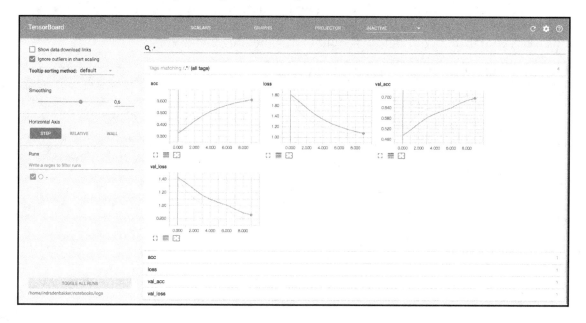

Figure 12.1: Example of a TensorBoard dashboard after 10 epochs

TensorBoard gives us a lot of flexibility in monitoring our training data. As you can see in the preceding screenshot, we are able to interactively adjust the smoothing parameter. This is just one of many advantages of working with TensorBoard. Another great feature of TensorBoard is the ability to visualize your training data with T-SNE or PCA. Switch to the **PROJECTOR** tab and your output should look something like this:

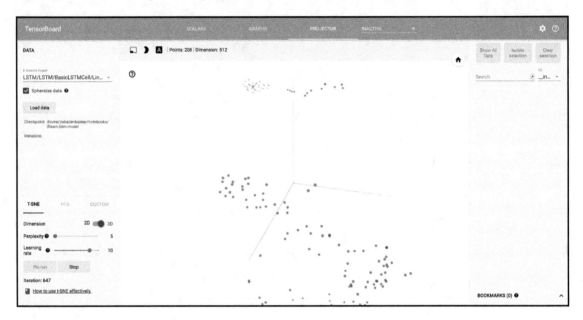

Figure 12.2: An example of training T-SNE on our training data

Working with batches and mini-batches

When training a neural network, we feed the training data to our network. Each full scan of the training data is called an epoch. If we feed all of the training data in one step, we call it batch mode (the batch size equals the size of the training set). However, in most cases, we divide the training data into smaller subsets while feeding the data to our model, just as in other machine learning algorithms. This is called mini-batch mode. Sometimes, we are forced to do this because the complete training set is too big and doesn't fit in the memory. If we look at the training time, we would say: the bigger the batch size, the better (as long as the batch fits in the memory). However, using mini-batches also has other advantages. Firstly, it reduces the complexity of the training process. Secondly, it reduces the effect of noise on the model by summing or averaging the gradient (reducing the variance). In mini-batch mode, the optimizer uses a balance of efficiency and robustness.

If the size of the mini-batch–also called batch size–is too small, the model can converge faster but is more likely to pick up noise. If the batch size is too large, the model will probably converge slower but the estimates of error gradients will be more accurate. For deep learning, when dealing with a lot of data, it's good to use large batch sizes. These batches are also great for parallelization on GPUs. In the following recipe, we will show you an example of steps to take when tuning the batch size.

How to do it...

1. Let's start with importing all the libraries, as follows:

```
from keras.datasets import cifar10
from keras.preprocessing.image import ImageDataGenerator
from keras.models import Sequential
from keras.layers import Dense, Dropout, Activation, Flatten
from keras.layers import Conv2D, MaxPooling2D
from keras.optimizers import Adam
from keras.callbacks import EarlyStopping, TensorBoard,
ModelCheckpoint
```

2. We will be using the `cifar10` dataset for our experiments. We load and pre-process the data like this:

```
(X_train, y_train), (X_test, y_test) = cifar10.load_data()

X_train = X_train.astype('float32')/255.
X_test = X_test.astype('float32')/255.
n_classes = 10
y_train = keras.utils.to_categorical(y_train, n_classes)
y_test = keras.utils.to_categorical(y_test, n_classes)
```

3. As model architecture, we use a straightforward convolutional neural network with convolutional blocks (both with two convolutional layers) and a fully connected layer before the output layer:

```
model = Sequential()
model.add(Conv2D(32, (3, 3), padding='same',
input_shape=X_train.shape[1:]))
model.add(Activation('relu'))
model.add(Conv2D(32, (3, 3)))
model.add(Activation('relu'))
model.add(MaxPooling2D(pool_size=(2, 2)))
model.add(Dropout(0.25))

model.add(Conv2D(64, (3, 3), padding='same'))
model.add(Activation('relu'))
model.add(Conv2D(64, (3, 3)))
model.add(Activation('relu'))
model.add(MaxPooling2D(pool_size=(2, 2)))
model.add(Dropout(0.25))

model.add(Flatten())
model.add(Dense(512))
model.add(Activation('relu'))
model.add(Dropout(0.5))
model.add(Dense(n_classes))
model.add(Activation('softmax'))
```

4. We define the `Adam` optimizer and compile our model:

```
opt = Adam(lr=0.0001)
model.compile(loss='categorical_crossentropy', optimizer=opt,
metrics=['accuracy'])
```

5. Because we want to make our model more robust, we will be using some data augmentation for training:

```
datagen = ImageDataGenerator(
    rotation_range=15,
    width_shift_range=0.15,
    height_shift_range=0.15,
    horizontal_flip=True,
    vertical_flip=False)

datagen.fit(x_train)
```

6. Next, we set our callback functions. We use early stopping to prevent overfitting, `ModelCheckpoint` to save our best model automatically, and TensorBoard for an analysis of our results:

```
callbacks = [EarlyStopping(monitor='val_acc', patience=5,
verbose=2), ModelCheckpoint('checkpoints/weights.
{epoch:02d}-'+str(batch_size)+'.hdf5',
save_best_only=True),  TensorBoard()]
```

7. Let's start training our first model with a batch size of 32:

```
batch_size = 32
n_epochs = 1000
history_32 = model.fit_generator(datagen.flow(X_train, y_train,
                            batch_size=batch_size),
            steps_per_epoch=X_train.shape[0] // batch_size,
            epochs=epochs,
            validation_data=(X_val, y_val),
            callbacks=callbacks
        )
```

8. Next, we recompile our model to make sure the weights are initialized:

```
model.compile(loss='categorical_crossentropy', optimizer=opt,
metrics=['accuracy'])
```

9. We can now start training our model with a batch size of `256`:

```
batch_size = 256
history_32 = model.fit_generator(datagen.flow(X_train, y_train,
                                 batch_size=batch_size),
                  steps_per_epoch=X_train.shape[0] // batch_size,
                  epochs=epochs,
                  validation_data=(X_val, y_val),
                  callbacks=callbacks
                  )
```

Here is the validation accuracy of both models against the number of epochs (with early stopping):

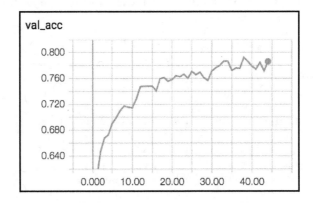

Figure 12.3: Validation accuracy for our model with batch size 32

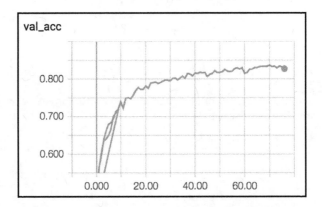

Figure 12.4: Validation accuracy for our model with batch size 256

So, we've noticed quite a few differences between the results of our two models. As expected, when using a bigger batch size, we need more epochs (in theory, the total number of steps/updates for converging should be the same regardless of the batch size). However, more interestingly, the validation accuracy of the model with a batch size of 256 is a bit higher: around 0.84%. Whereas the model with a batch size of 32 tops around 79%. When we train our model with a smaller batch size, the model might pick up a bit more noise. However, by fine-tuning our model further (for example, increasing the patience when using early stopping and decreasing the learning rate), the model with a batch size of 32 should be able to achieve similar accuracies.

Using grid search for parameter tuning

Tuning hyperparameters is a time-consuming and computation-expensive task. Throughout this book, we've paid limited attention to tuning hyperparameters. Most results were obtained with pre-chosen values. To choose the right values, we can use heuristics or an extensive grid search. Grid search is a popular method for parameter tuning in machine learning.

In the following recipe, we will demonstrate how you can apply grid search when building a deep learning model. For this, we will be using Hyperopt.

How to do it...

1. We start by importing the libraries used in this recipe:

```
import sys
import numpy as np

from hyperopt import fmin, tpe, hp, STATUS_OK, Trials

from keras.models import Sequential
from keras.layers import Dense, Dropout, Activation, Flatten
from keras.layers import Conv2D, MaxPooling2D
from keras.optimizers import Adam
from sklearn.model_selection import train_test_split
from keras.utils import to_categorical
from keras.callbacks import EarlyStopping, TensorBoard,
ModelCheckpoint

from keras.datasets import cifar10
```

2. Next, we load the `cifar10` dataset and pre-process the data:

```
(X_train, y_train), (X_test, y_test) = cifar10.load_data()
validation_split = 0.1
X_train, X_val, y_train, y_val = train_test_split(X_train, y_train,
test_size=validation_split, random_state=SEED)

X_train = X_train.astype('float32')
X_train /=255.
X_val = X_val.astype('float32')
X_val /=255.
X_test = X_test.astype('float32')
X_test /=255.

n_classes = 10
y_train = to_categorical(y_train, n_classes)
y_val = to_categorical(y_val, n_classes)
y_test = to_categorical(y_test, n_classes)
```

3. We can set the search space for different hyperparameters:

```
space = {
            'batch_size' : hp.choice('batch_size', [32, 64, 128,
            256]), 'n_epochs' : 1000,
        }
```

When using Hyperopt, you will have a lot of freedom with the settings you want to test. It's also possible to adjust the network architecture. For example, you can set the number of layers dynamically.

4. We will be using callbacks for early stopping, checkpoints, and visualization via TensorBoard:

```
def get_callbacks(pars):
    callbacks =[EarlyStopping(monitor='val_acc', p     atience=5,
verbose=2),
ModelCheckpoint('checkpoints/{}.h5'.format(pars['batch_size']),
save_best_only=True),
            TensorBoard('~/notebooks/logs-gridsearch',
write_graph=True, write_grads=True, write_images=True,
embeddings_freq=0, embeddings_layer_names=None,
embeddings_metadata=None)]
    return callbacks
```

5. Next, we define an objective function that we want to minimize. This function includes the network architecture, hyperparameters, results, and everything else you want to include. Make sure you include the status `STATUS_OK` in your return statement for successful runs:

```python
def f_nn(pars):
    print ('Parameters: ', pars)
    model = Sequential()
    model.add(Conv2D(32, (3, 3), padding='same',
input_shape=X_train.shape[1:]))
    model.add(Activation('relu'))
    model.add(Conv2D(32, (3, 3)))
    model.add(Activation('relu'))
    model.add(MaxPooling2D(pool_size=(2, 2)))
    model.add(Dropout(0.25))

    model.add(Conv2D(64, (3, 3), padding='same'))
    model.add(Activation('relu'))
    model.add(Conv2D(64, (3, 3)))
    model.add(Activation('relu'))
    model.add(MaxPooling2D(pool_size=(2, 2)))
    model.add(Dropout(0.25))

    model.add(Flatten())
    model.add(Dense(512))
    model.add(Activation('relu'))
    model.add(Dropout(0.5))
    model.add(Dense(n_classes))
    model.add(Activation('softmax'))
    optimizer = Adam()
    model.compile(loss='categorical_crossentropy',
optimizer=optimizer, metrics=['accuracy'])
    history = model.fit(X_train, y_train, epochs=pars['n_epochs'],
batch_size=pars['batch_size'],
                validation_data=[X_val, y_val],
                verbose = 1, callbacks=get_callbacks(pars))
    best_epoch = np.argmax(history.history['val_acc'])
    best_val_acc = np.max(history.history['val_acc'])
    print('Epoch {} - val acc: {}'.format(best_epoch,
best_val_acc))
    sys.stdout.flush()
    return {'val_acc': best_val_acc, 'best_epoch': best_epoch,
'eval_time': time.time(), 'status': STATUS_OK}
```

6. We can now initialize, start our grid search, and print the final results as follows:

```
trials = Trials()
best = fmin(f_nn, space, algo=tpe.suggest, max_evals=50,
trials=trials)
print(best)
```

If you want to parallelize training over multiple GPUs, you need to use MongoDB to create a database that handles asynchronous updates.

Learning rates and learning rate schedulers

It helps to avoid local optimas when using smaller learning rates. However, it often takes longer to converge. What can help shorten the training time is using a warm-up period. In this period, we can use a bigger learning rate for the first few epochs. After a certain number of epochs, we can decrease the learning rate. It's even possible to decrease the learning rate after each step, but this is not recommended, because you might be better off using a different optimizer instead (for example, if you want to use decay, you can specify this in as a hyperparameter). In theory, when the learning rate is too big during the warm-up period, it can be the case that you won't be able to reach the global optima at all.

In the following recipe, we demonstrate how to set a custom learning rate scheduler with Keras.

How to do it...

1. Let's start with importing all the libraries, as follows:

```
import math

from keras.models import Sequential
from keras.layers import Dense, Dropout, Activation, Flatten
from keras.layers import Conv2D, MaxPooling2D
from keras.optimizers import SGD
from sklearn.model_selection import train_test_split
from keras.utils import to_categorical
from keras.callbacks import EarlyStopping, TensorBoard,
ModelCheckpoint, LearningRateScheduler, Callback
from keras import backend as K
```

```
from keras.datasets import cifar10
```

2. Next, we load and pre-process the data:

```
(X_train, y_train), (X_test, y_test) = cifar10.load_data()
validation_split = 0.1
X_train, X_val, y_train, y_val = train_test_split(X_train, y_train,
test_size=validation_split, random_state=SEED)

X_train = X_train.astype('float32')
X_train /=255.
X_val = X_val.astype('float32')
X_val /=255.
X_test = X_test.astype('float32')
X_test /=255.

n_classes = 10
y_train = to_categorical(y_train, n_classes)
y_val = to_categorical(y_val, n_classes)
y_test = to_categorical(y_test, n_classes)
```

3. We can set the learning rate as follows:

```
learning_rate_schedule = {0: '0.1', 10: '0.01', 25: '0.0025'}

class get_learning_rate(Callback):
    def on_epoch_end(self, epoch, logs={}):
        optimizer = self.model.optimizer
        if epoch in learning_rate_schedule:
            K.set_value(optimizer.lr,
learning_rate_schedule[epoch])
        lr = K.eval(optimizer.lr)
        print('\nlr: {:.4f}'.format(lr))
```

Other than a custom callback function, Keras also provides a convenient `LearningRateScheduler` and `ReduceLROnPlateau` callback function. With these callbacks, you can implement an epoch-dependent learning rate scheme or reduce the learning rate if a monitored loss or metric reaches a plateau.

4. Let's, add our custom function to the callbacks list:

```
callbacks =[EarlyStopping(monitor='val_acc', patience=5,
verbose=2),
            ModelCheckpoint('checkpoints/{epoch:02d}.h5',
            save_best_only=True),
            TensorBoard('~/notebooks/logs-lrscheduler',
```

```
                    write_graph=True, write_grads=True,
                    write_images=True, embeddings_freq=0,
                    embeddings_layer_names=None,
                    embeddings_metadata=None),
                    get_learning_rate()
                    ]
```

5. We can now define and compile our model:

```
model = Sequential()
model.add(Conv2D(32, (3, 3), padding='same',
input_shape=X_train.shape[1:]))
model.add(Activation('relu'))
model.add(Conv2D(32, (3, 3)))
model.add(Activation('relu'))
model.add(MaxPooling2D(pool_size=(2, 2)))
model.add(Dropout(0.25))

model.add(Conv2D(64, (3, 3), padding='same'))
model.add(Activation('relu'))
model.add(Conv2D(64, (3, 3)))
model.add(Activation('relu'))
model.add(MaxPooling2D(pool_size=(2, 2)))
model.add(Dropout(0.25))

model.add(Flatten())
model.add(Dense(512))
model.add(Activation('relu'))
model.add(Dropout(0.5))
model.add(Dense(n_classes))
model.add(Activation('softmax'))
optimizer = SGD()
model.compile(loss='categorical_crossentropy',
optimizer=optimizer, metrics=['accuracy'])
```

6. Finally, we can start training. You will notice that the learning rate follows the set schedule:

```
n_epochs = 20
batch_size = 128

history = model.fit(X_train, y_train, epochs=n_epochs,
batch_size=batch_size,
            validation_data=[X_val, y_val],
            verbose = 1, callbacks=callbacks)
```

Comparing optimizers

In Chapter 2, *Feed-Forward Neural Networks*, we briefly demonstrated the use of different optimizers. Of course, we only used a test set of size 1. As for other machine learning algorithms, the most used and well-known optimizer for deep learning is **Stochastic Gradient Descent (SGD)**. Other optimizers are variants of SGD that try to speed up convergence by adding heuristics. Also, some optimizers have fewer hyperparameters to tune. The table shown in the Chapter 2, *Feed-Forward Neural Networks*, is an overview of the most commonly used optimizers in deep learning.

One could argue that the choice largely depends on the user's ability to tune the optimizer. There is definitely no ideal solution that works best for all problems. However, some optimizers have fewer parameters to tune and have proven to outperform other optimizers with default settings. In addition to our test in Chapter 2, *Feed-Forward Neural Networks*, we will perform another test to compare optimizers in the following recipe.

How to do it...

1. We start by loading the libraries as follows:

```
import numpy as np
import pandas as pd
from matplotlib import pyplot as plt

from sklearn.model_selection import train_test_split
from keras.models import Sequential
from keras.layers import Dense, Dropout
from keras.wrappers.scikit_learn import KerasRegressor
from keras.callbacks import EarlyStopping, ModelCheckpoint
from keras.optimizers import SGD, Adadelta, Adam, RMSprop, Adagrad,
Nadam, Adamax
```

2. For this test, we will create training, validation, and test sets and pre-process all the sets as follows:

```
(X_train, y_train), (X_test, y_test) = cifar10.load_data()
validation_split = 0.1
X_train, X_val, y_train, y_val = train_test_split(X_train, y_train,
test_size=validation_split, random_state=SEED)

X_train = X_train.astype('float32')
X_train /=255.
X_val = X_val.astype('float32')
```

```
X_val /=255.
X_test = X_test.astype('float32')
X_test /=255.

n_classes = 10
y_train = to_categorical(y_train, n_classes)
y_val = to_categorical(y_val, n_classes)
y_test = to_categorical(y_test, n_classes)
```

3. Next, we define a function that creates the model:

```
def create_model(opt):
 model = Sequential()
model.add(Conv2D(32, (3, 3), padding='same',
input_shape=x_train.shape[1:]))
model.add(Activation('relu'))
model.add(Conv2D(32, (3, 3)))
model.add(Activation('relu'))
model.add(MaxPooling2D(pool_size=(2, 2)))
model.add(Dropout(0.25))

model.add(Conv2D(64, (3, 3), padding='same'))
model.add(Activation('relu'))
model.add(Conv2D(64, (3, 3)))
model.add(Activation('relu'))
model.add(MaxPooling2D(pool_size=(2, 2)))
model.add(Dropout(0.25))

model.add(Flatten())
model.add(Dense(512))
model.add(Activation('relu'))
model.add(Dropout(0.5))
model.add(Dense(num_classes))
model.add(Activation('softmax'))
 return model
```

4. Also, we need to create a function that defines the callbacks we want to use during training:

```
def create_callbacks(opt):
    callbacks = [EarlyStopping(monitor='val_acc', patience=5,
verbose=2),
            ModelCheckpoint('checkpoints/weights.{epoch:02d}-
'+opt+'.h5', save_best_only=False, verbose=True),
            TensorBoard()]
    return callbacks
```

5. Create a `dict` of the optimizers we want to try:

```
opts = dict({
'sgd': SGD(),
'sgd-0001': SGD(lr=0.0001, decay=0.00001),
'adam': Adam(),
'adam': Adam(lr=0.0001),
'adadelta': Adadelta(),
'rmsprop': RMSprop(),
'rmsprop-0001': RMSprop(lr=0.0001),
'nadam': Nadam(),
'adamax': Adamax()
})
```

Instead of implementing our own script, we can also use Hyperopt to run different optimizers; see the *Using grid search for parameter tuning* recipe.

6. We train our networks and store the results:

```
n_epochs = 1000
batch_size = 128

results = []
# Loop through the optimizers
for opt in opts:
    model = create_model(opt)
    callbacks = create_callbacks(opt)
    model.compile(loss='categorical_crossentropy',
optimizer=opts[opt], metrics=['accuracy'])
    hist = model.fit(X_train, y_train, batch_size=batch_size,
epochs=n_epochs,
    validation_data=(X_val, y_val),
    verbose=1,
    callbacks=callbacks)
    best_epoch = np.argmax(hist.history['val_acc'])
    best_acc = hist.history['val_acc'][best_epoch]
    best_model = create_model(opt)
    # Load the model weights with the highest validation accuracy
    best_model.load_weights('checkpoints/weights.{:02d}-
{}.h5'.format(best_epoch, opt))
    best_model.compile(loss='mse', optimizer=opts[opt],
metrics=['accuracy'])
    score = best_model.evaluate(X_test, y_test, verbose=0)
    results.append([opt, best_epoch, best_acc, score[1]])
```

7. Compare the results:

```
res = pd.DataFrame(results)
res.columns = ['optimizer', 'epochs', 'val_accuracy', 'test_last',
'test_accuracy']
res
```

8. We obtained the following result:

	optimizer	epochs	val_accuracy	test_accuracy
0	sgd-0001	106	0.519531	0.53750
1	adam	112	0.589844	0.61250
2	sgd	0	0.000000	0.00000
3	adamax	213	0.578125	0.58750
4	rmsprop	600	0.597656	0.61250
5	adadelta	109	0.570312	0.58125
6	rmsprop-0001	38	0.539062	0.56250
7	nadam	84	0.597656	0.59375

Figure 12.5: Results of training with different optimizers on the cifar10 dataset

Determining the depth of the network

When we start building a deep learning model from scratch, it is hard to determine beforehand how many (different types of) layers we should stack. Generally, it is a good idea to have a look at a well-known deep learning model and use it as a basis to build further. In general, it is good to try to overfit to the training data as much as you can first. This ensures that your model is able to train on the input data. Afterwards, apply regularization techniques such as dropout to prevent overfitting and stimulate generalization.

Adding dropouts to prevent overfitting

The most popular method to prevent overfitting in neural networks is adding dropouts. In
Chapter 2, *Feed-Forward Neural Networks*, we introduced dropouts, and we've used
dropouts throughout the book. In the following recipe, we demonstrate, just like Chapter 2,
Feed-Forward Neural Networks, the difference in performance when adding dropouts. This
time, we will be using the cifar10 dataset.

How to do it...

1. We start by importing all libraries as follows:

```
from keras.models import Sequential
from keras.layers import Dense, Dropout, Activation, Flatten
from keras.layers import Conv2D, MaxPooling2D
from keras.optimizers import Adam
from sklearn.model_selection import train_test_split
from keras.utils import to_categorical
from keras.callbacks import EarlyStopping, TensorBoard,
ModelCheckpoint

from keras.datasets import cifar10
```

2. Next, we load the Cifar10 dataset and pre-process it:

```
(X_train, y_train), (X_test, y_test) = cifar10.load_data()
validation_split = 0.1
X_train, X_val, y_train, y_val = train_test_split(X_train, y_train,
test_size=validation_split, random_state=SEED)

X_train = X_train.astype('float32')
X_train /=255.
X_val = X_val.astype('float32')
X_val /=255.
X_test = X_test.astype('float32')
X_test /=255.

n_classes = 10
y_train = to_categorical(y_train, n_classes)
y_val = to_categorical(y_val, n_classes)
y_test = to_categorical(y_test, n_classes)
```

3. To monitor training and prevent overfitting, we introduce `callbacks`:

```
callbacks =[EarlyStopping(monitor='val_acc', patience=5,
verbose=2),
            ModelCheckpoint('checkpoints/{epoch:02d}.h5',
save_best_only=True),
            TensorBoard('~/notebooks/logs-lrscheduler',
write_graph=True, write_grads=True, write_images=True,
embeddings_freq=0, embeddings_layer_names=None,
embeddings_metadata=None),
            ]
```

4. Next, we define our model architecture and compile our model:

```
model = Sequential()
model.add(Conv2D(32, (3, 3), padding='same',
input_shape=X_train.shape[1:]))
model.add(Activation('relu'))
model.add(Conv2D(32, (3, 3)))
model.add(Activation('relu'))
model.add(MaxPooling2D(pool_size=(2, 2)))
# model.add(Dropout(0.25))

model.add(Conv2D(64, (3, 3), padding='same'))
model.add(Activation('relu'))
model.add(Conv2D(64, (3, 3)))
model.add(Activation('relu'))
model.add(MaxPooling2D(pool_size=(2, 2)))
# model.add(Dropout(0.25))

model.add(Flatten())
model.add(Dense(512))
model.add(Activation('relu'))
# model.add(Dropout(0.5))
model.add(Dense(n_classes))
model.add(Activation('softmax'))
optimizer = SGD()
model.compile(loss='categorical_crossentropy',
optimizer=optimizer, metrics=['accuracy'])
```

5. We start training:

```
n_epochs = 1000
batch_size = 128

history = model.fit(X_train, y_train, epochs=n_epochs,
batch_size=batch_size,
          validation_data=[X_val, y_val],
          verbose = 1, callbacks=callbacks)
```

6. Now, let's add `dropouts` to our model architecture. We do this after each convolutional block and after the fully connected layer:

```
model_dropout = Sequential()
model_dropout.add(Conv2D(32, (3, 3), padding='same',
input_shape=X_train.shape[1:]))
model_dropout.add(Activation('relu'))
model_dropout.add(Conv2D(32, (3, 3)))
model_dropout.add(Activation('relu'))
model_dropout.add(MaxPooling2D(pool_size=(2, 2)))
model_dropout.add(Dropout(0.25))

model_dropout.add(Conv2D(64, (3, 3), padding='same'))
model_dropout.add(Activation('relu'))
model_dropout.add(Conv2D(64, (3, 3)))
model_dropout.add(Activation('relu'))
model_dropout.add(MaxPooling2D(pool_size=(2, 2)))
model_dropout.add(Dropout(0.25))

model_dropout.add(Flatten())
model_dropout.add(Dense(512))
model_dropout.add(Activation('relu'))
model_dropout.add(Dropout(0.5))
model_dropout.add(Dense(n_classes))
model_dropout.add(Activation('softmax'))
optimizer = Adam()
model_dropout.compile(loss='categorical_crossentropy',
optimizer=optimizer, metrics=['accuracy'])
```

7. Let's start training from scratch again:

```
n_epochs = 1000
batch_size = 128

history_dropout = model_dropout.fit(X_train, y_train,
epochs=n_epochs, batch_size=batch_size,
        validation_data=[X_val, y_val],
        verbose = 1, callbacks=callbacks)
```

8. Let's plot the training and validation accuracy of our model without dropout:

```
aplt.plot(np.arange(len(history.history['acc'])),
history.history['acc'], label='training')
plt.plot(np.arange(len(history.history['val_acc'])),
history.history['val_acc'], label='validation')
plt.title('Accuracy of model without dropouts')
plt.xlabel('epochs')
plt.ylabel('accuracy')
plt.legend(loc=0)
plt.show()
```

In the following graph, we can see that the model clearly overfits on the training data:

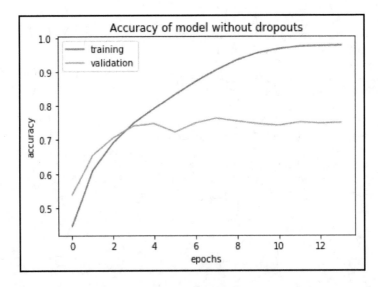

Figure 12.6: Accuracy of our model without dropouts

9. Finally, the training and validation accuracy of our model with dropouts:

```
plt.plot(np.arange(len(history_dropout.history['acc'])),
history_dropout.history['acc'], label='training')
plt.plot(np.arange(len(history_dropout.history['val_acc'])),
history_dropout.history['val_acc'], label='validation')
plt.title('Accuracy of model with dropouts')
plt.xlabel('epochs')
plt.ylabel('accuracy')
plt.legend(loc=0)
plt.show()
```

Now, we can see that, thanks to the dropouts, our model is able to generalize better and it doesn't overfit on the training data so much. However, there is still room for improvement:

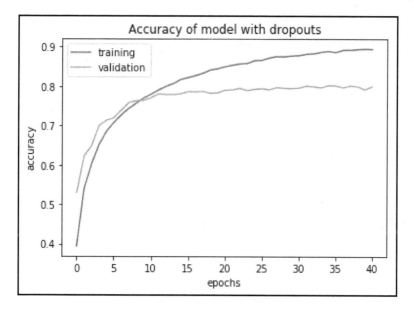

Figure 12.7: Accuracy of our model with dropouts

Making a model more robust with data augmentation

A popular method to boost the performance of a network for computer vision tasks is to add data augmentation. By using data augmentation during training time, you can increase the size of the training set. As a consequence, you make your model more robust to slight variations in the training data. In Chapter 7, *Computer Vision*, we demonstrated some data augmentation techniques. In the following recipe, we will be using Keras and its ImageDataGenerator for data augmentation.

How to do it...

1. We start by importing all libraries as usual:

```
from keras.preprocessing.image import ImageDataGenerator
from keras.models import Sequential
from keras.layers import Dense, Dropout, Activation, Flatten
from keras.layers import Conv2D, MaxPooling2D
from keras.optimizers import Adam
from keras.callbacks import EarlyStopping, TensorBoard,
ModelCheckpoint

from keras.datasets import cifar10
```

2. We load and pre-process the training and validation data as follows:

```
(X_train, y_train), (X_val, y_val) = cifar10.load_data()

X_train = X_train.astype('float32')/255.
X_val = X_val.astype('float32')/255.
n_classes = 10
y_train = keras.utils.to_categorical(y_train, n_classes)
y_val = keras.utils.to_categorical(y_val, n_classes)
```

3. Next, we define our model architecture:

```
model = Sequential()
model.add(Conv2D(32, (3, 3), padding='same',
input_shape=X_train.shape[1:]))
model.add(Activation('relu'))
model.add(Conv2D(32, (3, 3)))
model.add(Activation('relu'))
model.add(MaxPooling2D(pool_size=(2, 2)))
model.add(Dropout(0.25))

model.add(Conv2D(64, (3, 3), padding='same'))
model.add(Activation('relu'))
model.add(Conv2D(64, (3, 3)))
model.add(Activation('relu'))
model.add(MaxPooling2D(pool_size=(2, 2)))
model.add(Dropout(0.25))

model.add(Flatten())
model.add(Dense(512))
model.add(Activation('relu'))
model.add(Dropout(0.5))
model.add(Dense(n_classes))
model.add(Activation('softmax'))
```

4. We define the `Adam` optimizer and compile our model:

```
opt = Adam(lr=0.0001)
model.compile(loss='categorical_crossentropy',
optimizer=opt, metrics=['accuracy'])
```

5. In Keras, we can use `ImageDataGenerator` to easily set image augmentations, as follows:

```
datagen = ImageDataGenerator(
    rotation_range=15,
    width_shift_range=0.15,
    height_shift_range=0.15,
    horizontal_flip=True,
    vertical_flip=False)

datagen.fit(X_train)
```

6. Next, we set our `callback` functions:

```
callbacks = [EarlyStopping(monitor='val_acc', patience=5,
verbose=2), ModelCheckpoint('checkpoints/weights.{epoch:02d}-
'+str(batch_size)+'.hdf5', save_best_only=True),
TensorBoard('~/notebooks/logs-lrscheduler',
write_graph=True, write_grads=True, write_images=True,
embeddings_freq=0, embeddings_layer_names=None,
embeddings_metadata=None)
]
```

7. Let's start training our model:

```
batch_size = 128
n_epochs = 1000
history = model.fit_generator(datagen.flow(X_train, y_train,
                              batch_size=batch_size),
                 steps_per_epoch=X_train.shape[0] // batch_size,
                 epochs=epochs,
                 validation_data=(X_val, y_val),
                 callbacks=callbacks
                 )
```

Leveraging test-time augmentation (TTA) to boost accuracy

While data augmentation during training is a well-known and widely used technique, most people are less familiar with TTA. When using TTA, we can present our trained model with different views of, say, an image to classify. Maybe if we flip or slightly rotate the image, the trained model is able to make more accurate predictions. Using TTA can be seen as an ensemble of multiple models. We can choose to take the average of the probabilities or any other ensembling technique to combine the results of each individual prediction.

13
Network Internals

This chapter provides a collection of recipes regarding the internals of a neural network. This includes tensor decomposition, weight initialization, topology storage, bottleneck features, and corresponding embeddings.

We will cover the following recipes:

- Visualizing training with TensorBoard
- Analyzing network weights and more
- Freezing layers
- Storing the network topology and trained weights

Introduction

In this book, we have focused on providing building blocks for deep learning and hands-on solutions for real-world problems. In this chapter, we want to focus on what is happening under the hood of these powerful deep learning networks. For example, we will demonstrate how to analyze the trained weights and visualize the training process using TensorBoard.

Visualizing training with TensorBoard

In the previous chapter, we demonstrated how to set up **TensorBoard** with Keras. However, as already mentioned, TensorBoard can also be used with TensorFlow (among others). In this recipe, we will show you how to use TensorBoard with TensorFlow when classifying Fashion-MNIST.

How to do it..

1. Let's start by importing TensorFlow and a tool to load `mnist` datasets, as follows:

```
import tensorflow as tf
from tensorflow.examples.tutorials.mnist import input_data
```

2. Next, we specify the Fashion MNIST dataset and load it:

```
mnist = input_data.read_data_sets('Data/fashion', one_hot=True)
```

3. Let's create the placeholders for the input data:

```
n_classes = 10
input_size = 784

x = tf.placeholder(tf.float32, shape=[None, input_size])
y = tf.placeholder(tf.float32, shape=[None, n_classes])
```

4. Before we specify our network architecture, we will define a couple of functions we will be using multiple times in our model. We start with a function that creates and initializes the weights:

```
def weight_variable(shape):
    initial = tf.truncated_normal(shape, stddev=0.1)
    return tf.Variable(initial)
```

5. We create a similar function for the bias:

```
def bias_variable(shape):
    initial = tf.constant(0.1, shape=shape)
    return tf.Variable(initial)
```

6. In our architecture, we will be using multiple convolutional blocks that include a `max-pooling` layer:

```
def conv2d(x, W):
    return tf.nn.conv2d(x, W, strides=[1, 1, 1, 1], padding='SAME')

def max_pool_2x2(x):
    return tf.nn.max_pool(x, ksize=[1, 2, 2, 1],
    strides=[1, 2, 2, 1], padding='SAME')
```

7. Next, we define our complete network architecture. We will be using three convolutional blocks followed by two fully connected layers:

```
W_conv1 = weight_variable([7, 7, 1, 100])
b_conv1 = bias_variable([100])
x_image = tf.reshape(x, [-1,28,28,1])
h_conv1 = tf.nn.relu(conv2d(x_image, W_conv1) + b_conv1)
h_pool1 = max_pool_2x2(h_conv1)

W_conv2 = weight_variable([4, 4, 100, 150])
b_conv2 = bias_variable([150])
h_conv2 = tf.nn.relu(conv2d(h_pool1, W_conv2) + b_conv2)
h_pool2 = max_pool_2x2(h_conv2)

W_conv3 = weight_variable([4, 4, 150, 250])
b_conv3 = bias_variable([250])
h_conv3 = tf.nn.relu(conv2d(h_pool2, W_conv3) + b_conv3)
h_pool3 = max_pool_2x2(h_conv3)

W_fc1 = weight_variable([4 * 4 * 250, 300])
b_fc1 = bias_variable([300])
h_pool3_flat = tf.reshape(h_pool3, [-1, 4*4*250])
h_fc1 = tf.nn.relu(tf.matmul(h_pool3_flat, W_fc1) + b_fc1)
keep_prob = tf.placeholder(tf.float32)
h_fc1_drop = tf.nn.dropout(h_fc1, keep_prob)

W_fc2 = weight_variable([300, n_classes])
b_fc2 = bias_variable([n_classes])
y_pred = tf.matmul(h_fc1_drop, W_fc2) + b_fc2
```

8. Next, we need to extract `cross_entropy` as follows:

```
with tf.name_scope('cross_entropy'):
    diff = tf.nn.softmax_cross_entropy_with_logits(labels=y,
logits=y_pred)
    with tf.name_scope('total'):
        cross_entropy = tf.reduce_mean(diff)
tf.summary.scalar('cross_entropy', cross_entropy)
```

9. We will be using `AdamOptimizer` during training with a learning rate of `0.001`:

```
learning_rate = 0.001
train_step =
tf.train.AdamOptimizer(learning_rate).minimize(cross_entropy)
```

10. To track the progress, we want to extract the accuracy. We can do this as follows:

```
with tf.name_scope('accuracy'):
    correct_prediction = tf.equal(tf.argmax(y_pred, 1),
tf.argmax(y, 1))
    accuracy = tf.reduce_mean(tf.cast(correct_prediction,
tf.float32))
tf.summary.scalar('accuracy', accuracy)
```

11. We create an interactive TensorFlow session:

```
sess = tf.InteractiveSession()
```

12. Let's set up the summary writers for TensorFlow that we will be using for TensorBoard:

```
log_dir = 'tensorboard-example'
merged = tf.summary.merge_all()
train_writer = tf.summary.FileWriter(log_dir + '/train',
sess.graph)
val_writer = tf.summary.FileWriter(log_dir + '/val')
```

13. Next, we define some hyperparameters before we start training:

```
n_steps = 1000
batch_size = 128
dropout = 0.25
evaluate_every = 10
```

14. Finally, we can start training:

```
tf.global_variables_initializer().run()
for i in range(n_steps):
    x_batch, y_batch = mnist.train.next_batch(batch_size)
    summary, _, train_acc = sess.run([merged, train_step,
    accuracy], feed_dict={x: x_batch, y: y_batch, keep_prob:
    dropout})
    train_writer.add_summary(summary, i)
    if i % evaluate_every == 0:
        summary, val_acc = sess.run([merged, accuracy],
        feed_dict={x: mnist.test.images, y: mnist.test.labels,
        keep_prob: 1.0})
        val_writer.add_summary(summary, i)
        print('Step {:04.0f}: train_acc: {:.4f}; val_acc
        {:.4f}'.format(i, train_acc, val_acc))
train_writer.close()
val_writer.close()
```

15. To connect with TensorBoard, we open a new terminal window. If you're logged in to a server, make sure you start a new connection to your server and use a different port for SSH-tunneling, for example, when using GCP (replace instance-zone and instance-name with your own settings):

```
gcloud compute ssh --ssh-flag="-L 6006:localhost:6006"  --zone
"instance-zone" "instance-name"
```

16. After logging in, you can start the TensorBoard connection as follows:

```
tensorboard --logdir='~/tensorflow-example'
```

The terminal will output the location where you can connect with TensorBoard, for example, `http://instance-name:6006`. In our case, because we've enabled SSH-tunneling, we can go to our local browser and use the address `http://localhost:6006/` to access the dashboard. Within our TensorFlow dashboard, we can track the progress of our model. In the following figure, we can see the output after training is complete:

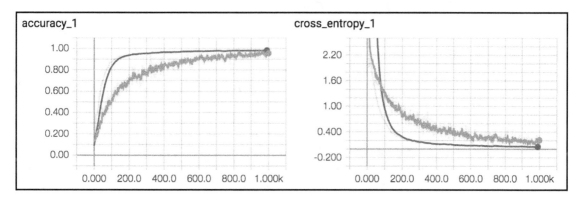

Figure 13.1: Training (orange) and validation (blue) results after 1,000 epochs

Visualizing the network architecture with TensorBoard

As we have demonstrated throughout the book, it is easy to output a simple summary of our network architecture when using the Keras framework. However, with TensorBoard, we are able to visualize our network architecture with different settings. In the following figure, you can see an example of such a visualization:

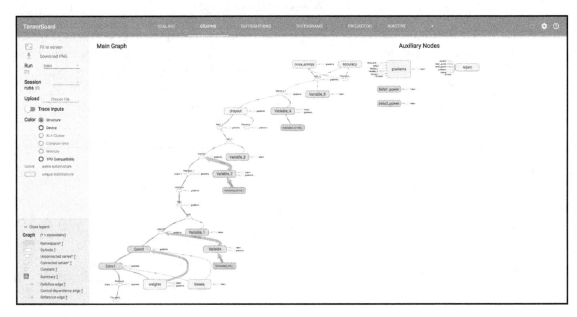

Figure 13.2: An example of TensorBoard graph visualization

Analyzing network weights and more

In the previous recipe, we focused on visualizing the loss and metric. However, with TensorBoard, you can also keep track of the weights. Taking a closer look at the weights can help in understanding how your model works and learns.

How to do it...

1. We start by importing TensorFlow, as follows:

```
import tensorflow as tf
from tensorflow.examples.tutorials.mnist import input_data
```

2. Now, we will be able to load the Fashion-MNIST dataset with just one line of code:

```
mnist = input_data.read_data_sets('Data/fashion', one_hot=True)
```

3. Before proceeding, we need to set the placeholders for our model:

```
n_classes = 10
input_size = 784

x = tf.placeholder(tf.float32, shape=[None, input_size])
y = tf.placeholder(tf.float32, shape=[None, n_classes])
keep_prob = tf.placeholder(tf.float32)
```

4. We define four functions that will help us build our network architecture:

```
def weight_variable(shape):
    initial = tf.truncated_normal(shape, stddev=0.1)
    return tf.Variable(initial)

def bias_variable(shape):
    initial = tf.constant(0.1, shape=shape)
    return tf.Variable(initial)

def conv2d(x, W):
    return tf.nn.conv2d(x, W, strides=[1, 1, 1, 1], padding='SAME')

def max_pool_2x2(x):
    return tf.nn.max_pool(x, ksize=[1, 2, 2, 1],
    strides=[1, 2, 2, 1], padding='SAME')
```

5. To write the statistics to TensorBoard, we define a function that extracts these values:

```
def summary_variable(var):
    with tf.name_scope('summaries'):
        mean = tf.reduce_mean(var)
        tf.summary.scalar('mean', mean)
        with tf.name_scope('stdev'):
```

```
            stddev = tf.sqrt(tf.reduce_mean(tf.square(var - mean)))
        tf.summary.scalar('stdev', stddev)
        tf.summary.scalar('max', tf.reduce_max(var))
        tf.summary.scalar('min', tf.reduce_min(var))
        tf.summary.histogram('histogram', var)
```

6. Next, we define our network architecture. For the first two convolutional blocks, we want to extract the weights and statistics during training. We do this as follows:

```
x_image = tf.reshape(x, [-1,28,28,1])
with tf.name_scope('weights'):
    W_conv1 = weight_variable([7, 7, 1, 100])
    summary_variable(W_conv1)
with tf.name_scope('biases'):
    b_conv1 = bias_variable([100])
    summary_variable(b_conv1)

with tf.name_scope('Conv1'):
    h_conv1 = tf.nn.relu(conv2d(x_image, W_conv1) + b_conv1)
    h_pool1 = max_pool_2x2(h_conv1)
    tf.summary.histogram('activations', h_conv1)
    tf.summary.histogram('max_pool', h_pool1)

with tf.name_scope('weights'):
    W_conv2 = weight_variable([4, 4, 100, 150])
    summary_variable(W_conv2)
with tf.name_scope('biases'):
    b_conv2 = bias_variable([150])
    summary_variable(b_conv2)

with tf.name_scope('Conv2'):
    h_conv2 = tf.nn.relu(conv2d(h_pool1, W_conv2) + b_conv2)
    h_pool2 = max_pool_2x2(h_conv2)
    tf.summary.histogram('activations', h_conv2)
    tf.summary.histogram('max_pool', h_pool2)
```

7. For the remaining layers, we don't store any information:

```
W_conv3 = weight_variable([4, 4, 150, 250])
b_conv3 = bias_variable([250])
h_conv3 = tf.nn.relu(conv2d(h_pool2, W_conv3) + b_conv3)
h_pool3 = max_pool_2x2(h_conv3)

W_fc1 = weight_variable([4 * 4 * 250, 300])
b_fc1 = bias_variable([300])
h_pool3_flat = tf.reshape(h_pool3, [-1, 4*4*250])
h_fc1 = tf.nn.relu(tf.matmul(h_pool3_flat, W_fc1) + b_fc1)
```

```
h_fc1_drop = tf.nn.dropout(h_fc1, keep_prob)

W_fc2 = weight_variable([300, n_classes])
b_fc2 = bias_variable([n_classes])
y_pred = tf.matmul(h_fc1_drop, W_fc2) + b_fc2
```

8. However, we do store the cross entropy and accuracy:

```
with tf.name_scope('cross_entropy'):
    diff = tf.nn.softmax_cross_entropy_with_logits(labels=y,
logits=y_pred)
    with tf.name_scope('total'):
        cross_entropy = tf.reduce_mean(diff)
tf.summary.scalar('cross_entropy', cross_entropy)

with tf.name_scope('accuracy'):
    correct_prediction = tf.equal(tf.argmax(y_pred, 1),
tf.argmax(y, 1))
    accuracy = tf.reduce_mean(tf.cast(correct_prediction,
tf.float32))
tf.summary.scalar('accuracy', accuracy)
```

9. Let's set the learning rate and define our optimizer:

```
learning_rate = 0.001
train_step =
tf.train.AdamOptimizer(learning_rate).minimize(cross_entropy)
```

10. Let's set up a session and create our file writers:

```
sess = tf.InteractiveSession()
log_dir = 'tensorboard-example-weights'
merged = tf.summary.merge_all()
train_writer = tf.summary.FileWriter(log_dir + '/train',
sess.graph)
val_writer = tf.summary.FileWriter(log_dir + '/val')
```

11. Next, we define our hyperparameters:

```
n_steps = 1000
batch_size = 128
dropout = 0.25
evaluate_every = 10
n_val_steps = mnist.test.images.shape[0] // batch_size
```

12. Let's start training:

```
tf.global_variables_initializer().run()
for i in range(n_steps):
    x_batch, y_batch = mnist.train.next_batch(batch_size)
    summary, _, train_acc = sess.run([merged, train_step,
    accuracy], feed_dict={x: x_batch, y: y_batch,
    keep_prob: dropout})
    train_writer.add_summary(summary, i)

    if i % evaluate_every == 0:
        val_accs = []
        for j in range(n_val_steps):
            x_batch, y_batch = mnist.test.next_batch(batch_size)
            summary, val_acc = sess.run([merged, accuracy],
            feed_dict={x: x_batch, y: y_batch, keep_prob: 1.0})
            val_writer.add_summary(summary, i)
            val_accs.append(val_acc)
        print('Step {:04.0f}: train_acc: {:.4f}; val_acc
        {:.4f}'.format(i, train_acc, sum(val_accs)/len(val_accs)))
train_writer.close()
val_writer.close()
```

See the *Visualizing training with TensorBoard* recipe for more information on how to connect with TensorBoard. The following graph shows an example output in TensorBoard:

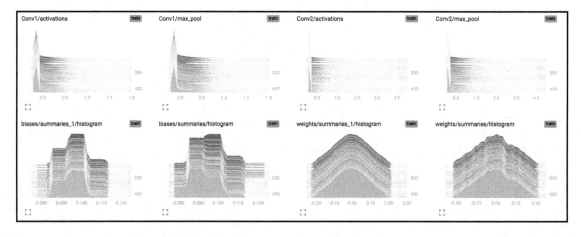

Figure 13.3: Weights and biasses visualized in TensorBoard

These statistics on your network weights can be extremely interesting and useful to understand what is happening under the hood. If you think your model isn't training properly, these visualizations can give you insights into the underlying causes in one of the layers.

Freezing layers

Sometimes (for example, when using pretrained networks), it is desirable to freeze some of the layers. We can do this when we're sure that some of the layers most of the time the first couple of layers, also known as the bottom of the network have proven to be of value as feature extractors. In the following recipe, we will demonstrate how to freeze a part of the network after training and only train the remaining subset of the network.

How to do it...

1. First, we load all libraries as follows:

```
import tensorflow as tf
from tensorflow.examples.tutorials.mnist import input_data
```

2. In TensorFlow, it's straightforward to load the MNIST dataset:

```
mnist = input_data.read_data_sets('Data/mnist', one_hot=True)
```

3. Next, we define the placeholders:

```
n_classes = 10
input_size = 784

x = tf.placeholder(tf.float32, shape=[None, input_size])
y = tf.placeholder(tf.float32, shape=[None, n_classes])
keep_prob = tf.placeholder(tf.float32)
```

4. We define some functions we want to use repeatedly in our network architecture:

```
def weight_variable(shape, name='undefined'):
    initial = tf.truncated_normal(shape, stddev=0.1)
    return tf.Variable(initial, name=name)

def bias_variable(shape, name='undefined'):
    initial = tf.constant(0.1, shape=shape)
    return tf.Variable(initial, name=name)
```

```
def conv2d(x, W):
    return tf.nn.conv2d(x, W, strides=[1, 1, 1, 1], padding='SAME')

def max_pool_2x2(x):
    return tf.nn.max_pool(x, ksize=[1, 2, 2, 1],
        strides=[1, 2, 2, 1], padding='SAME')
```

5. We are now ready to define our network architecture:

```
x_image = tf.reshape(x, [-1,28,28,1])

W_conv1 = weight_variable([7, 7, 1, 100], name='1st_layer_weights')
b_conv1 = bias_variable([100], name='1st_layer_bias')
h_conv1 = tf.nn.relu(conv2d(x_image, W_conv1) + b_conv1)
h_pool1 = max_pool_2x2(h_conv1)

W_conv2 = weight_variable([4, 4, 100, 150])
b_conv2 = bias_variable([150])
h_conv2 = tf.nn.relu(conv2d(h_pool1, W_conv2) + b_conv2)
h_pool2 = max_pool_2x2(h_conv2)

W_conv3 = weight_variable([4, 4, 150, 250])
b_conv3 = bias_variable([250])
h_conv3 = tf.nn.relu(conv2d(h_pool2, W_conv3) + b_conv3)
h_pool3 = max_pool_2x2(h_conv3)

W_fc1 = weight_variable([4 * 4 * 250, 300])
b_fc1 = bias_variable([300])
h_pool3_flat = tf.reshape(h_pool3, [-1, 4*4*250])
h_fc1 = tf.nn.relu(tf.matmul(h_pool3_flat, W_fc1) + b_fc1)
h_fc1_drop = tf.nn.dropout(h_fc1, keep_prob)

W_fc2 = weight_variable([300, n_classes])
b_fc2 = bias_variable([n_classes])
y_pred = tf.matmul(h_fc1_drop, W_fc2) + b_fc2

diff = tf.nn.softmax_cross_entropy_with_logits(labels=y,
logits=y_pred)
cross_entropy = tf.reduce_mean(diff)
correct_prediction = tf.equal(tf.argmax(y_pred, 1), tf.argmax(y,
1))
accuracy = tf.reduce_mean(tf.cast(correct_prediction, tf.float32))
```

6. Let's print the names of the trainable variables:

```
trainable_vars = tf.trainable_variables()

for i in range(len(trainable_vars)):
```

```
print(trainable_vars[i])
```

7. When defining our optimizer, we can set which variables should be included while training:

```
vars_train = [var for var in trainable_vars if '1st_' in var.name]

learning_rate = 0.001
train_step =
tf.train.AdamOptimizer(learning_rate).minimize(cross_entropy,
var_list=vars_train)
```

Instead of using the names of the variables, one can also decide to set the parameter `trainable` explicitly in TensorFlow.

8. Next, we can set the hyperparameters we want to use and start training:

```
n_steps = 10
batch_size = 128
dropout = 0.25
evaluate_every = 10

sess = tf.InteractiveSession()
tf.global_variables_initializer().run()
for i in range(n_steps):
    x_batch, y_batch = mnist.train.next_batch(batch_size)
    _, train_acc = sess.run([train_step, accuracy], feed_dict={x:
    x_batch, y: y_batch, keep_prob: dropout})
    print('Step {:04.0f}: train_acc: {:.4f}'.format(i, train_acc))
```

Storing the network topology and trained weights

In most deep learning frameworks, it is straightforward to store the network architecture and the trained weights. However, because this can be extremely important, we will demonstrate how to store your model with TensorFlow in the following recipe.

How to do it...

1. We start by importing the libraries:

```
import tensorflow as tf
from tensorflow.examples.tutorials.mnist import input_data
```

2. Next, we load the MNIST data:

```
mnist = input_data.read_data_sets('Data/mnist', one_hot=True)
```

3. We define the TensorFlow placeholders as follows:

```
n_classes = 10
input_size = 784

x = tf.placeholder(tf.float32, shape=[None, input_size])
y = tf.placeholder(tf.float32, shape=[None, n_classes])
keep_prob = tf.placeholder(tf.float32)
```

4. For convenience, we create functions to build our deep learning network:

```
def weight_variable(shape):
    initial = tf.truncated_normal(shape, stddev=0.1)
    return tf.Variable(initial)

def bias_variable(shape):
    initial = tf.constant(0.1, shape=shape)
    return tf.Variable(initial)

def conv2d(x, W):
    return tf.nn.conv2d(x, W, strides=[1, 1, 1, 1], padding='SAME')

def max_pool_2x2(x):
    return tf.nn.max_pool(x, ksize=[1, 2, 2, 1],
    strides=[1, 2, 2, 1], padding='SAME')
```

5. We can now define our full network architecture:

```
x_image = tf.reshape(x, [-1,28,28,1])

W_conv1 = weight_variable([7, 7, 1, 100])
b_conv1 = bias_variable([100])
h_conv1 = tf.nn.relu(conv2d(x_image, W_conv1) + b_conv1)
h_pool1 = max_pool_2x2(h_conv1)

W_conv2 = weight_variable([4, 4, 100, 150])
```

```
b_conv2 = bias_variable([150])
h_conv2 = tf.nn.relu(conv2d(h_pool1, W_conv2) + b_conv2)
h_pool2 = max_pool_2x2(h_conv2)

W_conv3 = weight_variable([4, 4, 150, 250])
b_conv3 = bias_variable([250])
h_conv3 = tf.nn.relu(conv2d(h_pool2, W_conv3) + b_conv3)
h_pool3 = max_pool_2x2(h_conv3)

W_fc1 = weight_variable([4 * 4 * 250, 300])
b_fc1 = bias_variable([300])
h_pool3_flat = tf.reshape(h_pool3, [-1, 4*4*250])
h_fc1 = tf.nn.relu(tf.matmul(h_pool3_flat, W_fc1) + b_fc1)
h_fc1_drop = tf.nn.dropout(h_fc1, keep_prob)

W_fc2 = weight_variable([300, n_classes])
b_fc2 = bias_variable([n_classes])
y_pred = tf.matmul(h_fc1_drop, W_fc2) + b_fc2
```

6. We need the following definitions to train our network and to determine the performance:

```
diff = tf.nn.softmax_cross_entropy_with_logits(labels=y,
logits=y_pred)
cross_entropy = tf.reduce_mean(diff)
correct_prediction = tf.equal(tf.argmax(y_pred, 1), tf.argmax(y,
1))
accuracy = tf.reduce_mean(tf.cast(correct_prediction, tf.float32))
```

7. Let's define our optimizer next:

```
learning_rate = 0.001
train_step =
tf.train.AdamOptimizer(learning_rate).minimize(cross_entropy)
```

8. We can now define our hyperparameters:

```
n_steps = 25
batch_size = 32
dropout = 0.25
evaluate_every = 10
n_val_steps = mnist.test.images.shape[0] // batch_size
```

9. To save our model during training, we need to create a TensorFlow `Saver` variable. We don't want to store too many models, so we set the variable `max_to_keep` to 5:

```
saver = tf.train.Saver(max_to_keep=5)
save_dir = 'checkpoints/'
```

10. We can now create our session and start training. We store the weights of our best model based on the validation accuracy:

```
sess = tf.InteractiveSession()
tf.global_variables_initializer().run()
best_val = 0.0
for i in range(n_steps):
    x_batch, y_batch = mnist.train.next_batch(batch_size)
    _, train_acc = sess.run([train_step, accuracy], feed_dict={x:
    x_batch, y: y_batch, keep_prob: dropout})
    if i % evaluate_every == 0:
        val_accs = []
        for j in range(n_val_steps):
            x_batch, y_batch = mnist.test.next_batch(batch_size)
            val_acc = sess.run(accuracy, feed_dict={x: x_batch, y:
            y_batch, keep_prob: 1.0})
            val_accs.append(val_acc)
        print('Step {:04.0f}: train_acc: {:.4f}; val_acc:
        {:.4f}'.format(i, train_acc, sum(val_accs)/len(val_accs)))
        if val_acc > best_val:
            saver.save(sess, save_dir+'best-model', global_step=i)
            print('Model saved')
            best_val = val_acc
            saver.save(sess, save_dir+'last-model'))
```

11. Now, if we want to use the weights of one of our stored models, we can load these from one of the checkpoints:

```
with tf.Session() as sess:
    new_saver = tf.train.import_meta_graph(save_dir+'last-
model.meta')
    new_saver.restore(sess, save_dir+'last-model')
    for i in range(35):
        x_batch, y_batch = mnist.train.next_batch(batch_size)
        _, train_acc = sess.run([train_step, accuracy],
        feed_dict={x: x_batch, y: y_batch, keep_prob: dropout})
```

14
Pretrained Models

This chapter provides a collection of recipes based on popular deep learning models such as VGG-16 and Inception V4:

- Large-scale visual recognition with GoogLeNet/Inception
- Extracting bottleneck features with ResNet
- Leveraging pretrained VGG models for new classes
- Fine-tuning with Xception

Introduction

During the last couple of years, a lot of game-changing network architectures have been proposed and published. Most of them open-sourced their code or published their weights. If the latter was not the case, others implemented the network architecture and shared the weights. As a result, many deep learning frameworks give direct access to popular models and their weights. In this chapter, we will demonstrate how to leverage these pretrained weights. Most of these models have been trained on large image datasets used in competitions, such as the ImageNet dataset. This dataset has been published for the **ImageNet Large Scale Visual Recognition Challenge (ILSVRC)**. By leveraging these pretrained weights, we can obtain good results and reduce training time.

Large-scale visual recognition with GoogLeNet/Inception

In 2014, the paper *Going Deeper with Convolutions* (`https://arxiv.org/abs/1409.4842`) was published by Google, introducing the GoogLeNet architecture. Subsequently, newer versions (`https://arxiv.org/abs/1512.00567` in 2015) were published under the name Inception. In these GoogLeNet/Inception models, multiple convolutional layers are applied in parallel before being stacked and fed to the next layer. A great benefit of the network architecture is that the computational cost is lower and the file size of the trained weights is much smaller. In this recipe, we will demonstrate how to load the **InceptionV3** weights in Keras and apply the model to classify images.

How to do it...

1. Keras has some great tools for using pretrained models. We start with importing the libraries and tools, as follows:

```
import numpy as np

from keras.applications.inception_v3 import InceptionV3
from keras.applications import imagenet_utils
from keras.preprocessing.image import load_img
from keras.preprocessing.image import img_to_array
```

 Note that you can replace VGG16 with any of the included pretrained models in Keras.

2. Next, we load the `InceptionV3` model as follows:

```
pretrained_model = InceptionV3
model = pretrained_model(weights="imagenet")
```

3. The `InceptionV3` model is trained on the ImageNet dataset, and therefore we should use the same input dimensions if we want to feed the model new images:

```
input_dim = (299, 299)
```

4. We will be using the default ImageNet preprocessing techniques included in Keras:

```
preprocess = imagenet_utils.preprocess_input
```

5. In the next step, we load an example image and preprocess it:

```
image = load_img('Data/dog_example.jpg', target_size=input_dim)
image = img_to_array(image)
image = image.reshape((1, *image.shape))
image = preprocess(image)
```

6. After these simple steps, we are ready to predict the class of our example image, as follows:

```
preds = model.predict(image)
```

7. To decode the predictions, we can use Keras's `imagenet_utils.decode_predictions` method:

```
preds_decoded = imagenet_utils.decode_predictions(preds)
```

8. Finally, let's print these values:

```
preds_decoded
```

9. Your output should look like this:

```
In [6]: preds_decoded
Out[6]: [[('n02109961', 'Eskimo_dog', 0.59557849),
          ('n02110185', 'Siberian_husky', 0.40070605),
          ('n02110063', 'malamute', 0.0032684309),
          ('n02091467', 'Norwegian_elkhound', 0.00015924724),
          ('n03218198', 'dogsled', 9.0920155e-05)]]
```

Figure 14.1: Predictions and probabilities of VGG16 on the example image

It's amazing how we are able to retrieve predictions on any image with just 16 lines of code. However, we can use this model only if the target class is actually included in the original ImageNet dataset (1,000 classes).

Extracting bottleneck features with ResNet

The ResNet architecture was introduced in 2015 in the paper *Deep Residual Learning for Image Recognition* (https://arxiv.org/abs/1512.03385). ResNet has a different network architecture than VGG. It consists of micro-architectures that are stacked on top of each other. ResNet won the ILSVRC competition in 2015 and surpassed human performance on the ImageNet dataset. In this recipe, we will demonstrate how to leverage ResNet50 weights to extract bottleneck features.

How to do it...

1. We start by implementing all Keras tools:

   ```
   from keras.models import Model
   from keras.applications.resnet50 import ResNet50

   from keras.applications.resnet50 import preprocess_input
   from keras.preprocessing.image import load_img
   from keras.preprocessing.image import img_to_array
   from keras.applications import imagenet_utils
   ```

2. Next, we load the ResNet50 model with the imagenet weights:

   ```
   resnet_model = ResNet50(weights='imagenet')
   ```

3. For this example, we will extract the final average pooling layer in the ResNet implementation; this layer is called avg_pool. You can look up the Keras implementation of ResNet50 at https://github.com/fchollet/keras/blob/master/keras/applications/resnet50.py if you want to extract the features from another layer:

   ```
   model = Model(inputs=resnet_model.input,
   outputs=resnet_model.get_layer('avg_pool').output)
   ```

4. We need to make sure the input dimensions of the example we want to test is 224 by 224, and we apply the default preprocessing techniques for ImageNet:

```
input_dim = (224, 224)
image = load_img('Data/dog_example.jpg', target_size=input_dim)
image = img_to_array(image)
image = image.reshape((1, *image.shape))
image = preprocess_input(image)
```

5. Let's extract the features of our example `image`:

```
avg_pool_features = model.predict(image)
```

6. The features extracted with this model can be used for stacking. For example, you can train an xgboost model on top of these features (and other features) to make the final classification.

Leveraging pretrained VGG models for new classes

In 2014, the paper *Very Deep Convolutional Networks for Large-Scale Image Recognition* (`https://arxiv.org/abs/1409.1556`) was published. At that time, both the models in the paper, VGG16 and VGG19, were considered very deep, with 16 and 19 layers, respectively. That included weights, in addition to the input and output layers, and a couple of max pooling layers. The network architecture of VGG stacks multiple 3×3 convolutional layers on top of each other. In total, the VGG16 network architecture has 13 convolutional layers and three fully connected layers. The 19-layer variant has 16 convolutional layers and the same three fully connected layers. In this recipe, we will use the bottleneck features of VGG16 and add our own layers on top of it. We will freeze the weights of the original model and train only the top layers.

How to do it...

1. We start by importing all libraries, as follows:

```
import numpy as np
import matplotlib.pyplot as plt

from keras.models import Model
from keras.applications.vgg16 import VGG16
```

```
from keras.layers import Dense, GlobalAveragePooling2D
from keras.optimizers import Adam

from keras.applications import imagenet_utils
from keras.utils import np_utils
from keras.callbacks import EarlyStopping
```

2. In this recipe, we will be using Keras' `cifar10` dataset:

```
from keras.datasets import cifar10
(X_train, y_train), (X_test, y_test) = cifar10.load_data()
```

3. We need to preprocess the data before we feed it to our model:

```
n_classes = len(np.unique(y_train))
y_train = np_utils.to_categorical(y_train, n_classes)
y_test = np_utils.to_categorical(y_test, n_classes)

X_train = X_train.astype('float32')/255.
X_test = X_test.astype('float32')/255.
```

4. We will be using the `VGG16` model and load the weights without the top dense layers:

```
vgg_model = VGG16(weights='imagenet', include_top=False)
```

5. The great thing about Keras is that when you use the weights for the first time, the weights will be downloaded automatically. This can be seen as follows:

```
In [*]:  pretrained_model = VGG16
         model = pretrained_model(weights="imagenet")

         Downloading data from https://github.com/fchollet/deep-learning-models/releases/download/v0.1/vgg16_weights_tf_dim_or
         dering_tf_kernels.h5
         155992064/553467096 [======>......................] - ETA: 23s
```

Figure 14.2: Keras automatically downloads the weights

6. On top of this `VGG16` model, we will add a dense layer and an output layer:

```
x = vgg_model.output
 x = GlobalAveragePooling2D()(x)
 x = Dense(512, activation='relu')(x)
 out = Dense(10, activation='softmax')(x)
```

7. We combine the two models as follows:

```
model = Model(inputs=vgg_model.input, outputs=out)
```

8. We can freeze the weights of our VGG16 model with the following code:

```
for layer in vgg_model.layers:
  layer.trainable = False
```

9. Next, we compile our model with the Adam optimizer and output a summary of our model:

```
opt = Adam()
model.compile(optimizer=opt, loss='categorical_crossentropy',
metrics=['accuracy'])
model.summary()
```

10. As you can see in the summary, in total our model has over 15 million parameters. However, by freezing the VGG16 layers, we end up with 535,562 trainable parameters.

11. We define a callback with early stopping to prevent overfitting:

```
callbacks = [EarlyStopping(monitor='val_acc', patience=5,
verbose=0)]
```

12. We are now ready to train our model:

```
n_epochs = 50
batch_size = 512
history = model.fit(X_train, y_train, epochs=n_epochs,
batch_size=batch_size, validation_split=0.2, verbose=1,
callbacks=callbacks)
```

13. Let's plot the training and validation accuracy:

```
plt.plot(np.arange(len(history.history['acc'])),
history.history['acc'], label='training')
plt.plot(np.arange(len(history.history['val_acc'])),
history.history['val_acc'], label='validation')
 plt.title('Accuracy')
 plt.xlabel('batches')
 plt.ylabel('accuracy ')
 plt.legend(loc=0)
 plt.show()
```

14. In the following figure, we can see that our model tops at a final validation accuracy of around 60%:

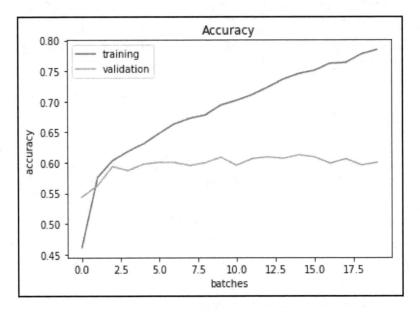

Figure 14.3: Training results after leveraging the VGG16 weights

Fine-tuning with Xception

The Xception network was made by the creator of Keras, François Chollet in *Xception: Deep Learning with Depthwise Separable Convolutions* (https://arxiv.org/abs/1610.02357). Xception is an extension of the Inception architecture, where the Inception modules are replaced with depthwise separable convolutions. In the previous recipe, we focused on training the top layers only while keeping the original Inception weights frozen during training. However, we can also choose to train all weights with a smaller learning rate. This is called **fine-tuning**. This technique can give the model a small performance boost by removing some biased weights from the original network.

How to do it...

1. First, we start with importing all the libraries needed, as follows:

```
import numpy as np
from keras.models import Model
from keras.applications import Xception
from keras.layers import Dense, GlobalAveragePooling2D
from keras.optimizers import Adam

from keras.applications import imagenet_utils
from keras.utils import np_utils
from keras.callbacks import EarlyStopping
```

2. Next, we load the dataset:

```
from keras.datasets import cifar10
  (X_train, y_train), (X_test, y_test) = cifar10.load_data()
```

3. We need to preprocess the data before feeding it to our model:

```
n_classes = len(np.unique(y_train))
y_train = np_utils.to_categorical(y_train, n_classes)
y_test = np_utils.to_categorical(y_test, n_classes)

X_train = X_train.astype('float32')/255.
X_test = X_test.astype('float32')/255.
```

4. Let's load the `Xception` model without the fully connected top layers from Keras:

```
xception_model = Xception(weights='imagenet', include_top=False)
```

5. Next, we define the layers we want to add to the `Xception` model:

```
x = xception_model.output
x = GlobalAveragePooling2D()(x)
x = Dense(512, activation='relu')(x)
out = Dense(10, activation='softmax')(x)
```

6. We combine this into one `model`:

```
model = Model(inputs=xception_model.input, outputs=out)
```

7. We need to make sure that the original weights of the Xception model are frozen. We will first train the top layers before fine-tuning:

```
for layer in xception_model.layers:
  layer.trainable = False
```

8. We can now define our optimizer and compile our model:

```
opt = Adam()
model.compile(optimizer=opt, loss='categorical_crossentropy',
metrics=['accuracy'])
model.summary()
```

9. To prevent overfitting, we use early stopping:

```
callbacks = [EarlyStopping(monitor='val_acc', patience=5,
verbose=0)]
```

10. Let's start training the top layers:

```
n_epochs = 100
batch_size = 512
history = model.fit(X_train, y_train, epochs=n_epochs,
batch_size=batch_size, validation_split=0.2, verbose=1,
callbacks=callbacks)
```

11. Afterwards, we can start fine-tuning. First, we need to know which layers we want to use for fine-tuning, so we print the names as follows:

```
for i, layer in enumerate(model.layers):
  print(i, layer.name)
```

12. Let's fine-tune the last two Xception blocks; these start at layer 115:

```
for layer in model.layers[:115]:
  layer.trainable = False
for layer in model.layers[115:]:
  layer.trainable = True
```

13. Afterwards, we train our model to train other layers as well. The learning rate is from great importance here, when the learning rate is too large we completely ignore the pretrained weights - which can be good if the original weights don't fit the task at hand:

```
opt_finetune = Adam()
model.compile(optimizer=opt_finetune,
loss='categorical_crossentropy', metrics=['accuracy'])
model.summary()
```

14. Finally, we can start fine-tuning our model:

```
history_finetune = model.fit(X_train, y_train, epochs=n_epochs,
batch_size=batch_size, validation_split=0.2, verbose=1,
callbacks=callbacks)
```

In this chapter, we demonstrated how to leverage pretrained deep learning models. The weights of these pretrained models can be used for similar image classification tasks or less related tasks.

Index

R

Reading comprehension (RC) 205
real-time detection frameworks 169
recurrent neural networks (RNNs) 153
regularization
  about 62
  generalization, improving with 61, 62, 63, 64, 66
reinforcement learning (RL) 117
ReLU 43
ResNet
  bottleneck features, extracting 302, 303

S

semantic segmentation 175
sentences
  translating 200
sentiment
  analyzing 197, 198
shallow neural network
  using, for binary classification 232, 233
simple RNN
  implementing 102, 103, 104
single-layer neural network
  implementing 34, 36, 37
Siri 212
speakers
  identifying, with voice recognition 215, 217, 218
speech recognition pipeline
  implementing 212, 213, 214, 215
speech-to-text (STT/S2T) 212
SSD (Single-Shot Multibox Detector) 169
stacking 219
state-of-the-art model
  building, with TensorFlow 16, 17
Stochastic Gradient Descent (SGD) 58, 271
stock prices
  predicting, with neural networks 224, 225, 227, 228
Street View House Numbers (SVHN) 52
strides 86
styles
  transferring, to images 190, 192
Super-Resolution GANs (SRGANs)
  resolution of images, upscaling with 145, 146,

149
Super-Resolution imaging (SR) 145

T

TanH 42
TensorBoard
  network architecture, visualizing 288
  training, visualizing 256, 258, 259, 260, 283, 284, 285, 286, 287
TensorFlow
  production-ready model, building 17
  production-ready model, creating 16
  state-of-the-art model, building 16, 17
test-time augmentation (TTA)
  about 154
  leveraging, for boosting accuracy 282
text
  1D CNN, applying to 98
  summarizing 205
tracking 178
trained weights
  storing 295
training
  visualizing, with TensorBoard 256, 258, 259, 260, 283, 284, 285, 286, 287

U

U-net
  classes, segmenting in images 170, 171, 172
Udacity's Self-Driving Car Simulator
  reference 236

V

vanishing gradients problem 42
videos
  with deep learning 219, 221
voice recognition
  speakers, identifying with 215, 217, 218
Voice Search 212

www.ingramcontent.com/pod-product-compliance
Lightning Source LLC
LaVergne TN
LVHW081515050326
832903LV00025B/1505